Mainstreaming the Headscarf

Gender and Islam Series

Mainstreaming the Headscarf

Islamist Politics and Women in the Turkish Media

Esra Özcan

I.B. TAURIS

LONDON • NEW YORK • OXFORD • NEW DELHI • SYDNEY

I.B. TAURIS
Bloomsbury Publishing Plc
50 Bedford Square, London, WC1B 3DP, UK
1385 Broadway, New York, NY 10018, USA

BLOOMSBURY, I.B. TAURIS and the Diana logo are trademarks
of Bloomsbury Publishing Plc

First published in Great Britain 2019

Cover design: Adriana Brioso
Cover image: Lawmakers of Turkey's AK Party attend a swearing-in ceremony at the
Turkish parliament in Ankara, 2015. (© ADEM ALTAN/AFP/Getty Images)

Bloomsbury Publishing Plc does not have any control over, or responsibility for, any
third-party websites referred to or in this book. All internet addresses given in this
book were correct at the time of going to press. The author and publisher regret
any inconvenience caused if addresses have changed or sites have ceased to exist,
but can accept no responsibility for any such changes.

A catalogue record for this book is available from the British Library.

A catalog record for this book is available from the Library of Congress.

ISBN: 978-1-7883-1401-5
eISBN: 978-1-8386-0081-5
ePDF: 978-1-8386-0080-8

Series: Gender and Islam

Typeset by RefineCatch Limited, Bungay, Suffolk

To find out more about our authors and books visit www.bloomsbury.com
and sign up for our newsletters.

Dedicated to
Atiye Nilgün Gökçek

Contents

Illustrations

Figures

Tables

Preface and Acknowledgments

This book is personal for me. I grew up among strong conservative women in Turkey: my grandmother, mother, aunts, and their circle of friends. They were highly educated, ardently studied religion, believed, and practiced. I heard the stories of conservative women from the 1960s firsthand and witnessed how this generation of conservative women shaped the coming generation. In that sense, I am writing not just from the position of an observer or researcher. Even though I am an outsider today, I feel part of the story when I try to make sense of the question that prompted me to write this book in the first place: Why have the vast majority of Turkey's strong, educated conservative women ended up supporting a repressive authoritarian regime? They were the ones who suffered most under Turkey's authoritarian secularism and challenged it on all fronts by resisting the headscarf ban in universities and questioning the anti-democratic practices of the state. What happened?

The conservative women I knew throughout my childhood were not actively engaged in party politics, yet they tended toward voting for the parties on the Right. Those who were politically active organized around Turkey's right-wing Islamist parties. They later became the carriers of the Justice and Development Party's (Adalet ve Kalkınma Partisi—AKP) ideological program to reshape Turkish society in religiously conservative terms. They became successful in mobilizing millions of other women to support the AKP. The conservative women's story in Turkey entered into a whole new phase with the rise of AKP to power in 2002.

The conservative women's story pre-AKP is a story of struggle, exclusion, and victimization. Although not all conservative women cover their hair, the story of the headscarf in Turkey has become an inseparable part of the story of conservative women. During the 1980s, wearing an Islamic headscarf was a stigmatizing decision that invited verbal insults and judgmental looks particularly in middle- and upper-middle-class neighborhoods. Not wearing a headscarf was the norm. I remember young conservative women's days of struggle at the gates of the university during the second half of the 1980s because of Turkey's notorious headscarf ban. The topic was close to the family, as many women around me wore the headscarf. I remember watching the news with my grandmother and her calm demeanor when Kenan Evren (1917–2015), the engineer of the 1980 military coup and the seventh president of Turkey (1983–90), referred to the ban in terms of cleaning the blood in our veins. It was common and pretty normal to refer to women wearing the headscarf (or the more extensive black çarşaf) as "cockroaches," to dehumanize them.

The headscarf ban continued on and off depending on the government and the political climate in the country. I attended university at the liberal Boğaziçi University in Istanbul and completed my BA and MA degrees while I was wearing a headscarf.[1] The ban was not in place when I started the university in 1992, but it came back in 1998 before I completed my MA degree. Boğaziçi University was famous for its resistance to the headscarf ban and allowed students like me, a very small minority at the time, to attend classes in spite of the ban. Still, after the reinstitution of the ban, I remember feeling the fear of exclusion each time I approached the gates of the university. That was discrimination. For students who were not allowed to attend classes in other universities, that was a traumatizing experience. I stopped wearing a headscarf a year after I graduated, in 2001. Hardships aside, my liberal education had convinced me that it was not God who wanted the headscarf for women. Many other women (and men) who spent their youth in conservative circles left conservatism (and the headscarf) for a variety of reasons. I am one of them.

This book grew out of my engagement with conservative women and leftist feminism, as well as my frustration and sadness about the rise of authoritarianism in Turkey and conservative women's role in it. As of this writing in 2018, and with my time wearing the headscarf long in the past, I am amazed by humans' endless capacity to find justification for inflicting on others the same pain that was once inflicted on them. It truly saddens me to see conservative women who once suffered from the headscarf ban defending repressive policies when these policies do not affect them anymore but do affect others. All the restrictions on the headscarf are now removed. Doors are wide open for young conservative women to participate fully in education, the economy, and politics. Yet, the removal of the ban went hand in hand with the suppression of dissent and the establishment of a conservative gender hegemony. Under Turkey's President Recep Tayyip Erdoğan's repressive regime, the headscarf moved to the mainstream and has become a symbol of desirable womanhood, pushing Turkey's secular feminists and their ideals of womanhood more and more to the margins. While conservative women cherish their new freedoms, for Turkey's secular population the headscarf has become one of the signifiers of increasing authoritarianism, adding a new layer to the already-complex meanings of the garment.

The rise of authoritarianism in a number of other countries,[2] and politicians like Recep Tayyip Erdoğan and Donald Trump have made me wary of conservatism and the exclusionary discourses it produces without regard to a specific religion in question. In that sense, I came to see more similarities than differences between the "East" and "West." The debates on religion and secularism are not unique to Turkey. Controversies over school curricula (i.e., teaching Darwin or not), sexual rights, and definitions of the "family," have been taking place in both national and international forums throughout the world. The old categories between the East and the West are breaking down. Poverty, wealth inequality, corruption, racism, and exclusion characterize both wealthy and poor nations. Turkey's modernizers saw the West as a model to look up to and imitate. The "West" was (and still is) a number of things: colonizer, an intimidating power center, source of inspiration in the search for equality, and a successful model for democratization. Under globalized neoliberalism, the West has lost its promise to be a model for equal citizenship and democracy. Situated within this broader context, this book questions some of the established categories that we have been using in academia to make sense of "Islamist" politics, women, and the media in Turkey. My narrative challenges the established naming practices employed to tell the story of Turkey's conservative women, particularly in academic literature written in English, and evaluates the basic assumptions behind these practices.

Writing this book was painful and challenging. As I was trying to capture the moment and document it, others' writings documenting the same moment have started to disappear day by day, both from the digital and material world, because of the campaign against the media in Turkey. At international conferences, I met colleagues from smaller Anatolian universities who were afraid of writing about media censorship in Turkey for fear of losing their jobs. After the failed coup attempt of July 15, 2016, I just stopped counting the number of journalists, writers, and academics that went to jail, and the number of newspapers that were shut down. The newspapers that I used as sources were not there the next morning. Throughout the process of writing this book, I spent a lot of time saving and archiving news stories or articles that crossed my path for fear that they might disappear at any point because of the AKP's crackdown on the media.

I am indebted to a number of very beautiful people and institutions in the process of writing this book. Carol Lavin Bernick Faculty Grants of Tulane University provided generous funding for editorial support for the completion of the book. Tulane University's Newcomb College Institute (NCI) provided funding to present my findings at the International Communication Association's (ICA) 2017 Conference in San Diego, and invited me to give a talk at their Fridays at Newcomb lecture series in April 2017. I'd like to thank Sally J. Kenney, Zülal Fazlıoğlu Akın, Claire Daniel, and all the other colleagues and students who came to this talk, and asked stimulating questions. Tulane's School of Liberal Arts made grants from the PoP Travel Fund twice in 2018 to make it possible to discuss the book's arguments with colleagues at ICA's 2018 Conference in Prague, and the European Communication Research and Education Association's (ECREA) 2018 Conference in Lugano. NCI generously supported me to be able to participate in ECREA's 2018 Lugano conference as well.

Kenan Çayır has accompanied me in a very long journey since my years in Boğaziçi University. I am indebted to him, both as a friend and colleague, in numerous ways. I continued to engage with the ideas of my early mentor Nilüfer Göle, and the Boğaziçi professors who worked on feminism, gender, and the media: Nükhet Sirman and Yeşim Arat have remained as significant influences on my thinking, even when I have questioned their ideas and approaches. Soli Özel introduced me to the theories on power and never ended his support throughout my intellectual journey. The same is true of Faruk Birtek and Ayşe Öncü. I am truly grateful to my doctoral mentor, Marion G. Müller from Jacobs University Bremen, for introducing me to visual communication and analysis. I would not have been able to undertake this project without the training that I received from her. Michael Griffin, another great scholar of visual communication, was always there for me when I needed his advice. I would like to thank Özen Odağ and Christina Ogan for their conversations on the changes in women's rights in Turkey and for collaborating with me to prepare a panel for the ICA's San Diego Conference in 2017. I was incredibly lucky to have them always within my reach when I needed their expertise on methodological issues. Özen joined me next year for another panel at ECREA Lugano to discuss the current state of gender equality in Turkey. This panel would have been impossible without the selfless support and participation of colleagues from a number of Turkish universities: Eser Selen and Esin Paça Cengiz from Kadir Has University, Esra Ercan Bilgiç from Bilgi University, and Feyda Sayan-Cengiz from Celal Bayar University. I'd like to thank them all for their participation against all the odds. Murat Akser, Ognyan Seizov, and Ece Algan shared their much appreciated comments and criticisms on my work during and after the conference.

I would like to thank Handan Koç for patiently listening to my project and helping me find the old issues of feminist publications. Nazlı Eda Noyan from Bahçeşehir University regularly encouraged me to deepen my research and write this book. Along with her, Şule Dikmendinç Fırat, Ümit Fırat, and Suncem Koçer helped me to figure out copyright clearance for the images I wanted to use in the book. During my Istanbul visits, the conversations I had with them and with my other colleagues and friends helped me to keep things in perspective and test my arguments. For that, I am grateful to Nadire Mater from Bianet; Güldem Baykal Büyüksaraç from Istanbul University; İncilay Cangöz from Anadolu University; Deniz Bayrakdar, Melis Behlil, Levent Soysal, and Banu Baybars Hawks from Kadir Has University. The encouragements coming from my friend and colleague Berk Esen, from Bilkent University, was a source of relief, helping me renew my energy to go on. I am thankful to Marwan Kraidy and Michael X. Delli Carpini of Annenberg School for Communication for carefully listening to my project in the aftermath of the ICA 2016 Conference in Fukuoka and share their comments with me. Mehdi Semati, from Northern Illinois University and Yeşim Kaptan from Kent State University encouraged me at every opportunity and helped me think about new ideas while working on the book. My conversations with Meyda Yeğenoğlu helped me fine-tune my argument on how conservative women have appropriated the language of postcolonial feminism in favor of right-wing politics. Mahmut Mutman helped me to look at the Turkish Left from a different angle.

I want to express much gratitude to my fantastic friends from Istanbul: I simply cannot find words to describe Berrin Yenice's and Mehtap Meydan's never-ending, selfless support. Their positivity in spite of heavy repression in Turkey and their intellectual exchanges have become a source of inspiration. I thank Nihan Akdoğan Uçar, Dilge Gözgü, the whole IUB Tayfası, and Gönül Aykuter for their warm friendship and support. I am blessed to have Sona Öcal in New Orleans. Life would be much more difficult without her cushioning support and comforting, delicious food.

I am grateful to my colleagues from Tulane University's Department of Communication for their support and encouragement. It was great to find Mauro Porto and Vicki Mayer by my side whenever juggling with teaching, writing, and service felt overwhelming. Michele White regularly gave invaluable advice that helped me to steer and manage the process of writing. My conversations with Mohan Ambikaipaker over lunch in the department's kitchen always energized me to think in new directions. Synchronizing multiple academic tasks while writing this book would be impossible without Marie Davis and Ava Lherisse's skilled logistical support. I would like to thank Connie Balides, LZ Humphreys, Eric Herhuth, and Betsy Weiss (Communication), Nancy Maveety (Political Science) and Michele Adams (Sociology) for making themselves available whenever I needed them and for their invaluable friendship. It felt like a blessing to have Kaarina Nikunen, Karina Horsti, Stefan Gendler, Sofia Rodriguez, Toby Miller, Jonathan Ong, Radha Hedge, and Kaya Şahin visiting New Orleans and/or Tulane's Department of Communication during the course of my writing. Their lovely presence made a heavy task lighter and enjoyable. I would like to thank Regina Marchi from Rutgers University for her wonderful support and encouragement. Her visit to New Orleans was another blessed moment.

I would like to thank my editor from I.B. Tauris, Sophie Rudland, for her kindness, patience, and belief in this project. Katie Van Heest took care of upstream editing, and her editing skills made this a better book. The comments of anonymous reviewers helped me to rethink some of my arguments. Any shortcomings of this book are solely my own.

Last, but not least, I cannot overstate my colleague and husband Ferruh Yılmaz's contribution to this book, both emotionally and intellectually. In addition to his unending comforting support, he helped me realize the intricate ways that those in power justify their positions. Thanks to him, I appreciate the explanatory power of hegemony theory more than ever. He introduced me to rhetorical analysis and argument analysis. Without years of endless conversations with him, I would not have been able to develop the perspective to write this book in this way.

One paragraph from the introduction appeared in my PhD dissertation published online by Jacobs University Bremen in 2010.[3] Parts of Chapter 3 were previously published in *European Journal of Communication* (*EJC*) in 2015.[4] I greatly revised and expanded that article here by focusing on image analysis and qualitative discussion.

Introduction

May 3, 1999: Merve Kavakçı, an elected representative of the Turkish parliament, refused to take off her headscarf during the oath-taking ceremony. Kavakçı was forced out of the parliament under heavy protests and was never able to return.

August 27, 2015: Ayşen Gürcan, the first female minister to wear a headscarf, assumed her office as the head of the Ministry of Family and Social Policies. The Justice and Development Party established this ministry in 2011 to minimize the role of institutions that worked toward eliminating all forms of discrimination against women.

July 29, 2017: Merve Kavakçı was appointed as the Turkish ambassador to Malaysia.

On July 27, 2005 *Hürriyet*, one of the most prominent high-circulation dailies in Turkey, published a photograph that stirred wide public discussion in the following days. The photograph showed a woman cheerfully dancing in a concert—with part of her belly visible, and wearing a headscarf. The entire image seemed like a contradiction in terms when considered within the religious rationale for covering the hair: modesty and self-control. Yet the image seemed to defy expectations. The implied contradictions were difficult to comprehend for both the Turkish readers and the editors who received the image. Ertuğrul Özkök, then editor in chief of *Hürriyet*, wrote a commentary on the photograph.[1] Departing from a modernist analysis, he interpreted the image as depicting the new sociological reality of the country and predicted the eventual demise of the headscarf along with increasing modernization and urbanization.

Özkök's prediction could not have been proved more wrong. Within twelve years, instead of disappearing, the headscarf has gone mainstream. It has become more and more visible in private and public television, in newspapers, in politics, and in everyday life. Anchorwomen, journalists, politicians, policewomen, judges, and ministers wearing the headscarf have taken their place at the center of Turkish media and politics. Media and politics are not the only spaces where the headscarf has gone mainstream. A short walk in Istanbul proves that the garment has become part of the cityscape, appearing in huge billboards on the streets and in commercials running on subway and bus stops—places both expected and unexpected. The headscarf commercials have become common even in neighborhoods like Nişantaşı, which symbolized upper-class secular modernity. The images of the headscarf in these neighborhoods do not just make a commercial statement by promoting a product; they also make a political statement by reminding the residents of who is now in power under the Justice and Development Party's (Adalet ve Kalkınma Partisi—AKP, 2002–present) "new" Turkey.

Representations are not just innocent reflections of society. They are part of an ongoing struggle for power, inseparable from individuals' actions and practices. Controlling the representations of desirable womanhood sets the parameters within which women are allowed or not allowed to enjoy their basic rights. The history of women's rights in modern Turkey is characterized by this struggle to gain the power to control the image and to define what constitutes women's rights. The headscarf has become the most visible, elusive, and distracting symbol of this struggle for power. Under the AKP, the struggle that has been taking place over the meanings of women's headscarves in Turkey has taken a new turn, and the pro-AKP media have succeeded in recasting the garment as a new source of power and prestige.

Turkey, traditionally known for its staunch secularism, has gone through an enormous transformation between 2002 and 2018 under the rule of the AKP. The party has pushed the secular establishment out of power and implemented restrictive gender policies by continuously endorsing misogynist views and practices, vilifying feminism, openly rejecting the idea of equality between men and women, and defining a woman's role mainly in relation to family and motherhood. *Mainstreaming the Headscarf: Islamist Politics and Women in the Turkish Media* looks at this new phase of conservative gender politics in Turkey through the prism of the images of women's headscarves in secular and Islamist news media. The book provides an analysis of newspaper photographs from four newspapers collected between 2002 and 2012 during the election periods, and also analyzes the columns of conservative women journalists wearing the headscarf published between 2006 and 2014. Although the headscarf is analyzed and theorized from a variety of perspectives, an analysis of the transformation of visual culture under the AKP governments with a focus on images of the headscarf in news media has not been done. *Mainstreaming the Headscarf* aims to fill that void and contribute to feminist scholarship on Muslim women from the perspective of visual culture and communication.

In this book, I argue that the AKP has created a new gender hegemony and has transformed the image of women in Turkey. My aim is to show how this transformation in visual culture has been taking place and in what ways a new hegemonic image of desirable womanhood has been established since the AKP came to power. Based on my analysis, I argue that during the AKP regime, the headscarf has moved from the margins to the mainstream in the media—and the women wearing it, from victimhood to success. The representations of the headscarf, as signifiers of the new ideal woman, are part of the new gender hegemony that the AKP wants to establish (and so far has succeeded in doing so). The Islamist newspapers in particular have been skillfully using the images of middle-class conservative women wearing the headscarf in creating and reinforcing a new conservative gender hegemony.

Following the changes in news photographs, I observe what I call "the rise of the conservative female journalist" as an important phenomenon and I examine the role of conservative women journalists in the creation of the AKP's hegemony. I argue that the conservative, or right-wing, female journalists wearing the headscarf have become part of a new elite that plays a significant role in legitimating the AKP's grip on power and reinforcing its anti-secular and antifeminist hegemony in Turkey. The AKP's new hegemony could not have been sustained without the support of the elite conservative women in Turkey's new, pro-Erdoğan media. As Ayşe Çavdar convincingly argued, although Erdoğan has parted ways with all the leading conservative men since he came to power, he has never parted ways with the conservative women.[2] Conservative women in return have never ended their support for him.

Mainstreaming the Headscarf has three unique contributions. First, it focuses on the transformation of the visual culture and the image of the headscarf in Turkey. Second, it looks at how conservative women journalists wearing the headscarf gained positions of power in the media and have become engineers of the AKP's new hegemony, legitimating the party's policies at all crossroads that gradually led to the rise of authoritarianism. Third, the book addresses the issues that the change in the image of women and the rise of a new class of conservative women to positions of power have generated for progressive feminists in Turkey. Among these issues are the imposition of restrictive gender roles by the government supported by a significant majority of conservative women and an increasing Islamophobia and anti-Muslim sentiment in a Muslim-majority country.

Along these lines, this book has three main arguments. First, as mentioned above, I argue that the headscarf has moved from the margins to the center, becoming one of the visual symbols of a new gender hegemony, and an essential part of the image of desirable womanhood. Second, I propose that describing women wearing the headscarf as "Islamists" in post-1980 academic literature turned out to be misleading. The dominant academic literature on the headscarf[3] focuses only on the aftermath of 1980s and looks at women wearing the headscarf as "new" actors of Islamism. Yet this approach undermines women's connections to earlier generations of conservative women's activism and writing.[4] Framing the headscarf within the context of Islam versus secularism has overshadowed women's involvement in right-wing politics before the 1980s. I argue that the story of conservative women columnists should be situated not just as part of the history of Islamism but also as part of the history of women's right-wing activism in Turkey.

Third, I propose that feminism in Turkey has to develop a new language and a new strategy to push back the AKP's new gender hegemony. Turkey's new gender conservatism is complex and conservative women are among the leading actors who redefine "women's rights" in conservative terms. The "mainstream" has been redefined in Turkey, and conservative women have become powerful actors of the new mainstream. This has been a challenging and divisive process for Turkey's feminists too, particularly on the question of whether or not pro-AKP conservative women could still be considered allies on women's issues. I address this question in Chapter 5, and lay out the opportunities for new strategies, alliances, and drawbacks for Turkey's feminists in their struggle to push the conservative gender hegemony back.

This book aims to problematize designators such as "Islamist women" or "Islamic feminists" to describe Turkey's conservative women. I use Deniz Kandiyoti's approach to hegemony theory as my main framework[5] and I attempt to reframe the debate on "Islamist" women along the lines of Left versus Right and progressive versus conservative, thereby dissociating "Islam" from the conservative women's movement. Using the word "Islam" to describe conservative women's politics has long exoticized them and presented their position as if it were qualitatively different from the other religiously conservative women's movements in the West. I do not claim to have a depoliticized or an "objective" position as a researcher-scholar here. Within Turkey's political climate, no one is apolitical, and neither am I a depoliticized or "objective" subject. I am aware that this reframing attempt itself is political and aims to push back religious and social conservatism that has been consolidating itself in Turkey. I hope in the coming chapters it will become clear why I argue for a reframing of the axes of political conflicts in Turkey.

Islamist women, pious women, or conservative, right-wing women?

I would like to explain the word choice in describing women as conservative, or right-wing. The women I prefer to call "conservative female journalists" in Chapter 4 have been named in various ways in the literature so far: Islamist women,[6] Islamic (or Muslim) feminists,[7] pious women,[8] conservative women,[9] or, very rarely, right-wing women.[10] This applies to naming practices of women themselves. Women have named themselves as Islamists and conservatives, and also positioned themselves on the Right. Among all these, I believe the designations that best describe this set of women's political standing are conservative and right-wing. I argue that focusing on Islam and Islamism diverted attention from the right-wing nature of Islamist activism and women's role in it. I will elaborate on this argument in Chapter 4, where I analyze women's columns. The AKP's long tenure in government and its turn to authoritarianism since 2011 calls for the rethinking of the categories used to understand and explain various actors' role in Turkish politics. In addition, I argue that resistance to authoritarianism entails questioning the categories that might have contributed to its rise in the first place and then producing a new language that would help reframe the authoritarian power center and its allies to push them back.

The term "Islamist women" is the most widely used signifier for women wearing the headscarf who actively campaigned against the headscarf ban in Turkish universities. It refers to women active in Islamist politics. Defining these women with reference to Islam emphasizes their difference, and calls to mind Islam's distinctiveness from the "West." The phrase situates the women primarily within a conflictual realm between "Islam and secularism" and "Islam and the West." Framing women in this context is a legacy of modernization theory, which has fallen short of explaining the role of religion in right-wing politics and women's engagement in them. Within the framework of modernization theory, the position of "Islamist" women demanding a "secular" education without leaving "tradition" or religion behind, seemed unexpected and "surprising" and called for research projects. It was "surprising" to see Islamist women engaging with the ideas of Western feminists and philosophers. Scholars who analyzed the headscarf via the framework of the "Islam vs. secularism" binary focused on women's relationship to secularism and saw women's adoption of secular language on a number of women's issues as promising for women's rights.[11]

Yet, when the assumptions of modernization theory (the idea that there is linear progress and women will eventually leave their "backward" religion/ tradition behind) are abandoned, the "surprise" element immediately disappears. Turkey's conservative women attended secular education institutions like everyone else because these schools were the ones available in their cities and neighborhoods while they were growing up. There is nothing surprising about the fact that young conservative women have sought success and upward social mobility, and enrolled in secular education institutions in a country where secular education was the norm.

There is nothing surprising about the fact that Turkey's conservative, or right-wing, women (named Islamist women in the literature) have internalized the gains of Turkish modernism and secularism when it comes to women's rights. They have also internalized some of the gains of feminism. As a result, their stance on women's issues often conflicts with the strict interpretations of Islam. "Islamist women" were seen as transformative agents who could change the Islamist movement from within[12] because of their criticisms of patriarchal interpretations of Islam by using secular arguments.[13] Expecting Islamist women to behave in line with the strict interpretation of the Qur'an, scholars have regularly approached conservative women as feminists, and have given their position in Turkish politics a progressive connotation even though the same women have continuously supported an authoritarian and misogynist politician and helped him to concentrate power in his own hands. This dilemma, having conservative women who adopt a language of women's rights and at the same time support a misogynist leader who pushes for a gender-conservative regime, cannot be explained with reference to "Islam versus secularism," or by attributing a "feminist voice"[14] to women who have regularly distanced themselves from feminism.

Tracing "religious" or "secular" arguments in women's writing does not mean anything in itself, as secularism and Islam are used within specific contexts and in relation to other actors of Turkish politics for strategic purposes to gain power or legitimize claims for power. In that sense, looking only at women's position in relation to gender issues has misled scholars into attributing a transformative role to conservative women. As I will illustrate in Chapter 4, women's position can best be analyzed with reference to certain issues and their relationship vis-à-vis the other actors in Turkish politics. In this book, I therefore argue that women's political standing today can best be explained with reference to their commitment to right-wing politics and the antifeminist strand within right-wing politics. Ronnee Schreiber's truly inspiring book *Righting Feminism: Conservative Women and American Politics*[15] gives a number of clues for understanding conservative women's position in contemporary Turkish politics as devout supporters of Erdoğan and the AKP. Schreiber eloquently explained how conservative women in the United States have appropriated the language of feminism to undermine it. Her framework opens up new ways of understanding the position of conservative female journalists in Turkey and their ongoing support for the AKP.

Therefore, I approach the women journalists whose work I analyzed as strong actors of Turkey's conservative Right, as subjects who actively have taken part in an ongoing struggle to define the meaning of the headscarf and reshape the political landscape in their favor, even when it meant eliminating democratic institutions and supporting an authoritarian leader. In addition, the term "Islamist" conceals the similarities between conservative women from different religions who support similar agendas across borders. For example, conservative women who support Erdoğan in Turkey and conservative women who support Donald Trump in the United States use the same right-wing arguments on a series of issues ranging from economy and foreign policy to education. The term "Islamist" amplifies religion, which is in fact a minor difference between women supporting conservative politics in these two countries.

Having Islam as the main explanatory framework restricts the possibilities to compare similar women's movements across so-called Western and non-Western countries. Yet when we look at women's movements in terms of the political alliances they engage in, it becomes clear that conservative, right-wing women's movements carry numerous similarities independent of whether they are located in Muslim or non-Muslim countries: alliance with their respective countries' conservative, right-wing political parties and active engagement with them to delegitimate the Left; emphasis on religion (whether Islam, Christianity, Judaism, Hinduism, or Buddhism); emphasis on the family, accompanied by activism against LGBT rights and abortion; active development of agendas countering feminist demands; and engagement in imperialist projects to influence the international public sphere and extend their gender vision globally.[16]

Following Tanıl Bora, I approach Islamism as one of the "main pillars of the Turkish Right."[17] Conceptualizing Islamism as separate or detached from right-wing politics has led Turkey's liberal democrats to underestimate Islamism's regressive potential. Liberal democrats situated the Islamists as an oppressed group, rather than as followers of a right-wing movement who aim to gain legitimacy by inserting their point of view into the mainstream discourse. I argue that de-emphasizing the term "Islamist" and situating women within the history of right-wing conservative politics in Turkey creates more possibilities to understand the present. In that sense, the history of so-called Islamist women should be rewritten as the history of conservative, right-wing women's activism, which significantly overlaps with the history of antifeminism in Turkey. In this book, I confine the use of the term "Islamist" to the discussions about the liberal democrats' perspective on the headscarf.

Another term that carries similar issues is "Islamic feminist." Other variants are "Muslim feminist" and "Islamist feminist." The underlying concept exoticizes Turkey's conservative women even further, making their position unique. The term "Islamic feminist" also carries modernist and orientalist biases in framing women's activism primarily within the realm of Islam and finding their engagement with feminism unexpected or paradoxical. The conservative women's relationship with feminism is complex. On the one hand, conservative women appropriate ideas from feminism but they also regularly distance themselves from feminism (with few exceptions). Politically, Turkey's conservative women have engaged with feminism in a highly selective manner.[18] Even though they have regularly criticized conservative men, they preferred to have the misogynist conservative men, not the feminist sisters, as their allies at critical junctures. In addition, as I have argued elsewhere,[19] the term "Islamic feminist" attaches a progressive connotation to conservative women's activism and therefore is misleading.

I argue that Turkey's "Islamic feminism" is a form of right-wing feminism,[20] and it has to be distinguished from the "Islamic" feminisms observed in some other Muslim-majority countries. In Malaysia, Islamic feminism, as embodied in Sisters in Islam, is blended with Marxist philosophy and used to open up space for women. In Malaysia, Islamic feminists are allies of the Left. In Turkey, women branded as Islamic feminists have been involved in right-wing politics, and as of 2018 allied with Erdoğan's repressive and authoritarian regime with few exceptions. In other Muslim countries, "Islamic feminism" refers to the efforts of women activists who, in the absence of a secular option, look for alternative religious arguments to bend and challenge the oppression of the Islamic law from within.[21] Women in Turkey, conservative or not, used to be born into an environment where they naturalized the rights and opportunities that women in other Muslim countries have been missing and fighting for: the right to drive a car, the right to vote, the right to contraception and access to abortion, the right for legal guardianship of children, the right for equal inheritance, the right to have her own money and bank account, the right to initiate divorce, the right to travel in and outside of the country without a male guardian, the right to open up a practice, the right to not to wear a headscarf, and the right to reject gender segregation, among many others. In spite of all its democratic deficiencies, Turkey's political system made it possible for a vibrant secular feminism to develop. Conservative women's activism has contributed to the marginalization of the secular in Turkey and the loss of rights and freedoms for millions of women who do not want to live a conservative religious life in Turkey. The country's conservative women leaders who are seen as "Islamic feminists" work toward marginalizing secular feminism,[22] religionize everyday life, and establish a new gender hegemony. In other words, their politics should not be confused with "Islamic feminists" elsewhere, and should be named differently.

Another term used to characterize the conservative women in academic literature is "pious."[23] This is a term women regularly use to name themselves in addition to "conservative." The problem is, the term makes their political involvement invisible and depoliticizes these strong political actors. Women also actively debate what counts and does not count as "pious" as part of their politics. Other Muslims can be included or excluded depending on the boundaries of "piety." Conservative women columnists strive to maintain control over what constitutes piety, which is based on the religious practices of educated, middle- or upper-middle-class women wearing the headscarf. They actively take part in the process of defining and policing piety.[24] This means that practices of Muslims who follow different or unfavorable religious orders, Muslims who are lower class, or the women who reject the headscarf yet continue to practice religion in the privacy of their homes are not defined or acknowledged as pious. For example, following the coup attempt in July 2016, Fethullah Gülen and his followers were quickly pushed out of "piety" and placed within the realm of "treason" and "terrorism." İhsan Eliaçık, the leader of "The Anti-Capitalist Muslims"[25] was pushed out of piety because of his critical attitude toward the AKP governments.[26] In other words, "piety" is contested and competing Muslim groups have competing interpretations of piety.

The other strength of the term "conservative," or "right-wing," to describe women's standing is that the terms "Islamist women," "Islamic feminists," or "pious women" invariably refer to the women wearing the headscarf. Although I focus on women wearing the headscarf in this work as well, I'd like to create space for the very fact that a number of conservative, right-wing women do not wear the headscarf and they continue to support the AKP's authoritarian regime.[27] On the other hand, other women wearing the headscarf (although a minority) have allied with leftist politics and strongly opposed the AKP's authoritarianism. Hüda Kaya, a member of the Turkish parliament from the leftist, pro-Kurdish party HDP (Halkların Demokratik Partisi/People's Democratic Party), is an important case in point. Similarly, groups like Anti-Capitalist Muslims and Hak ve Adalet Platformu (Platform for Rights and Justice) actively challenge the AKP's authoritarianism and neoliberal economic policies. In that sense, the term "conservative" or "right-wing" detaches women's political standing from the headscarf and opens up more analytical possibilities.

The questions and concerns that are raised in this book are similar to those raised in the literature on right-wing, or conservative, women. In *Rethinking Right-Wing Women: Gender and the Conservative Party, 1880s to the Present,* Clarisse Berthezène and Julie V. Gottlieb point out that "Conservative women have been under-researched for the paradoxical reason that they have not been of much interest to androcentric historians of the Tory Party, while they have never been embraced by women's historians because of their presumed reactionary views and their complicity with the patriarchal establishment."[28] Conservative women in Turkey, in fact, have been over-researched due to the fact that the majority of them wear headscarves. Because of the distraction caused by the debates over the headscarf ban there, Turkey's conservative women have been conceptualized as Islamist women and are rarely seen as right-wing or conservative women even though the women themselves position their activism within right-wing politics and ally with right-wing parties. As a result, the strong similarities between their and other right-wing women's political activism in Latin American countries,[29] Britain,[30] Germany,[31] India,[32] Canada,[33] the United States,[34] and Africa[35] have been overlooked, and connections between them have rarely been established.[36] In fact, the absence of research on right-wing or conservative women in Muslim-majority societies reflects the larger academic trend of treating everything Muslim as a unique case. This book aims to enter into dialogue with the research on right-wing and conservative women from other corners of the world. I believe researchers in this area will find Turkish conservative women's discourses very similar to conservative, right-wing women's discourses elsewhere. I hope readers also find insight into the specific circumstances that trigger and sharpen right-wing arguments.

Scholars have drawn attention to right-wing parties' exploitation of feminism in Europe and women's rights discourses against Muslim immigrants living in those societies.[37] As this book aims to show, the exploitation of women's rights discourses is not unique to right-wing parties in Europe. Conservative women on Turkey's religious right have provided ideological grounds for the AKP's redefinition of ideal womanhood in conservative terms. The AKP's nationalism is based on pushing half of Turkey's population outside of the nation, by embracing only those Muslims who do not challenge or threaten the party's hegemony. Conservative women have played a big role in carrying the party to power and in legitimating its nationalist and authoritarian policies.

I have to emphasize that I do not see Turkey's conservative women as a homogenous entity. There are factions and ongoing disputes among conservative women as well. I categorize these differences among conservative women into three groups: the mainstream wing, the radical wing, and the critical wing. The mainstream wing of conservative women is pro-AKP, and they are the ones who are the most visible in Turkey's new mainstream media. This book focuses on them, particularly in Chapter 4, while talking about the rise of the conservative female journalist. The radical wing disagrees with the mainstream conservative women particularly on how to interpret Islam when it comes to women's issues, and prefers a stricter male-dominated interpretation of Islam.[38] Finally, what I call the critical wing of conservative women departs from the mainstream with its critical attitude toward the AKP government. This wing has held this stance since 2010 but raised the volume of its criticisms in the aftermath of the failed coup attempt on July 15, 2016. Some of the women from this wing actively campaigned against the further concentration of power in Erdoğan's hands by supporting the No vote in the April 2017 referendum. Although they share commonalities with the mainstream conservative women on feminism, they are ready to criticize the AKP policies that marginalized feminism. There are crossovers between this critical wing and the Turkish Left, similar to the crossovers between the Turkish Right and the wing of the Left that stands close to the Right. I touch upon this group of women when I talk about potential allies against authoritarianism in Chapter 5.

Organization of the book

The first chapter provides background for debates in Turkish politics and aims to challenge the narrative that focuses on secularism versus Islamism as the main source of division in Turkey. The chapter also narrates the landmark events during the AKP's time in power to make it easier for the reader to follow the controversies picked up by the conservative female journalists whose columns are analyzed in Chapter 4.

Chapter 2 tells the story of the headscarf from the perspectives of different actors in Turkey and summarizes the most common rhetorical strategies used to defend or question the headscarf. Chapter 3 introduces the visual culture of gender depictions in Turkish newspapers and situates the discussions of the headscarf within the field of visual culture and news. In this chapter, I analyze the news photographs in four newspapers (Islamist and secular) between 2002 and 2012 and introduce three major results that have emerged from the analysis: (1) Within ten years, stories of poor women disappeared in Islamist newspapers and have been replaced by the stories of successful middle-class women wearing the headscarf. (2) Secular newspapers have become less confrontational in their depictions of the headscarf, yet they have kept their modernist narrative. (3) Female columnists wearing the headscarf have moved from the margins to the center. They have become prominent figures not only in newspapers but also on television, with their own talk shows and debate programs. They have also moved from being the critiques of establishment to the defenders of the new establishment. The chapter explains these points with examples from the data.

Chapter 4 looks at the rise of the conservative female journalists by analyzing their columns. Here, I analyze the argumentative strategies used by conservative women to justify Erdoğan's and the AKP's authoritarianism. I look at how conservative female journalists have approached a series of controversial events and issues that have deepened the polarization in Turkish society: the Gezi protests of May 2013, the peace process with the Kurds, and the restrictions on alcohol consumption. Finally, I analyze women's break with Turkey's liberal democrats as part of a hegemonic struggle to gain the power to define what counts as common sense. In this chapter I explain the process by which conservative women journalists have become part of the new establishment, legitimating not only the AKP's conservative gender vision but also the party's policies in a number of other realms.

In Chapter 5, I interpret the implications of these transformations in the image of the headscarf and in the role of the conservative female journalists for the leftist and progressive feminist movements in Turkey. How should the progressive feminist movements interact with the conservative women in a political climate in which feminism and feminists are constantly demonized by the AKP and President Erdoğan? What are the possibilities for the future of feminism in Turkey? Progressive feminists in Turkey are increasingly wary of

Islam and religion. How can they fight misogyny and Islamophobia at the same time? This chapter links the debates raised in the previous chapters to broader questions within feminism.

In Chapter 6, I discuss the potential for a new "gender equilibrium" under the AKP in Turkey. This concluding chapter sums up the findings and debates raised in the book and tries to gauge the future directions of the headscarf debates in Turkey.

1

Old Versus New Turkey

Let's look at the political background within which a significant shift in Turkey's gender regime took place. According to the Justice and Development Party's public relations terminology, Turkey's modern history is divided into two phases: old Turkey and new Turkey. Over the past sixteen years, the AKP has sought to discredit the old Turkey by framing it as a period of oppression, a period governed by a sold-out Westernized elite alienated from their own people's culture and values. Repression of religious expression is flagged as the lead characteristic of this period. In contrast, the new Turkey represents to the AKP freedom of religion, wealth, self-confidence, and power in the world. To its opponents, the new Turkey represents widescale corruption, elimination of the rule of law and democratic institutions, and a slide toward dictatorship (one-man rule). Both terms—"old Turkey" and "new Turkey"—have become part of the everyday political language in the country.

Let's start with the "old" Turkey and its main actors. How did it look for the members of an ethnically, religiously, and culturally diverse society? In the following section, I argue that the old Turkey was far more complex than how Islamist and AKP propaganda has represented it. I also question the construction of secularist-versus-Islamist divide as a lead category for analyzing society and politics in pre-AKP Turkey. The secularist-versus-Islamist divide has become "a national obsession,"[1] dominating the academic literature on Turkey particularly since the 1980s as a major explanatory axis. Kandiyoti eloquently questioned this narrative by emphasizing the alternative accounts that underlined the "long-term reincorporation of Islam into state ideology and into politics more broadly"[2] in Turkey. In the coming section, I follow up on Kandiyoti's convincing suggestion that "the secular–Islamic divide is of dubious utility from an analytic point of view"[3] and I argue that the secularist-versus-Islamist division is a convenient yet insufficient and reductive categorization for depicting the dynamics of old Turkey and what life looked like for its constituent groups.

"Old Turkey"

So-called old Turkey (1923–2002) was a project of the Enlightenment and of Western modernity. It was a response to colonialism and the growing power of Europe over the Ottoman Empire and other Muslim lands. It was a response to defeat following the First World War and the disintegration of the Ottoman Empire. The founder of modern Turkey, Mustafa Kemal, and the other Turkish modernizers thought that only with the implementation of Westernizing reforms could the new nation catch up with the West. Their ideas are similar to other modernizing and Westernizing movements at the time in Egypt, Iran, Pakistan, and Afghanistan. Qasim Amin's ideas about Western modernism, the role of religion, and the status of women in Muslim lands are very similar to Mustafa Kemal's ideas.[4] Educated in Europe and having internalized the orientalist perspective of Western powers at the time, these modernizers blamed Islam as the main reason for their defeat and their submission to colonial powers.

At that particular juncture in history between the two World Wars, the modernizers in Turkey succeeded in defeating the supporters of other political projects, Islamism among them, that vied for hegemony to shape the future of the nation. "Kemalism," in very general terms, refers to the Turkish modernizing and nation-building project led by Mustafa Kemal. It is the official ideology of the so-called old Turkey that ended the Ottoman constitutional monarchy, abolished the Caliphate, implemented the Westernization/modernization reforms in all conceivable areas of life, established a secular constitution, and marginalized the role of religious conservatism in Turkey. To this day, Turkey is the only Muslim-majority country that does not have an official religion.

Turkish modernizers cherished scientific thinking, reason, and rationality as the motor of development and progress. They made secularism, based on the French model that required the leaving behind of religious differences, a precondition for membership in the nation and political participation. Religion had to be part of private life and had to be practiced at home. Signs of religious expression for both men (beards) and women (headscarves) were not welcome in the Kemalist public sphere. Even the religious personnel were not allowed to wear their religious garb except in places of worship. For them, religion was the main source of ignorance and backwardness and, as a result, had to be kept under control.

Kemalism restructured the whole society and all its institutions (education, media and cultural institutions, political institutions, the constitution, the military) on the principle of secularism and, over time, created a powerful elite class who saw themselves as the guardians of secularism, an elite class that scholars later referred to as the "secular establishment":[5] important and powerful actors of the Kemalist secular establishment included the Republican People's Party (Cumhuriyet Halk Partisi—CHP), the party that was the driver of modernization and secular reforms and the single party until the 1950; mainstream parties on the Right and the Left; an established Westernized bureaucracy socialized into modernism and internalized secularism; the judiciary; schoolteachers committed to educating new generations on the basis of Kemalist ideals; a dedicated class of social and natural scientists and theologians at the universities; professionals such as doctors, architects, musicians and engineers; and, last but not least, the Turkish military.

For the secular establishment, backed by the military, keeping Islamism under control basically meant keeping public expressions of religion under control and suppressing those expressions they deemed related to radical Islamism. Obviously, identifying what is radical and undesirable can be a very difficult and even arbitrary task. Turkish modernizers used three major mechanisms to execute that difficult task: centralizing religious services aimed for the Sunni-Hanafi majority under the Directorate of Religious Affairs, the Diyanet; controlling religious education and knowledge production on Islam; and controlling the media through state television (Turkish Radio Television—TRT) until the early 1990s. The AKP would later use all three mechanisms, the Directorate of Religious Affairs, the education system, and the media system, to propagate its own vision of society. I will briefly mention the significance of each institution within Turkish secularism.

The directorate, whose role and function has been controversial throughout the history of modern Turkey,[6] appoints imams and other religious staff to the mosques. Established as a government branch in 1924 with a centralized structure, the directorate aimed to make sure that imams did not stray, particularly during the Friday sermons, from the versions of Islam that were sanctioned and authorized by the secular state. Imams were made the paid employees of the state and were required to preach only the approved sermons. During the 1990s, both the religious conservatives and the liberal democrats problematized the role of the directorate. Religious conservatives were not happy because of the directorate's passive role in religious affairs, and the liberal democrats were not happy because of its Sunni nature. Both groups saw the directorate as proof that the Turkish state was not truly secular: for liberal democrats, because the state did not have an equal distance from all religions and sects, and for Islamist groups it was because the state kept religion under control and limited religious expression instead of protecting religious freedom. The Directorate of Religious Affairs did not comment on the headscarf controversy and stayed neutral on this debate, which was additionally frustrating for the religious conservatives.

Institutional control of religion also meant the control of knowledge production about Islam. Institutionalized in faculties of theology, the scientific study of religion produced modernized interpretations of Islam. It should come as no surprise that it was a professor from the Faculty of Theology in Ankara who first refused a student for wearing a headscarf in his class in 1967.[7] This was the first known publicized case of a student being rejected because of the headscarf. The Faculty of Theology in Ankara interpreted the Qur'an's verses on women's veiling and modesty in a liberal way. As these verses are ambiguous, the faculty took a lenient view, and argued that the Qur'an required women to cover their chest and bosoms, not their hair. The faculty's well-known women theologians, Bahriye Üçok (1919–90) and Beyza Bilgin (1935–), argued against approaching the headscarf as a religious requirement. Both scholars drew attention to the ways in which the headscarf demarcated the boundaries between the enslaved and free Muslim women, slave Muslim women being deterred from wearing the headscarf during the early decades of Islam.[8] According to Bahriye Üçok, the headscarf was mentioned in the Qur'an within a specific context and could not be universally applied to all Muslim women as a religious requirement. Üçok became a target of threats after she expressed her views on the headscarf in a television program in 1988, and she was assassinated at the age of seventy-one by an explosive sent to her house in 1990. Her killers were never found. Islamists were the usual suspects, yet they argued that the secularists framed them for Üçok's murder.

Religion on television was controlled, too. TRT, established in 1964, was the only broadcaster until the beginning of 1990s. Although it was initially built to emulate the BBC, TRT was never able to achieve autonomy and act as an impartial public service broadcaster; it fell under the control of the governing party or parties. TRT's half-hour religious program, *İnanç Dünyası*, broadcast weekly on Thursday evenings, was a good example of both the control over religion and the concessions given to the religious conservatives following the 1980 military coup.[9] The program started with a reading of Qur'an and its translation, followed by a talk given by a religious scholar either from the Directorate of Religious Affairs or from one of the theology schools. The scholars who appeared were carefully selected to reflect a state-sanctioned and sanitized interpretation of Islam.

In spite of these institutional mechanisms, it is hard to talk about a complete and total control of religion by the secularists in Turkey. Turkish secularists' power was limited, as they had to play within a democratic political structure that, in spite of deficiencies, had instituted the separation of powers, electoral politics, and checks and balances. For example, in contrast to the Faculty of Theology in Ankara, the Faculty of Theology at Marmara University in Istanbul was religiously conservative, and its scholars played important roles within the religious right and, later, in justifying the AKP's conservative gender policies.[10] The Imam Hatip Schools that trained imams were a persistent source of controversy and a realm of struggle between the Turkish modernists and conservatives as well.[11] The modernists wanted to keep these schools limited to training imams, while the conservatives wanted to extend them in numbers, including girls in their enrollment (even though girls could not be appointed as imams). The struggle over the status of these schools within the Turkish education system entered a whole new phase after the AKP came to power in 2002.

The Turkish state's control of religion was disturbing for the members of various right-wing Islamist groups that remained a political minority in Turkey throughout the twentieth century. According to the Islamist narrative, the majority in Turkey suffered under secularist oppression. Yet a number of popular counter-narratives challenge this claim.[12] Elif Batuman's story[13] exemplifies the eclecticism that was common under the secular republic. Batuman's grandfather was both a staunch secularist and a devout Muslim who was against the headscarf. More interestingly, even the Islamist women's personal narratives challenge their political claim that the majority suffered under secular oppression and could not practice Islam. Ayşe Böhürler, a conservative Islamist journalist born in 1963, described the culture in her youth in terms similar to Batuman's story. In her account, women in Kayseri and Konya, two conservative cities in middle Anatolia, never approved of gender segregation: they were equally against overcovering and undercovering, miniskirts and long skirts, tight clothes and loose clothes. Women in these conservative cities did not tolerate the extremes. When Böhürler covered her hair and body in Islamist style, her mother did not approve of her decision, and she was also reprimanded by the women in Kayseri, who always partially covered their hair as part of their traditional attire. They said, "This may be nice in religious terms, but you should also follow the times."[14] Similar stories can be encountered all over Turkey. For the generation of women who are now in their eighties, whether they lived in rural or urban areas, the most important thing was to get an education. And the women were ready to take off the headscarf as soon as their fathers or male elders agreed to send them to school. The Islamist claim that women suffered because of the headscarf ban is only partially true. Many women who could not get an education blamed their fathers and early marriages, not the headscarf ban. Commitment to this practice was a nonissue for many women of that generation.

Religious pragmatism characterized the practice of Islam in "old" Turkey. Practicing Islam in everyday life is a demanding task: praying five times a day amid a busy schedule, with all the attendant pre-ritual preparations and covering the hair, were not seen as practical in modern life. For many Turks, enjoying life together as men and women, responsibilities to the workplace, and family came before responsibilities to God. The best time to take care of responsibilities to God was after retirement and before death. Many Turks took their pilgrimages in old age to repent for their sins. In pre-1990s Turkey, when a young woman covered her hair, the elder women who themselves wore the headscarf used to object by saying, "But you're so young, religion is not for the young. You can do that later when you get older."[15] During the 1980s many families, urban and rural, did not understand when their daughters wanted to cover their hair with the headscarf.[16] For these older generations of women, youth represented a period full of wishes, whereas the headscarf meant the repression of these desires, leaving them unfulfilled.

Under Kemalism, people were able to find a balance between everyday life and religious practice. It was quite common to meet people who would practice religion only during religious holidays and Ramazan—consuming alcohol the whole year except for the holy month, for instance. Anatolian Muslims practiced a mixture of Sunni and Alevi Islam, shamanism (the religion Turks practiced before Islam), and Christianity. During the Christian religious holidays, churches are filled with Muslims who want to obtain some holy water, even today. Lived Islam in Turkey did not follow "the book" and did not care much about what was in the book, either. Many Turks revered the Qur'an, showed it great respect and hung it on the best place on their wall as an object of worship and adoration, not to be touched again. Considering that the Qur'an was translated into Turkish only during the 1930s, which is also the period of mass literacy for Turkish citizens, this kind of disinterest in the content of the book is not surprising. The term "Anatolian Islam" refers to this laidback attitude toward religion. Yet this nonchalant and relaxed attitude to religious practice was not acceptable for the Islamist right-wing. The followers of these movements studied the Qur'an and Hadith and argued that good Muslims had to follow the book. While accusing the secularists of oppressing the Muslim majority, conservative writers like Böhürler denigrated the forms of Islam practiced by the same majority, and associated those practices with ignorance and tradition. Religiously conservative women have actively redefined "Muslim" as a "political subject."[17]

As a result of these struggles, the meaning of the term "Muslim" constantly shifts in Turkey, making its referent elusive. The ambiguity of the term creates slippages in the meaning. For example, consider the following sentence that I heard frequently from religious conservatives throughout my childhood: "This is a Muslim country, but Muslims are oppressed here." The term "Muslim," used twice, refers to two different populations in each instance. The first one, used as an adjective, refers to the whole Muslim population in Turkey, many of whom do not even primarily identify themselves as Muslims, and experience secularism not as an oppressive but as an emancipatory ideology. The second instance of the term refers to only those Muslims who claim that they are oppressed under Turkish secularism. Turkey's religious conservatives have reworked the meaning of the term "Muslim" by utilizing such slippages in their political claims. They also reworked the meaning of "secular." According to Kandiyoti, since the 1990s "the 'secular' has accrued a new layer of meaning as a term of derision when it does not carry the more sinister overtones of *putschist* or authoritarian tendencies."[18]

A neglected aspect of Kemalism is that, in spite of its anti-Islamism, it produced varieties of new interpretations of Islam that easily blended with secularism, some on the basis of Islamic mysticism, known as Sufism. This Kemalist version of religiosity emphasizes the importance of the inner world and sees any emphasis on the outside appearance as a distraction from the spiritual journey. Some famous women representatives of these interpretations included Nezihe Araz (1920–2009), who extensively wrote about Islam, Mohammad, and women spiritual leaders of Anatolia, and who was also a strong defender of the Atatürk reforms. Araz never adopted nor defended the headscarf. Today, a famous spiritual woman leader, Cemalnur Sargut, who does not cover her hair in public, represents this Kemalist-Sufi trend. According to her interpretation, the hijab (*tesettür*) should be in the heart. With followers mainly among educated upper-class secular people, Sargut is a common guest in secular television stations.[19] Another famous Kemalist interpretation of Islam was Yaşar Nuri Öztürk's approach, which became immensely popular among secular circles during the 1990s.[20] Fulya Atacan's important work on the Cerrahi sect shows another instance of religious practice interpreted through a Kemalist framework.[21] The scholarly work emphasizing these interpretations of Islam remained in the shadows and rarely received attention because of the overemphasis on Islamism during the 1990s.

By the 1990s, Kemalist ideology and the secularism of the republic were internalized by the masses and had become common sense in Turkey. Contrary to what the AKP's leadership propagates, Turkish modernizers were not simply a detached, Westernized, alienated elite. On the contrary, their ideas have resonated broadly and become the new normal and mainstream in Turkish society into the twenty-first century. A Tesev study conducted in February 1999[22] showed widespread support for the modernization reforms, particularly in the area of civil code and the family. Eighty percent of Turks said they were against marriage as defined by Islamic law, against Islamic inheritance laws, and against polygamy.[23] Only those who defined themselves as very religious supported a civil code based on Islam. The majority said they were against the restrictions on the headscarf, but they did not like it when this issue was used by the Islamist parties for political ends.[24]

Turkey's modernizers have successfully transitioned the country to a multiparty parliamentary democracy. In spite of deficiencies, they have institutionalized both the separation of powers and checks and balances into the system. In addition to the modernizers' success in creating a democratic system in a highly volatile region full of dictatorships, they made women's basic rights the norm. Universal mandatory elementary coeducation for boys and girls was probably their most significant achievement. Women were able to get a good education, equal to men's at all levels. Kemalism succeeded in creating a new professional class of women, putting Turkey ahead of many European countries in terms of its educated women professionals (the number of women in prestigious professions such as law and medicine in particular).[25] Both secular and religious women, women with or without the headscarf, benefited immensely from the Kemalist reforms because these changes made the idea of equality between men and women the new normal. Although Kemalism closed off a number of opportunities for conservative women wearing the headscarf, the opportunities it provided to all women (making girls' education an important norm, rather than the exception) opened the way for these women's primary education too, making religious texts accessible to them and helping them to develop a critique of Kemalism.

This does not mean that Turkish modernists eliminated patriarchal domination and sexism altogether. Structural problems remained for women's rights, but important gains were made, thanks to the Kemalist and feminist women's activism throughout the 1980s and 1990s. The system had a number of other significant issues as well: Kurds were marginalized, leading to the emergence of the PKK (Partiya Karkerên Kurdistanê—The Kurdistan Workers' Party) and armed conflict in 1984. In spite of the institutionalization of democratic mechanisms, the democratic process was interrupted several times by military coups and interventions since the 1960s, giving the Turkish military overwhelming power over the parliamentary system, particularly after the 1980 military coup.

The military coup of 1980 was pivotal in reshaping the political system for decades to come. The military regime rewrote the Turkish constitution to limit democratic rights and freedoms considerably. The constitution was approved by popular vote in 1983. The military regime also institutionalized the role of the military in civil politics and installed the mechanisms that situated the military beyond civil control or oversight.[26] Deeply untrusting of politicians, military generals were placed in a position to keep an eye on politics and make sure the government did not stray from the nationalist Kemalist ideals. The military oversight of politics meant the tight control of Kurdish demands for cultural rights and Islamist demands for more religious rights.

Paradoxically, the 1980 military coup is also credited with the rise of the religious right, also called Islamist movements in Turkey because the coup makers were interested in creating a new synthesis between Islam and Turkish nationalism to suppress and decimate the leftist movements in the country. Kandiyoti draws attention to how the conservative right in the 1960s used Islam as an "ideological counterforce" against socialism.[27] The 1980 military coup took this approach to new heights and provided new opportunities and restrictions for Turkey's Islamists. The military approached the Islamist parties that were the AKP's predecessors with suspicion, yet the Welfare Party from the religious far right eventually filled the vacuum created by the 1980 coup's suppression of the Left. The ban on the headscarf in universities, implemented officially for the first time, was one of the major restrictions that appeared under the presidency of Kenan Evren, the military general who led the coup. Within the new opportunity structures, and the ensuing economic liberalization under Turgut Özal's center-right government, religious conservatives were able to insert their voices and vision of society into the political discourse.

In the 1990s, Islamism in Turkey could be grouped into two major strands: Islamism that followed a top-down strategy aiming at seizing the power of the government using party politics, versus Islamism that followed a bottom-up strategy. The Fethullah Gülen movement was a typical representative of the bottom-up strategy. Instead of focusing on parliamentary politics, they focused on education, schooling, media power, and publicity strategies to give Islam a friendly face and expand the role of religion in society from the ground up. In addition to extensive public relations, Fethullah Gülen's movement also focused on secretly placing its trained members into key positions in the Turkish bureaucracy and military. These different groups within the Islamist right-wing did not necessarily get along with each other, yet they shared a critical attitude toward Kemalism and the Westernization reforms of the early republic.[28]

Although Islamism can be seen as a major critique of Kemalism, Kemalism also produced its secular critiques, based on leftist, socialist, and liberal democratic approaches. By the 1990s, Turkey's liberal democrats and academics in the social sciences at leading universities in Istanbul considered Kemalism a successful project that had accomplished its mission in the country. The founding ideology had become like an old dress that could not fit society anymore. Many from the Left argued that Kemalism had completed its course with its accomplishments and failures and it was now time to move on to a more inclusive, participatory democracy that incorporated the Islamists and the Kurds into the system through peaceful means. Some scholars argued that it was time for a new phase in Kemalism, for the Second Republic.[29] In its first phase, Kemalism succeeded in mobilizing large masses, providing coeducation, mass literacy, and opportunities to very different groups of people on the condition that they leave their differences behind. Now, they argued, it was time to move forward by eliminating the repressive aspects of the system and its democratic deficiencies. They defined the creation of a new civil constitution that broadened individual rights and freedoms as one of the most urgent tasks in the country.

When the AKP came to power in 2002, many secular critiques of Kemalism had long been arguing that the democratic mechanisms had to be restored by curtailing the continuing impact and the role of the military in Turkish politics. They argued for a new social and inclusionary contract for the people of Turkey. They were also more or less convinced that right-wing Islamist politicians had reevaluated their position in relation to democracy, seeing it not just as a means to an end. The country had been experimenting with religiously conservative politicians for a while in many cities' municipalities, and Erdoğan in particular had been seen successful in creating an open persona. His temper and authoritarian personality were seen as minor issues at the time, a reflection of the macho neighborhood culture in which he grew up. The main problems for further democratization were seen as the role of the military in politics, and the structures that prevented the full inclusion of the Alevis, Kurds, Islamists, and other ethnic and religious minorities in the system via representation in the parliament. One important impediment to inclusive participation was the 10 percent threshold that prevented the small parties representing diverse views from getting into the parliament. The threshold for a majority government was also set low, at 35 percent, making it possible for a party to dominate the parliament with a relatively small share of votes. The reshaping of the electoral system to create a more inclusive parliament that represented diverse views was among the agendas and subjects of debate. Eliminating the restrictions on freedom of expression, as well as broaching taboo topics such as Armenian genocide and the Kurdish issue in public discussion, were also on the agenda. Recep Tayyip Erdoğan himself had served jail time for four months because he had read aloud a nationalist poem during a public rally. The Turkish judiciary system based on Kemalist principles had interpreted this as a case of hate speech.[30] According to Turkish liberal democrats, such mechanisms of political repression had to be eliminated.

The AKP came to power in a political climate where both secular and Islamist critiques of Kemalism were loud with demands for more freedoms and democratization and where the previous parties and coalitions had failed to bring comprehensive change. European Union entry reforms were on the horizon. Public opinion polls indicated widespread support for EU candidacy to facilitate change, even though there was resistance from some parts of the Kemalist establishment and the military. Democratization entailed tackling a series of issues head on: ending the armed conflict with the PKK through peaceful means and expanding freedoms and individual rights for the Kurds, rethinking the meaning of secularism in Turkey, and restructuring the media system to secure freedom of expression and protect research and free speech, guarding academics and journalists from prosecution. When the AKP came to power, Kurds, tired of violence in the region, were waiting for solutions, women in favor of the headscarf were waiting for the elimination of the ban, liberal democrats were pushing for a more inclusive democracy, and feminist organizations were pushing for the elimination of gender discrimination in all areas of life and had succeeded a great deal prior to 2002.

Let's see how the AKP responded to all these challenges by looking at the major developments and relevant yardstick events under the AKP in Turkey. Table 1.1 recounts the history of the AKP in a chronological manner, following the timeline of elections and other major significant events. Having these events in mind will be helpful to the reader as we analyze the images of headscarf in the newspapers, and the conservative women's columns. The images analyzed in Chapter 2 come from the national elections of 2002, 2007, and 2011.

Table 1.1 Timeline of AKP rule, 2002–18

Date		Event
2002	November 3	National elections; the AKP comes to power
2004	December 16	EU starts accession negotiations with Turkey
2007	January 19	Armenian journalist Hrant Dink murdered
2007	July 12	Ergenekon investigations start to end military tutelage[a]
2007	July 22	The AKP wins elections following the crisis over Abdullah Gül's nomination to presidency; the AKP faces a closure trial by the Constitutional Court
2010	September 12	Constitutional referendum; the AKP gains control over the judiciary
2011	June 12	National elections; the AKP wins for the third time
2011	December 28	Roboski/Uludere Massacre; Turkish armed forces kill 34 Kurdish smugglers at the Turkish–Iraqi border; the AKP government defends the armed forces
2012	February 7	Conflict between Fethullah Gülen and the AKP erupts for the first time over Turkey's National Security Agency
2013	February 15	Negotiations with the Kurdish PKK gains momentum after Erdoğan names it a "solution process" (also called "peace process")[b]
2013	May 31	Gezi protests erupts
2013	December 17–25	Gülenists leak tape recordings of conversations involving top AKP representatives, including Erdoğan. Corruption scandals about the AKP government erupt
2014	August 10	National elections for the new president; Erdoğan becomes president after Abdullah Gül
2015	June 7	National elections; the AKP loses its majority in the parliament, the coalition attempts fail
2015	November 1	National elections; the AKP regains the parliamentary majority
2016	July 15	Coup attempt against Erdoğan takes place and fails; Erdoğan holds the Gülenists responsible
2017	April 16	Constitutional referendum takes place to change the Turkish political system from parliamentary democracy to a presidential system, giving Erdoğan extraordinary powers over the executive, legislative, and judicial branches
2018	June 24	National snap elections (scheduled originally in 2019) put the new presidential system into effect

a *BBC Türkçe*, "Dokuz Soruda Ergenekon Davası," February 17, 2013. Available online: https://www.bbc.com/turkce/ozeldosyalar/2013/02/130217_rengin_ergenekon (accessed December 8, 2018).

b According to Tanıl Bora, *Cerayanlar*, and others, this process started earlier, in 2009 when Turkey's National Intelligence Organization (MIT) had started secret talks with the PKK in Oslo. I prefer to take 2013 as a landmark where the AKP started its "sensible people" PR initiative to explain the "peace process" (also called "solution process") to the masses.

"New Turkey" under the Justice and Development Party

The Justice and Development Party (Adalet ve Kalkınma Partisi, the AKP) came to power with a parliamentary majority of 36 percent on November 3, 2002. This majority gave the party executive power as a single party (without a coalition partner) within the electoral system that has been problematized by the liberal democrats. In its initial years, the AKP was described by some as a "Muslim democrat"[31] party and by others as a "conservative democrat"[32] or "moderate Islamist."[33] The party itself used "Muslim Democrats" to describe themselves with reference to Christian Democrats in Europe. Esen and Gumuscu argue that at the moment competitive authoritarianism best characterizes the AKP. Within this model, the elections take place on a playing field so skewed in favor of the incumbent party that the opposition parties do not stand a chance of winning elections. By this measure, Turkey fits the competitive authoritarian model in all indicators and "no longer satisfies even the minimum requirements of democracy."[34]

In its first term, the AKP tried to appease the secular elite and prove their fears unjustified. The AKP focused its energy on a goal that many thought was unlikely to be pursued by a party with an anti-Western discourse: candidacy for the European Union. The party passed major democratic reform packages on December 16, 2004 that gained them the support of the liberal democrats in the years to come. In these initial years, the AKP and Erdoğan repeatedly mentioned their commitment to secularism and their endorsement of the current system of government. One important way of appeasing the secularist fears was to keep the debate on the headscarf out of focus. The issue came to the surface again not because of the headscarf ban in the universities but because of the exclusion of the AKP representatives' wives from official receptions.[35] In these initial years, where the secular establishment was still in power, AKP representatives tended to keep their wives, with headscarves, behind the scenes.

The AKP did not bring the headscarf issue to the fore until the end of its first term, when Abdullah Gül's presidency had become a major point of contention. Gül's appointment meant that the headscarf would be carried to the very top of the Turkish state and would be part of how Turkey was represented to the outside world. For the secular establishment, this represented a big blow to Turkey's secular image in the West. They were also worried that the AKP's having the control of both the parliament and the president's office would shift the balance of power in the country,[36] and they protested. In 2007, with the leadership of the Republican People's Party, huge rallies were held in Turkey's largest cities, to protest against the AKP. Around the same time, the military issued a statement on its webpage, a statement that was interpreted by many as an electronic coup, emphasizing the military's commitment to Turkish secularism. This was followed by a lawsuit aimed at the AKP's closure because of the party's violations of the main principles of secularism in the Turkish Republic. National elections took place within this tense environment.

The national elections on July 22, 2007 revealed that the majority of Turkish voters did not approve of these secularist pressures or dictates by the military. The AKP increased its vote by 12 percent and consolidated its power. Seen as an approval by the electorate, and with the majority in the parliament to elect Gül as president, the AKP sent Gül to Çankaya, with Hayrünnisa Gül as First Lady wearing a headscarf. With their second victory, the AKP decided to focus on the headscarf problem in its second term. In 2008, the party wanted to solve this problem once and for all by making wearing the headscarf a constitutional right. This move created one of the first major cracks in the alliance between the AKP and the liberal democrats. The liberal democrats interpreted this move as trying to circumvent the problem by using a back door. Instead of defending all types of clothes, and removing other possible restrictions and discriminations, focusing only on the headscarf by changing a foundational document was not the proper way to remove the ban.

During the Justice and Development Party's second term, concerns started to appear over the party's democratic performance and Erdoğan's behavior toward the media. Armenian journalist Hrant Dink was murdered in front of his newspaper's (*Agos*) building in Istanbul in 2007. Not only was the case never brought to justice but the government also seemed to protect the nationalist suspects, bringing up significant questions about the AKP's commitment to the rule of law. The observers who closely followed the AKP's politics started to warn about the party's clientelism and the structural changes that the party had been undertaking.[37] The party aggressively replaced the cadres in important government institutions with its own committed members. The AKP's clientelist policies and all the other structural changes constantly created controversies and gave enough fodder to both the opponents and the supporters. The Ergenekon trials, where a group of ultranational secularists (military officials and journalists) were accused of plotting a coup against the AKP government, were a case in point. While some saw this as an opportunity to genuinely curb the power of the military, for others it was a tactic to replace one form of authoritarianism with another, as many journalists and military officials on the opposition side were linked to the coup plot without evidence and sent to jail. So, were these trials a move toward democratization or a move by the AKP to silence the opposition?

During these trials, the AKP had the support of Fethullah Gülen's movement, which was very well organized within government institutions and bureaucracy. The Gülen movement provided the AKP with a skilled public relations machine both inside and outside of Turkey and helped Erdoğan to keep a positive image. The AKP later blamed the Gülen movement for wrongdoings in these trials.

The party's approach to the Kurdish issue created similar questions over the party's program of "democratization." The AKP lifted the ban on broadcasting in the Kurdish language in June 2008, but monopolized Kurdish-language broadcasting and kept it limited to the state television, TRT, not allowing any private broadcasters to offer programs in the Kurdish language. Having the Kurdish language on air was something to celebrate for many, yet for others TRT's monopoly revealed the AKP's limited approach to "democracy" and was a point of concern. An institute that included the study of the Kurdish language at the graduate level was opened in Mardin, a development which was seen as revolutionary by many, yet the institute faced tremendous bureaucratic difficulties that made it difficult to function in practice.[38]

On September 12, 2010, a year before the national elections, a very divisive constitutional referendum took place. The date was a direct reference to the anniversary of the 1980 military coup. The AKP proposed a number of amendments to the 1982 constitution made by the military. Under the revised constitution, the trial and sentencing of Kenan Evren, the general who led the 1989 coup, would be possible. The amendments included changes in the judicial system and changes in the role of the president. The presidents in the Turkish system were elected by the parliament and had a limited, symbolic role. Amendments proposed the election of the presidents by popular vote. These proposals were early signs that deeper structural changes were on the way.

Three major campaigns were organized in favor or in opposition to the amendments. The Yes campaign by the AKP supported and promoted the changes. The No campaign opposed the amendments on very important grounds: that instead of securing independent courts, the changes proposed for the judiciary would bring it under total control of the AKP as the executive power. Even though No campaigners had legitimate concerns about the amendments, they voiced their opposition mostly in the language of secularist nationalism that made it easy for the AKP to frame them as the representatives of "old" Turkey who opposed the democratization process. Tired of the secular establishment's constant recourse to secularist nationalism, the liberal democrats supported the proposed constitutional amendments with their "not enough but yes" campaign. Even though the amendments fell short of making structural changes for further democratization (for example, the AKP defended the controversial 10 percent threshold), the campaigners still saw some potential in the amendments.

The AKP was able to pass the proposed amendments in the referendum. In the aftermath of referendum, the country experienced a brief, deceptive, period of democratic opening. Books about the Armenian genocide appeared on bookshelves. Kurdish perspectives on the Kurdish issue became visible on television. For the first time in years, Labor Day (May 1) was celebrated at Taksim Square in Istanbul in 2011 with the participation of numerous leftist groups, Kurds, gays, and lesbians. Charges, although symbolic, were brought against Kenan Evren. The debate programs on television discussed the Dersim massacre at length, as part of the atrocities committed during the Kemalist nation-building process. Yet the debates on Dersim in particular were not part of an honest project of coming to terms with the past; they were part of a process of political delegitimation aimed at Turkish Kemalists and modernizers, as the AKP was careful in selecting only those events that would work against the Republican People's Party, the AKP's main opponent.

The AKP's power was tested in another national election in June 2011 that brought another victory for the AKP. By then, it had become clear to many liberal democrats that the AKP had not proposed the constitutional amendments with democratization in mind. The amendments helped the AKP to establish control over the judiciary with the majority power to appoint the judges. Erdoğan's language became more divisive, and concerns about increasing authoritarianism became common among the opposition. Controversies over high taxes on alcohol, religious education, restrictions on the media and the internet, and restrictions on abortion followed. Peace negotiations with the Kurds went hand in hand with large-scale imprisonment of Kurdish representatives from municipalities. The party regularly passed new legislature without much discussion and made decisions that violated the law. One major example was the construction of a new presidential residence, the White Palace, in an area with high symbolic power: a forest donated by the founder of modern Turkey, Atatürk. The construction continued against the court decisions. Besides the construction of White Palace, almost all the other construction work sanctioned by the AKP was problematic, too, particularly in Istanbul. Mega-construction projects that overhauled the city were undertaken mostly by pro-AKP businesses, creating a new conservative wealthy class.[39] Erdoğan imposed the building of a third bridge in Istanbul and named it after one of the brutal Ottoman Sultans, Yavuz Sultan Selim, famous with the massacre of Alevis in the 1500s, in spite of strong opposition coming from the Alevi population in Turkey. He also revitalized the controversial project of building a mosque at one of the cosmopolitan centers of Istanbul, at Gezi Park in Taksim Square.

During May 2013, the restlessness caused by the authoritarian attitude of the party tipped over. In this extremely tense environment, the unending police brutality toward young students who wanted to protect a small park triggered the largest mass demonstration in Istanbul in the history of modern Turkey. Gezi Park protests pushed millions of people, young and old, out onto the streets. People who would otherwise never come together ran onto the streets to protest against Erdoğan's government in spite of the heavy use of gas and water cannons. Gezi also exposed how the pro-AKP media had turned into a propaganda machine, with numerous pro-AKP newspapers having exactly the same headlines during the protests. It also became clear that the AKP had succeeded in taming the secular media through fines and business relations. Aydın Doğan's CNN Türk became the iconic example of this when the news channel broadcast a documentary on the reproduction patterns of penguins during the height of Gezi protests, when millions in Istanbul were on the streets. It took hours for the main news stations to start reporting about the protests at the heart of the country. During Gezi, media organizations throughout Istanbul became targets of protests.

The AKP government's brutal response to the Gezi protests and Erdoğan's uncompromising attitude were a wake-up call for many who had supported the AKP for more democratization (the remaining liberal democrats, who were still unsure about the AKP's authoritarian nature). During the Gezi protests, instead of calming down the masses and listening to them, Erdoğan increased the tension and called the protests a coup against the AKP. Coupled with the fear of a coup similar to the one that took place in Egypt around the same time, Erdoğan tightened his grip day by day. In the months following Gezi, the AKP did not address the public's concerns but turned to even more authoritarian politics. Erdoğan's heavy-handed policies tightened the controls over the media and silenced critical voices more and more. Since 2013, the AKP passed new legislation that gave enormous powers to the police and de facto annulled the right to protest.

December 17, 2013 witnessed a major breakdown between the AKP and its long-time supporter Fethullah Gülen, the leader of the most powerful Islamist community in Turkey. The Gülen movement, very powerful and secretive, had organized within the government and bureaucracy and had provided the main public relations support for the AKP both inside and outside of Turkey. In December, public prosecutors connected to the movement revealed scandalous corruption cases that involved Erdoğan, his family, and other top AKP ministers.

At the end of the same year, *Zaman*, the major publication of the Gülen movement, which is also analyzed in this book, turned against the AKP, creating a big turning point in Islamist media in Turkey. Gülen supporters in the government and bureaucracy started to leak phone conversations—illegally obtained, yet showing the degree of Erdoğan's control over the media bosses and editors with direct phone calls and threats. Erdoğan named the organization of his former ally "the parallel government." The rift between the two culminated in a coup attempt in July 2016.

In 2014, the presidential term of Abdullah Gül, who was elected by the parliament in 2007, came to its end. The amendments made to the constitution required that the new president be elected by popular vote. Erdoğan was among the three candidates for the office. The election period witnessed the rise of the Kurdish opposition leader Selahattin Demirtaş, a rival that could threaten the AKP's right-wing populism with populism from the Left within the Turkish political scene. Yet neither he nor the other candidate from the Republican People's Party, Ekmeleddin İhsanoğlu, were able to defeat Erdoğan, who tapped into all the resources of his party and the government to silence and marginalize his opponents in this very significant election. TRT, which is supposed to stay neutral during elections, gave overwhelming coverage to Erdoğan at the expense of the other candidates.[40] Istanbul municipality is run by the AKP, who changed the whole city's visual landscape with Erdoğan's elections posters, leaving no room for the posters of the opposition candidates.

Following his victory, Erdoğan moved to the White Palace, built in violation of court orders, and never accepted to be an impartial figure above politics as stated in the constitution. Although Erdoğan won the presidential elections, Selahattin Demirtaş and his party, People's Democratic Party (Halkların Demokratik Partisi—HDP), emerged as a strong opposition to the AKP during the elections. Demirtaş not only made the Kurdish voice heard in the western provinces of Turkey but also presented himself as the representative of all the oppressed people who suffered from the AKP's authoritarian and neoliberal policies. In the June 2015 national elections, the pro-Kurdish HDP increased its vote significantly, passing the threshold of 10 percent for the first time, and entered the parliament, making the AKP lose its parliamentary majority for the first time since 2002. This was a very important opportunity for all the parties in opposition to challenge AKP and Erdoğan in their authoritarian policies and corruption. With no party having the majority, a coalition government had to be formed. This is where things went awry, as the ultranationalist Nationalist Movement Party (Milli Hareket Partisi—MHP) rejected any collaboration at all with the pro-Kurdish HDP. The Republican People's Party (Cumhuriyet Halk Partisi—CHP) also had the problem of containing the anti-Kurdish wing of the party. The general anti-Kurdish sentiment of the Turkish political establishment gave the AKP a great opportunity. As the coalition talks failed, President Erdoğan decided to renew the elections in November the same year. Using an attack on the Turkish police by the PKK (preceded by the Suruç attacks) as a pretext, the AKP ended peace talks with the Kurds and started to crack down on the Kurdish regions in the east while engaging a heavy anti-HDP propaganda in the mainstream pro-AKP media. This strategy paid off. In the November 2015 elections, both the HDP and the nationalist MHP lost votes to the AKP, giving the party a parliamentary majority again.

The failed coup attempt on July 15, 2016 gave a new momentum to increasing authoritarianism in Turkey. Turkish scholars are still developing a language to talk about the coup itself, most aspects of which remained in the dark, and about its aftermath. Following the coup, Erdoğan declared a state of emergency and tightened his grip. The media entered into a new phase of repression.[41] Since July 2016, around 150 media outlets have been closed[42] and around five thousand academics, many of whom did not have any relations or ties with the Fethullah Gülen movement, have lost their jobs by executive decree.[43] The repression of press freedom impacted even foreign journalists.[44] Between the summer of 2016 and the summer of 2018, the AKP, under the state of emergency, prepared the country for the transition to the "Turkish style" presidential system where the legislative, executive, and judicial powers could be united under Erdoğan's rule. A constitutional referendum took place on April 16, 2017 to change the constitution to fulfill that vision; and the new system was put into place following the national snap elections on June 24, 2018. These elections were originally scheduled to take place on November 3, 2019.

The country has stayed under the state of emergency with rights and freedoms severely curbed until after the June 24, 2018 national snap election where Erdoğan consolidated his power fully. The 2018 election ended the parliamentary system in Turkey and instituted a "presidential" system modified to give Erdoğan extraordinary powers over all branches of government.[45] According to the opposition, the lifting of the state of emergency did not mean going back to "normal." On the contrary, it signified the completion of the process that had made the state of emergency and repression of dissent the country's new normal.[46]

In 2012, Erdoğan had spoken against the "separation of powers."[47] The 2018 elections signified the realization of his dream to put an end to the separation of powers which he long saw as an impediment to do whatever he wanted to "serve" the people. The elections signified the realization of his other dream to rule the country like a company, in a managerial style.[48] Yet, the party had not stayed in power merely because of its success in receiving popular support: Cenk Aygül documented how the AKP manipulated the 2014 local elections through redistricting that put the main opposition party at a great disadvantage. He argued that "the election success of the AKP significantly depended on a radical overhaul of the election system in Turkey."[49]

The party, especially in the aftermath of 2011, can be characterized as neo-authoritarian, as many have pointed out the similarities between Erdoğan and Russia's Putin. According to Yılmaz, the AKP's Islamist populist language is similar to the right-wing populist parties in Europe and the leftist popular parties in Latin America.[50] As populist parties imagine a divide between the elites and the masses, the elite that the AKP targets in Turkey is the secular, Westernized, educated elite that established the modern Turkey. The AKP presents this elite as corrupt and not part of the culture, like a foreign element.

Erdoğan and the AKP members have reduced the concept of democracy to a simple equation. Democracy in their lexicon is equal to the ballot box. The majority that comes from the ballot box represents the "national will" and as 45–50 percent of the votes go to the AKP, it is the AKP that represents the national will. Erdoğan's rhetoric does not define Turkish citizens who do not support the AKP as part of the "nation." The picture in Turkey looks very grim, particularly for those who do not support AKP. Scholars and journalists on the opposition increasingly describe the situation as the rise of fascism and totalitarianism in Turkey.[51] In the new Turkey there is no autonomous institution at the moment that could keep the AKP under control and push the party to be accountable. All the democratic institutions that were in place to control those in power were framed as impediments to the actualization of the national will. Institutions that had at least some autonomy, such as the judiciary and the Higher Committee of Elections, have lost their autonomy altogether. The major institutions that checked those in power and controlled the budget and spending of the government were shot down and eliminated.

The mechanisms that were used by the Kemalists to control religion were adopted by the AKP and used for the propagation of religion at an unprecedented level. The AKP gave increasing power to the Directorate of Religious Affairs, the Diyanet, and extended its budget. The directorate became a more visible actor in Turkish media and politics and has even established its own television channel.[52] Religion has become more noticeable and visible in the daily lives of Turks, particularly in Istanbul. Istanbul has always been an important battleground for right-wing Islamist politics. In addition to the symbolic Taksim Mosque project, another controversial grand-mosque project has been in progress in Çamlıca, one of the highest hills in the city, making the mosque visible from very different parts of the city. At the moment, Istanbul is home to more than three thousand mosques. In addition to the construction of new mosques in a city already full of them, the calls to prayers were adjusted to a much higher volume, making the sound of religion greater and more present in the daily life of the city. The morning call to prayer in particular, which is very early before dawn, wakes up residents who do not practice religion at odd hours.

Similar to Kemalists, the AKP aimed for control over knowledge production. The higher education institutions have also had their share of the transformation taking place in the country. The AKP appointed a pro-AKP chair as the head of the Higher Education Council (YÖK). Throughout the AKP's rule, the Middle East Technical University (ODTÜ), which is known for its tradition of protest, has repeatedly become the target of Erdoğan's and the AKP's attacks. The university's resources were diminished, and its rector and faculty were insulted openly by Erdoğan. One final attack on academia took place when the Academics for Peace Initiative called on the government on January 11, 2016 to end their siege of the Kurdish towns in southern Turkey. Erdoğan called these 1,128 academics traitors and asked the judiciary to take action against them. As a result, academics were arrested, lost their jobs, and were put on trial for charges of supporting terrorism. Boğaziçi University also became one of the targets.[53]

The AKP had a total overhaul of the education system in Turkey and reinserted the conservative perspective into schools and curricula. In line with the Erdoğan's project of educating "pious" generations, a Sunni nationalist rhetoric that glorifies the Ottoman past has become part of the curriculum. High schools that provide secular education were converted into Imam Hatip Schools that provide religious education. The number of Imam Hatip Schools has more than doubled since 2003[54] and the number of students enrolled in these schools has increased tenfold.[55] According to Erdoğan's own claim, the number of students enrolled in these schools has jumped from sixty thousand to more than one million.[56] Education in Imam Hatips encourage conservative gender relations, they separate boys and girls, and they encourage female students to wear the headscarf in all classes.[57]

I took a photograph of a billboard, in the summer of 2015, in Sefaköy, Istanbul (Figure 1.1). This is an advertisement for a private school showing a small girl with a headscarf beside a boy. This picture would have been unthinkable in

Figure 1.1   Billboard advertising a pre-K and K–12 school in Istanbul. Photograph by the author.

Turkey in 2002. A huge shift has taken place: the headscarf has become mainstream even for young schoolgirls in Turkey. In a visit to Atatürk Airport in Istanbul in 2018, four out of five policewomen in my sight were wearing a headscarf. Nobody would believe that could be possible in Turkey sixteen years previously. In sixteen years, the AKP had changed the structure of politics, culture, and society in Turkey.

Finally, the AKP has, through multiple means, succeeded in turning mainstream newspapers and television into a pro-AKP propaganda machine that pumps only the party's version of events into homes every night. It is to this point that I turn next.

Media under the AKP

In 2002, when the AKP came to power, the Turkish media constituted a complex scene. The extent of media production under private ownership and the accompanying diversity were simply incomparable to the 1980s, when television and radio broadcasts were still under the monopoly of the state. The print media were highly diversified, ranging from Islamist right-wing newspapers to the Left, from more serious papers to tabloids. In other words, a broad range of views were able to find outlets for expression. The mainstream media were secular by default, with high circulation rates. Right-wing Islamist newspapers catered to niche audiences who were devout Muslims or political Islamists.

In spite of a pretty diverse media environment, there were still significant restrictions on the freedom of the press. Turkey ranked as "partly free" in the Freedom House index until 2014 (when it changed to "not free")[58] and was constantly criticized by international media watch organizations. Repression of the Kurds, the Armenian genocide, and the cult of Atatürk were taboo topics and led to the prosecution of journalists from time to time, depending on the political conjuncture. The increasing concentration of ownership in the media sector was yet another significant problem.[59] Aydın Doğan, the owner of the Hürriyet Group, had become a media mogul, owning around 40 percent of the newspapers and magazines on the market as well as radio and television stations.[60] Aydın Doğan owned the high-selling catch-all tabloids (*Hürriyet* and *Posta*) on the one hand, and the left-wing *Radikal* on the other. Doğan owned large shares in the non-media sector, compromising the ability of journalists working for his newspapers to report on the practices of companies owned by him. Doğan's main competitor, Dinç Bilgin, was the owner of *Sabah*, and it was common to find them campaigning against each other. As a result, the journalists faced pressure both from the government and the owners, and sometimes they themselves failed to follow the ethics of the profession. In other words, re-regulation of the media sector was needed in Turkey, both to prevent conflict of interests due to cross-ownership and to remove the restrictions on the freedom of the press, instituting the role of the media as a democratic agent and as the fourth estate.

The AKP came onto the scene with the full support of the right-wing Islamist newspapers: *Anadolu'da Vakit* (formerly *Akit*), *Yeni Şafak*, and *Zaman*. Erdoğan was very quick to understand the power of the media and to use the opportunities to reshape the media structure in Turkey to the party's advantage.[61] AKP re-regulated and restructured the Turkish media system as a whole, not to strengthen the media's role as the fourth estate, but to turn the mainstream media into a propaganda machine for the party. The AKP was able to diminish the power of the big media owners, yet the result was not more diversity but the elimination of criticism and opposition. In 2007, the government confiscated Dinç Bilgin's Sabah Media Group because of its debts, and the newspaper was sold to a pro-AKP business group run by Erdoğan's in-laws, making this a yardstick event that shifted the powers in the media.[62] In 2009, Aydın Doğan received the highest tax fine in Turkish history that pushed him to sell his media assets, again, to Demirören Holding, a pro-AKP business group. With these big shifts in ownership, a considerable amount of mainstream media passed to businesses that are closely linked to Erdoğan and benefit from the AKP's policies. These media companies eventually laid off in high numbers journalists who were critical of the AKP and the Erdoğan regime. While the critical newspapers were silenced and intimidated and their journalists not accredited, the AKP-friendly Islamist newspaper *Yeni Şafak* received tax cuts and was rewarded for its unconditional allegiance to Erdoğan.[63] In March 2018, Aydın Doğan, once Turkey's media mogul, sold all his remaining media assets to the pro-AKP Demirören. This transfer, probably the largest in the history of Turkey, made Demirören the biggest media owner in the country, and increased the market share of the print media that give "full support to the government" to 66 percent.[64]

Dividing the Turkish media into two camps, secular versus Islamist, has been the dominant way of categorizing newspapers in both the academic literature and popular parlance.[65] Yet the AKP's policies toward the media and changes in the ownership structures made the usual categorization of the Turkish media secular and Islamist redundant. Many secular-seeming newspapers (without religious content, featuring images of scantily clad women) could continue only as far as they supported the AKP or toned down their criticisms. Newspapers known as secular are now under the control of pro-AKP owners and cannot publish oppositional content.

What complicates the picture is that newspapers may shift positions depending on the AKP's policies on controversial issues, particularly the Kurdish question. "Left" and "Right" are indeed more meaningful categories to understand the newspapers' position on the government's policies toward the Kurds. The secular-right media *looks* progressive because of its critical attitude toward religion and its liberal attitude toward women's dress and sexuality. Yet, anti-Kurdish racism runs deep among many Turkish secular people and they start speaking the language of nationalism and right-wing politics as soon as the Kurds' demands for equal rights becomes the topic of conservation. Racism toward Syrian refugees is another point dividing the secular right and secular left in Turkey. In other words, "secular" does not mean "progressive" when it comes to the coverage of a number of key issues in Turkish media.

As of 2018, Turkish media may better be categorized as pro-AKP media versus oppositional media, as opposed to Islamist versus secular. Oppositional media, mostly the ones on the Left, have become marginalized and pushed to the internet in a country where television is the most widespread medium of mass communication. At the moment of this writing, *Cumhuriyet* is the main opposition print newspaper. In May 2016, the newspaper's editor in chief, Can

Dündar, and Erdem Gül, the Ankara bureau chief, received five-year jail sentences because of a news report about the weapons sent to Syrian rebels by the AKP government.[66] *Radikal*, the left-wing newspaper of Aydın Doğan's media group, could not survive the political pressure and closed in April 2016. A number of news websites that remain critical of the AKP government can still reach relatively small audiences.[67] *T24*, *Diken*, *Artı Gerçek*, and *Gazete Duvar* are among these outlets. *Bianet*, established to strengthen local news and journalists' network with financial support from the European Union, is also an important source of online news that has remained in the Turkish media scene. Yet the impact of these small outlets is minimal compared to pro-AKP propaganda.

Under the AKP, press freedom declined to an unprecedented extent. According to the Committee to Protect Journalists' report, "Turkey, Iran and China accounted for more than half of all journalists imprisoned around the world in 2013."[68] By 2014, after Erdoğan became president, around two thousand journalists and citizens were arrested for insulting Erdoğan.[69] In its 2014 *Enemies of the Internet* report, *Reporters Without Borders* listed Turkey among the countries that have turned Internet Service Providers into "instruments of censorship and surveillance."[70] Facebook, Twitter, and YouTube have become the target of the AKP regime, especially during and after the Gezi protests. Currently, as anyone traveling to Turkey will readily notice, a large number of websites are not accessible to Turkish internet users. Turkey blocked access to Wikipedia (the whole website, in all languages) on April 29, 2017.[71] On March 21, 2018, the AKP government passed new legislation that brought more restrictions on the internet.[72] The new restrictions place not only the content of the oppositional online news sites, but also the entertainment content offered in platforms such as Netflix under the government's heavy thumb.[73] Turkey's Radio and Television Higher Committee already censors the content of radio and television. The new law expands the committee's power to monitor internet broadcasts.[74]

The AKP's time in power introduced a new term to the lexicon for debates on Turkish media: "the pool media." The term describes "corporate owners whose media properties are in service of the government."[75] In *Hürriyet* journalist Murat Yetkin's words, "The 'pool media' is the name given to those media companies with no transparent ownership and financed by a number of construction companies that win huge government tenders."[76] According to Gülseren Adaklı (*Bianet*), pool media is characterized by centralized management of news policies and finances, accompanied by constant shifts in ownership and a lack of transparency that makes it very difficult to trace who owns what.[77]

In addition to the "pool media," two state institutions play a critical role in this propaganda effort. Both the Anadolu Agency, the state's news agency, and TRT, the Turkish Radio and Television Corporation, were restructured to frame current events and history from the perspective of the leading party, making them into government mouthpieces.[78] During the presidential elections in 2014, TRT gave tremendous coverage to Erdoğan at the expense of the other two candidates.[79] The content of TRT was also reshaped to include more religious and nationalistic programming, making the station an important propaganda tool in the AKP's project of creating new pious generations for the future. Big productions glorifying the Ottoman past and religious figures have become part of TRT's regular programming.[80] As opposed to the half-hour religious programming of the 1980s, TRT now contains a great deal of religious programming.[81] In violation of the remaining regulations, a close friend of Bilal Erdoğan (the president's son) was appointed as the director of the television station in 2017.[82] Following the June 2018 elections, a Directorate of Communication was established under the president, with authority over TRT and the budget of Anadolu Agency. The directorate, controlled directly by Erdoğan, also has the authority to issue service passports for journalists.[83]

Theologians and scholars of religion who are famous for their misogynist interpretations of religion have become common guests of talk shows on TRT. Their sexist views about women are not only tolerated but also respected. A famous example is Ömer Tuğrul İnançer, a religious leader who is notorious for his sexist comments. While on one such program, he criticized feminine hygiene commercials, and argued that pregnant women should not go outside of their homes, as they do not look aesthetically pleasing, and also implied that it is shameful to walk outdoors with a pregnant belly. His comments pushed the women out onto the streets, yet the protests did not have any impact on İnançer's status as a respectable guest for TRT screens. İnançer is part of the environment that has made open misogyny the new mainstream in Turkey.

What happened to the representations of the headscarf in the media while all these changes have been taking place in Turkey? What changes have occurred in women's image and women's representations? What does ideal womanhood look like in contemporary Turkey? Before turning to these questions, let's first look at the meanings of the headscarf for Turkey's different constituents.

The Headscarf as a Contested Terrain in Turkish Media and Politics

The connotations of wearing a headscarf in Turkey are multiple, complex, and part of an ongoing hegemonic struggle. Depending on the shifting positions in this ongoing struggle, the headscarf has been defined in relation to culture, religion, and politics, or simply to basic human rights. The meanings of the headscarf have always been in the making. In some moments, it is the anti-headscarf position that emphasizes the "religious" meanings of the headscarf to delegitimate it. At others, it is the Islamists who de-emphasize religion in the debates and define the headscarf with reference to the "Turkish" or "Anatolian" culture. The religious, cultural, or political meanings of the headscarf all depend on what different actors in this struggle want to do with those meanings, how they utilize them toward what end, and what is at stake for them. In that sense, even innocuous "cultural" or "religious" meanings of the garment have been heavily politicized. I placed "culture" and "religion" in quotation marks here because defining the boundaries of culture or religion, and what falls within each, is inherently a political process that has mobilized competing actors and constituents in Turkey.

In what follows, I talk about the headscarf's different connotations in post-1980 Turkey for four different groups: secularists, Islamists, feminists, and liberal democrats. The meaning of the headscarf is elusive and hard to fix. Each group tried to define and fix the meaning to make its own understanding of the headscarf the hegemonic, commonsensical one in Turkey. There are numerous types and styles of headscarf in Turkey, and naming different styles has also been part of a rhetorical battle that try to legitimate, or delegitimate, the headscarf. The most controversial style, known as the "Islamic" style, covers all of the hair and the neck. Here, I talk about this particular style popularized by the Islamist right-wing during the 1980s in Turkey. In this chapter, I introduce different connotations of the headscarf in Turkey, and lay the ground for situating them within the field of visual culture of news.

Why universities? The headscarf, conservative families, and the control of women's sexuality

In 1992, on the day of my enrollment at Boğaziçi University in Istanbul, my uncle, who is an alumnus, gave me a campus tour. In the 1980s, before the coup, he was among the tiny group of conservative students who organized a club against alcohol (Yeşilay Club). He was in the same cohort as the later-to-be Prime Minister Ahmet Davutoğlu.[1] During the campus tour, I pointed at a building and asked what it was. He said, "the girls' dormitory." And he continued: "You know what? You could find aborted babies in women's restrooms over there." For my uncle, that building was the hotbed of immoral behavior. I lived in Istanbul and I was ineligible for residence at the dormitory. It was clear that I was not going to stay there. But what would my uncle think about me if I had?

In France, the headscarf problem arose in high schools; in Germany, it appeared when the teachers wearing the headscarf wanted to work at schools. In Turkey, it was the university that was the hotbed of the complex debates on the headscarf. The connotations attaching to university education itself provide clues for understanding the secular justification for the headscarf ban in Turkish universities.

Higher education represents an important turning point in the modern life cycle, shaping not only the professional future of young people but also their private lives. Young people start looking for future partners and experiment sexually during their college years. Most modernized and urbanized families in Turkey during the 1960s and 1970s took it for granted that their sons and daughters would meet their future spouses during their four years at the university. Yet the university was an ambiguous space for many conservative families and their adult children—a desirable and a feared space at the same time. The Turkish education system had girls-only or boys-only high schools, but the same was not applicable to the universities.

Binali Yıldırım's story, recounted by himself at an alumni gathering, is a typical example of the dilemmas these families and their children experienced with regard to university education. Yıldırım (b. 1955 in Refahiye, Erzincan) became prime minister on May 24, 2016 following Ahmet Davutoğlu, and he is a loyal supporter of Erdoğan. After high school, Yıldırım had to choose between two universities: Istanbul Technical University, a prestigious engineering school with an overwhelming majority of male students, or Boğaziçi University, with diverse disciplines and a more balanced number of male and female students. When Yıldırım visited Boğaziçi University, he saw young men and women sitting on the grass, socializing and talking, and he said to himself, "I would stray away from the path here,"[2] and he preferred the male-dominated technical university, even though both universities offered high-quality engineering education. This choice exemplifies the typical conservative attitude: cautious of mixed-gender socializing, keeping some distance from the opposite sex, standing against flirting and sex outside marriage, and looking for the approval of the family in the choice of spouse.

The conservative anxiety toward the university played out differently for sons and daughters and was at times expressed in misogynistic terms, negatively stereotyping young female students who moved away from their towns of origin to get an education. In provincial areas in particular, young female students were seen as sexually available, posing a threat to local sexual morals in spite of the fact that the dormitory administrations severely restricted the girls' ability to move in and out whenever they wanted. Despite stereotypes about young female university students, many conservative families sought university education for their daughters as a kind of insurance policy to make sure that their daughters could make ends meet in case of divorce or loss of spouse. University education for girls was like a "golden bracelet," something given to the bride during a Turkish wedding ceremony as an asset to be used in hard times, the idea being that a woman could resort to her diploma if things went wrong in her marriage. Aware of the stereotypes that stigmatize college women, most families moved together with their daughters during their university education, requiring whole families to go through major transitions to make college possible for young women.

As a result, the prospects offered by the university were both desirable and undesirable for conservative families living in small cities and towns. University education brought prestige and facilitated upward social mobility, but the social life that accompanied attendance at university was seen as decadent and seductive. Conservative families, who wanted to have stronger control over their children's choice of spouse, did not like the idea of sending their daughters and sons to a social space they perceived as sexually permissive. They did not like the idea that their daughter might date someone and lose her virginity, endangering her prospects of a good marriage. On the other hand, they feared their sons might fall in with morally lax girls instead of the good girls who might merit the full approval of the parents. This created a dilemma for many families. Even though they wanted to send their daughters to the university, they did not want their sons to meet girls from the university. How then, could they make sure that their own daughters would differ from the others who, they feared, might seduce their sons? How would they prevent their daughters from being seduced by a permissive environment? In time, asking their daughters to wear the headscarf seemed like a solution for some of these families. Also, with the influence of rising Islamist right-wing activism (during the 1980s), more girls adopted the headscarf. Seeing this as an option, some families started to offer this to their daughters as a precondition for sending them to university.

The rise of the Turkish Left in the 1970s and the ensuing feminist wave also contributed to conservative anxieties about women's sexuality. The leading feminists from the Left during the 1980s defended flirting and women's sexual empowerment and questioned the virginity cult. The egalitarian gender socializing among leftist movements and the accompanying leftist feminism greatly disturbed the followers of the Islamist right-wing, and feminism has become a major target for these groups. Islamist male and female writers constantly attacked the feminist struggle for women's economic, social, and sexual empowerment, depicting feminism as a corrupt Western influence. Their antifeminist propaganda, which framed feminism as a foreign ideology that asks women to turn into men, strengthened the image of the promiscuous female college student. This is the context that produced the urban legend of "aborted babies" to which my uncle referred.

The Islamist right-wing was able to speak to the anxieties of gender-conservative families. The possibility of sexual experimentation before marriage made the universities a dangerous zone where young men and women could be seduced to transgress the borders imposed on them by two forceful institutions: religion and the family. The desire for the headscarf, by the families or by the girls themselves, should be placed within this context. This context is also crucial to understanding the secular justification for the headscarf ban. These conservative anxieties played out their role again when Erdoğan justified his attacks on co-ed dormitories in 2013 with reference to the concerns about the universities in Anatolian towns.[3]

The headscarf, Islamism, and the secular establishment

The secular establishment has a complex relationship with the headscarf. There are numerous types of female headgear in Turkey, totally or partially covering the hair in various ways. Within the modernist framework, the different types of headgear worn in rural areas were mostly seen as a sign of underdevelopment. Turkish secular establishment assumed that as the girls get their education and move up on the social ladder, they would naturally give up the headscarf. But things did not develop as they assumed. Some of the girls never adopted the headscarf, but some others did.

The type of headscarf that has become common today was introduced to Turkey during the 1960s and 1970s under the influence of the Islamist movements in Egypt and the larger Middle East[4] and became increasingly more popular with the activism of leading conservative women in the 1960s. The secular establishment saw this as a sign of rejection of the Atatürk reforms,[5] yet the professors and the university administrations did not exactly know what to do about it. My own mother started university in 1968 wearing a headscarf that covered all her hair. She had realized that this decision would please her father. In those years, this decision branded her as a student on the Right. She recounts only one instance in five years where a professor kicked her out of class, calling her an "enemy of Atatürk," only to apologize and accept her again the next day. She said that they simply did not know, did not understand why a woman would cover her hair. When she said that this was in the Qur'an, most professors tended to abide it. In fact, many women themselves whose fathers told them to cover did not understand it either. Practice came first, only later did they start to explore why.[6] My mother, who graduated in 1973, on the fiftieth anniversary of the declaration of the Turkish republic, was one of the few women in her class.

During the same years, there were a few other female students wearing the headscarf, and much more involved in Islamist right-wing politics than my mother. My mother clearly remembers one of them as the girl who used to place her prayer mat at the top of the stairs to pray in public, blocking the way and letting no one pass: a form of Islamic activism to protest the lack of prayer rooms in the university.[7] According to my mother's account, even in those instances nobody stopped the praying student who blocked the path that all the other students used to go to their classes. In other words, in spite of occasional outbursts (as in the Faculty of Theology in Ankara)[8], the Islamic headscarf was not on the radar of the state to be perceived as a significant threat in the 1960s and 1970s.

For the secular establishment, the meaning of the headscarf as a threat to secularism was crystallized after the Iranian Revolution in 1979 and the ensuing imposition of the headscarf for all women under Khomeini in Iran. It is difficult to exaggerate the impact of the revolution on the Turkish secular establishment and its perception of the headscarf in Turkey. A revolution taking place next door greatly influenced the ways Turkish secularists saw the women's headscarf in Turkey. To the Turkish secularists' horror, Iran had initiatives to import the

Figure 2.1   Graduation ceremony, Istanbul University, Faculty of Dentistry, 1973 (the fiftieth anniversary of the declaration of the Turkish Republic). Part of the accompanying news story reads, "among the graduates, who will continue the fight to bring [the nation] to the level of the civilized world, was also a female dentist who tightly covered her hair." *Cumhuriyet*, September 16, 1973. Image credit: Türk Haberler Ajansı (THA, now defunct), photographer unknown. Courtesy of *Cumhuriyet*.

revolution to other Muslim-majority countries. Furthermore, Turkey's Islamist men and women viewed the revolution in positive terms, as resistance to American imperialism, and they widely read the books by Ali Shariati, the ideologue of the Iranian Revolution.[9] As a result, following a widespread rumor, many in secularist circles came to believe that women wearing the Islamist headscarf in Turkey were on the payroll of the Iranian government. This has become a long-standing urban legend among many secular people.[10]

The 1979 Iranian Revolution was a traumatic moment in Turkish politics, and it is followed by another trauma, the 1980 military coup in Turkey. Within that climate, the complex reasons for which the girls had adopted (or had been pushed to adopt) the headscarf, and the subtle meanings of the garment, disappeared. It is therefore not so surprising that the first official headscarf ban came about in 1982 during the military regime in Turkey.[11] In spite of its rather lenient attitude toward the Islamist right-wing, the military still found women's headscarves intolerable, as a violation of the modernist commitment to the Turkish republic. The overlap of these two highly traumatizing moments is also reflected in academic literature on the headscarf: the "rupture"[12] approach has become dominant in academic discourse. Feyda Sayan-Cengiz has criticized the assumed "rupture" between "traditional" and "new" veiling. I am critical of the "rupture" approach for another, additional reason though. This approach has eclipsed the connections between pre- and post-1980s conservative women's activism in Turkey, brought new naming practices by labeling the women "Islamists," and made it appear as if "Islamist" women's activism did not exist before the 1980 military coup.[13]

The basic connotation of the headscarf for the Turkish secular establishment has then clearly become "the threat to Turkish secularism" and Islamist militancy. The headscarf has come to represent the political commitment to overthrow the secular constitution of Turkey either by instrumentalizing democratic institutions or by sheer force, with the eventual goal of establishing an Islamic state similar to Iran, where the Islamic headscarf would be mandatory for all women. The headscarf in that sense is seen as a symbol of an anti-systemic challenge, part of a repressive, totalitarian, and extremist project. Identifying the headscarf as a threat, the Higher Education Council banned the headscarf from all universities (it was already forbidden in high schools). Students wearing the headscarf were not allowed to attend classes in some universities; neither were women (even MPs) allowed to wear the headscarf in parliament, government offices (women with a headscarf could receive services but could not work while wearing a headscarf), and military premises (no woman wearing a headscarf was allowed on the premises). The crystallization of the headscarf as a threat accompanied a struggle over how to name the garment: the Islamist groups preferred the name "headscarf" because of its local and sympathetic connotations, linking it to indigenous Anatolian culture. Secularists, on the other hand, reworked the meanings of an existing term that simply referred to a style of head-covering: "turban."[14] In the secularist language, the term "turban" marked the headscarf as foreign and political.

The first generation of women raised in modern Turkey (mostly born during the 1920s and 1930s) were staunch defenders of the nation and its founder,

Mustafa Kemal Atatürk, as they obtained their most basic rights as parts of Westernization reforms (coeducation, right to higher education, right to divorce, equal inheritance, travel, right to vote, and right to be elected). This generation of women appreciated the opportunities given to them, and they were committed to authoritarian secularism. From their perspective, demanding the right to cover the hair was inexplicable. How come women could want limited rights on the basis of religion instead of all the opportunities that were offered to them by the new regime? Most of these women reacted very strongly to other women's demands to wear a headscarf in the universities. Türkan Saylan (1935–2009)[15] was probably the epitome of this generation.[16] Raised as a typical republican woman, Saylan was a medical doctor specializing in leprosy who chaired the World Leprosy Association until 2006. She established one of the largest NGOs in Turkey (Çağdaş Yaşamı Destekleme Derneği) to educate girls for modern life. Yet she was also famous for her strong rejection of the Islamist headscarf as a symbol of backwardness, darkness, and women's oppression. This point of view found its voice in the Republican People's Party, whose primary mission had become the protection of a narrowly defined secularism in Turkey after the 1980s.

For secular people, the headscarf debate was also part of a lifestyle debate, and about defending the right not to practice religion or believe in any religion. Opposing the headscarf meant protecting a particular secular urban lifestyle that is embedded in the work–life cycle and in socializing. Lifestyle issues included the freedom to consume alcohol throughout the year, including the holy month of Ramazan, wearing short skirts, going to mixed beaches, and wearing bikinis without being disturbed. For seculars, the elimination of the threat of violence toward those who do not practice religion was a serious issue. The month of Ramazan in particular has been a period of tension as radical groups could, but did not often, attack those who did not observe fasting. Secular people were afraid that, once in power, an Islamist party would not respect their rights not to practice or believe in religion, would not protect them from potential attacks, and would interfere with women's dress, imposing the headscarf.

Contrary to what the Islamist right-wing has argued, Turkish secularists were not simply a detached elite, alienated from their people. On the contrary, they knew very well how conservatism played out in girls' education, coming from provincial towns. Turkish secular people were also well aware of the conservative family dynamics in their country. For some, the ban aimed to break the power of conservative families over young women who did not want to cover their hair but were coerced by their families to adopt the headscarf. In that sense, the ban provided a space for women who were pushed into wearing the headscarf against their will. These girls could use the ban as a pretext to escape from their families' impositions until they were empowered by their own economic independence and stand for their own preferences, following university education. This was in fact a stronger argument in favor of the ban, although not utilized very often. Unsurprisingly, Turkey's conservatives never accepted or admitted such repressive aspects of headscarf.

Although 1982 marked an important yardstick for the ban, throughout the subsequent fifteen years, during which time the center-right governments were primarily in power, the headscarf ban was enforced on and off and was left to the discretion of the rectors and the deans at the universities.[17] As a result, different universities developed different responses to the headscarf ban on the basis of their own tradition. Boğaziçi University, for example, was like a safe haven for girls wearing the headscarf. According to the university's stance, all students had the right to secular education, regardless of their cultural or religious background. Believing in the transformative power of a secular, liberal arts education, they hoped to give a new perspective to students, particularly in the social sciences. Indeed, a number of conservative, Islamist students of my generation who studied in the liberal arts departments at Boğaziçi University eventually changed their position and distanced themselves from religious conservatism during the 1990s.

On the way to February 28, 1997

The 1990s witnessed two important parallel developments in Turkey: the rise of liberalism and the rise of Islamism as a new branch of the Turkish Right. Throughout the decade, the consequences of the economic liberalization and privatization reforms that the center-right government of Turgut Özal had implemented became visible in the media sector. The monopoly of Turkish Radio Television, TRT, came to an end with the introduction of ratings-based commercial media. This made controversial Islamist actors, who were not able to get through the filter of TRT's sanitized religious programs, much more visible on Turkish television in forums and debates. Gradually, Islamist groups started to have their own television and radio stations.

Within this environment, the Islamist groups and women wearing the headscarf gained greater visibility in the media. Even though they usually faced a hostile environment in the mainstream secular media, they had the chance to insert their arguments and their vision of the world into the political debate. They challenged the negative connotations of the headscarf as a threat to secularism and tried to prove the secularist fears ungrounded. They emphasized their own interpretation of the garment as a symbol of religious observance, chastity, piety, submission to God, and adherence to a religious lifestyle. At the same time, they constantly tried to distinguish their style from the traditional styles of covering that they deemed "un-Islamic." These traditional styles from rural Anatolia and villages had also been devalued by the secular establishment as a sign of undereducation, poverty, and underdevelopment.[18] Conservative women tried to detach themselves from these negative connotations by reinventing the headscarf and by carefully choosing different fabrics and designs.[19] Paradoxically, as they distinguished their style from the local (and lower-class) forms of the headscarf, conservative women also worked to sustain the argument that their headscarf was not political but cultural, part of Turkey's local and authentic culture.[20] In other words, conservative women tried to naturalize the headscarf with reference to local practices and culture, while the Kemalists tried to denaturalize it with reference to religious extremism, women's rights, and political Islam.[21]

At the same time, a new Islamist right-wing party started to increase its votes. In a landmark 1994 local election, the Welfare Party (Refah Partisi—RP) succeeded in winning the Istanbul Municipality, introducing Recep Tayyip Erdoğan—then the party's Istanbul chair—to the scene of Turkish politics as the mayor of Istanbul. The party's mobilization of conservative women to support its cause helped greatly in the local election wins. Organized street by street, the women members of the party walked from door to door trying to persuade women to cast their ballots for the party. The party's ensuing success in distributing municipal services in Istanbul and in the other cities prepared the ground for its ascension to the government as a coalition partner in 1996.

In 1996, Necmettin Erbakan, the head of the Welfare Party, and Erdoğan's mentor, established a coalition government with the center-right True Path Party (Doğru Yol Partisi—DYP) and became Turkey's first prime minister from the Islamist Right. During his term, Erbakan's attempts to incorporate radical Islamist groups into Turkish politics generated a strong reaction from the secular establishment and the military. Erbakan's invitation of the radical Islamist groups to the prime minister's residence received extensive coverage and became a visual symbol of the Islamist threat in the media.[22] Erbakan's term in office led to the imposition of the February 28 directives, where, in a routine national security meeting in 1997, the military pressured Erbakan to sign a series of extreme measures to contain the Islamist activities. The enforcement of the headscarf ban was among the most important measures proposed in the document.

Following February 28, 1997, the headscarf ban was implemented in a very aggressive manner, closing all potential channels for women wearing the headscarf to pursue higher education. During this period, Istanbul University took the application of the ban to new heights. The university's administration decided to create rooms next to the entry gates at the beginning of the academic year to persuade the girls wearing the headscarf to take it off. Conservative writers regularly pointed to these "persuasion rooms" to define this practice as the epitome of secularist oppression.[23]

The Welfare Party was closed down by the Constitutional Court in 1998 for violating the secular principles of the constitution, and Necmettin Erbakan was banned from politics for five years. Soon after, the Virtue Party (Fazilet Partisi—FP) was born as its successor. In 1999, the party nominated a woman wearing the headscarf to parliament for the first time, making Merve Kavakçı Turkey's first MP with the headscarf. Merve Kavakçı encountered strong protests from the members of the other parties and had to leave the parliament without taking her oath. The ensuing events led to Kavakçı's expulsion from Turkish citizenship on the grounds that she had accepted American citizenship without notifying Turkish authorities. The Merve Kavakçı incident became another symbolic landmark in the story of the headscarf in the aftermath of February 28 in Turkey.[24]

February 28 opened a new chapter in the story of the Islamist right-wing in Turkey. The period between 1998 and 2002 is significant for a number of reasons. First, banning Erbakan from politics opened the way for the establishment of the AKP under a new young leader, Recep Tayyip Erdoğan. He and his closest colleagues, who established the AKP with him, adopted a new discourse that emphasized the expansion of democratic rights and freedoms in Turkey, creating a series of contradictions with their previous Islamist discourse.[25] The AKP emphasized its differences from the Welfare Party and argued that—taking its lessons from the February 28 period as to the importance of rights and freedoms—the party was committed to expansion of democratic rights for all people in Turkey.

Second, this new discourse eventually persuaded Turkey's liberal democrats, who constantly criticized the Kemalists for their lack of commitment to democratic participation, of the AKP's potential to implement democratic reforms that the country needed. The liberal democrats supported the AKP out of the belief that it represented a significant break from the radical Islamist politics of the former Welfare Party. Third, AKP created a new symbol of victimization on the basis of February 28. The aggressive enforcement of the headscarf ban in the aftermath of February 28 provided the AKP with an invaluable opportunity to create new symbols and stories of oppression. During their time in power, the AKP and its supporters on the religious right reconstructed this period as a symbolic era, casting secularism as a source of oppression for women. Numerous documentaries and books were produced by various Islamist groups about February 28 and the "persuasion rooms," making them a symbolic landmark justifying the AKP's authoritarian practices and its narrative of the "new Turkey." The leading secularist actors of the February 28 period also took their share from the AKP's retributive policies. While suffering from cancer at the age of seventy-three, Türkan Saylan was accused of supporting a coup attempt against the AKP government as part of Ergenekon trials in 2009. The accusations later proved to have been forged.[26]

The process of February 28 changed the relations between Turkey's liberal democrats and conservative women (and men), bringing them up more closely against the oddities of Kemalist secularism. A number of leading liberal democrats criticized the process and the extreme measures taken against Islamism and the headscarf, forging new relations with conservative circles. For example, Nuray Mert, a leading female liberal democrat, supported headscarf-wearing women during this phase. A number of other liberal intellectuals lost their jobs in secular newspapers, and conservative Islamist newspapers invited them to write columns on their pages.[27] Conservative Islamist newspapers benefited a lot from this period of interaction: their radical edge seemed to disappear and they were able to present themselves as capable of tolerating different views (something the Kemalists could not) and as open to conversation and dialogue. This rather exceptional phase came to a close around 2011, when the AKP started to consolidate its power and attack the liberal democrats for their criticisms. Interestingly, Nuray Mert was among the first to become a target, a case that I will talk more about in Chapter 4, where I analyze conservative women's columns. All the liberal democrats were eventually pushed out of the conservative Islamist newspapers, as these newspapers became the mouthpiece of the AKP government.

In short, in spite of their legitimate concerns about the rise of Islamism in Turkey, the secularists could not succeed in creating a language to express these concerns within an inclusive, nonauthoritarian, nonpolarizing, nondiscriminatory, and democratic language. They also failed to address the disenchantment and frustration caused by economic liberalization and wealth inequality. Trapped into the language of modernization that approached large masses as underdeveloped and backward, they provided fuel for the AKP's discourse that cast the secularists as an alienated Westernized elite who look down upon "the people." Sticking to a dogmatic language of protecting Atatürk reforms and Turkish secularism, the secular establishment failed to explain its own rationale about the headscarf ban to the masses. The AKP, on the other hand, has become very successful in using the secular obsession with the headscarf to its own advantage, redefining the garment as a symbol that stands for the oppression of the "people."

The secularist approach to the headscarf remained hegemonic until the early 2000s.[28] The meanings given to the headscarf by the secularists were questioned not only by the Islamist groups on religious grounds but also by the liberal democrats and the Turkish feminists.

The headscarf and the liberal democrats

Liberal democrats in Turkey can be considered a diverse group of intellectuals and writers in the media and academia. Even though they mostly underwent their early intellectual formation in leftist movements, Turkey's liberal democrats constituted the wing of the Left that leaned toward the Right. They celebrated Turgut Özal's center-right government's economic liberalization, deregulation, and privatization reforms during the 1980s and saw the market economy as a precondition for democratization.[29] Their approach blended modernization theory and economic liberalization.

Liberal democrats argued for the expansion of individual rights and freedoms. They linked the question of the headscarf with the question of democracy in Turkey, arguing that the exclusion of women wearing headscarves from the public sphere was a clear sign of the deficiencies of democracy in the country. They saw the headscarf ban as a consequence of authoritarian secularism in Turkey, which repressed not only headscarf-wearing women and Islamist parties but also Kurds, Alevi Islam, leftist movements, and all the other ethnic and religious minorities. For them the meaning of the headscarf was linked to individual choice and to limiting the power of the state on personal lives. They emphasized dialogue, conversation, and building bridges between the secular and the Islamic camps in Turkey. For them, the secularists' fears about Turkey turning into Iran were unwarranted and out of proportion. Liberals argued that, in spite of its deficiencies, secular democracy in Turkey was strong enough to prevent a totalitarian project of transforming Turkey into an Islamic state. What the Turkish state had to do was to give up its fears and welcome an inclusive democracy, they argued.

Within the liberal democratic camp, sociologist Nilüfer Göle's work on young Islamist women in universities became widely influential and popular during the 1990s. Göle approached the headscarf as part of an adaptation strategy in a society characterized by internal migration from the rural areas to the urban centers from the 1950s onward.[30] The headscarf was the link between tradition and modernity. In her view, women did not want to give up either their tradition or their rights to education and access to employment. They wanted to stay rooted in tradition, yet they also transformed tradition by blending it with modernity. Göle suggested the concept of "non-Western modernities" to understand the headscarf in Turkey. Taking a modernist approach, she and her team of young students (including myself)[31] supported the thesis that the women in Islamist movements would transform the movements from within and would eventually lead to the Islamist movements' integration into Turkey's secular democracy by pushing Turkish secularism to allow more diversity into the system. Even though Göle's approach was critical of the modernization theory per se, she still departed from the theory's main assumptions to figure out what did not work in the theory and to modify it. The concept of non-Western modernities was a product of this effort to modify the modernization theory.[32] Her framework relied on binaries between the East and the West, and Islam and secularism, and left the basic assumptions of the theory unquestioned: from this perspective, Muslim women wearing the headscarf and referring to Western philosophers instead of Islamic sources seemed like a significant observation. Göle read this as "Islamist" women creating their own version of "modernity." Yet the same observation could also be read in the following terms: right-wing, or conservative women mobilizing multiple rhetorical resources and argumentative strategies to insert their point of view into the discourse.[33]

Liberal democrats in academia and the media[34] have consistently pointed at the democratic failures of the Turkish state and the contradictions within the system. The liberal democrats (and feminists) emphasized the ways the ban on the headscarf unfairly disadvantaged Islamist women, but not Islamist men. Nothing prevented male Islamist students from getting access to higher education. Although the regulations problematized men's beards as well, it was not a problem for male Islamists to shave their beards (if they had any) to get into university.

Liberal democrats worked tirelessly to expose the discriminatory logic behind some secularist arguments in favor of the ban. According to some in the secularist camp, wearing a headscarf in the university was pointless anyway, as these women would not be able to find jobs after graduation. For the secularists, it was pointless to demand a degree in physics if the woman in the end was going to stay at home as a housewife. Yet the secularists did not ask the same question of women who did not wear headscarves and who could also end up being housewives because of a lack of jobs, gender discrimination in the job market, or sheer personal preference. Liberals argued that the jobs must be available for women wearing the headscarf. Yet, there was also a great deal of disagreement in the liberal camp about the types of jobs that should be available to such women. Many liberal democrats were unwilling to see women wearing the headscarf in certain jobs that demanded neutrality and adherence to secular principles: schoolteachers, officials in government bureaucracy, judges, police, and so forth. As a result, some liberals distinguished between service givers and takers: a university student is demanding a service as a citizen, so she should be allowed to wear a headscarf in class. Yet a professor is providing a service and, as a sign of her equal distance from all students, she should not wear a headscarf. This distinction was also contested by other liberals, who argued that not wearing a headscarf did not guarantee equal distance from all students, as many Kemalist female professors did not shy away from showing open hostility to their students wearing the headscarf.

Most of these liberal intellectuals would not be happy if the headscarf were demanded for girls under eighteen. They saw the headscarf ban in the universities as a violation of an adult individual's right to wear whatever she prefers. But for girls younger than eighteen, they would see it as ideological indoctrination and would be concerned about the restrictive role of the family on the young women. Liberals also believed that, as much as the state has to protect rights and freedoms, it also has to protect its young citizens from exposure to the restrictive ideologies at a young age. Some liberals objected to the headscarf ban not because they sympathized with it but because they thought eliminating the ban would curtail its symbolic power and eliminate the discourse of victimization that mobilized Islamists around the headscarf.

The 1990s were also a period during which theories on identity politics became popular. For Turkish academics like Göle, the headscarf was an extension of identity politics, expanding democratic possibilities, much as other social movements based on identity claims had done in the West. Islamist movements were compared with leftist movements (particularly with respect to their imagining of a utopian future), the US civil rights movement, and the feminist movement.[35] The terms "white Turks" and "black Turks" have become common in talking about democracy and inclusion. The distinction does not have much to do with the color of the skin. The term "white Turks" referred to those with privilege (secular, Westernized, educated, middle class, and born in the cities) whereas "black Turks" referred to Turks without privilege (all the other Turks with the opposite characteristics that seem undesirable within a modernist framework). Women wearing the headscarf were seen as black Turks because of their exclusion from the university and the parliament. Islamists loved this comparison: Comparing religious identity with racial identity as if the two were the same helped them to make their own religious and political preferences seem natural, inevitable, immutable, and unquestionable. This comparison removes the headscarf from the realm of choice and presents it as something as deep as skin color, which a person cannot do anything about. On the other hand, many Islamists would not like the headscarf to be compared to miniskirts: a form of dress worn to fulfill God's wishes cannot be seen as equal to other forms of dress.[36]

Liberal democrats and conservative women

Leading women writers in the conservative camp have become instrumental in convincing liberal democrats about the "moderate" nature of the Islamist movements in Turkey and their potential for democratic transformation in the 1990s and early 2000s. Major left-wing academic publishers published books about women wearing the headscarf, talking about their exclusion from the system.[37] Conservative women were invited to academic panels and, defining themselves as an oppressed group, made their voices heard with the help of intellectuals who argued for democratic expansion.[38] These publications and appearances gradually paved the way for more positive coverage about conservative women in mainstream secular media and their further inclusion in the public debate.

Liberal democrats saw women wearing the headscarf as the victims not only of the secular establishment but also of Islamist men. These women were not able to find jobs in regular corporate firms; neither were they able to find jobs in workplaces run by the Islamists—because the Islamist men, first, did not want to be stigmatized with the image of the headscarf and, second, they believed that a woman's place was primarily at home. Things got worse in the aftermath of February 28, when women within Islamist circles did not receive support from the men in their own circles. For Islamist men, Islamist women had done enough for the movement and now they could go back where they belonged: home.

While asking women to go back home, these men preferred to marry women without headscarves; this way, they could escape stigmatization, but their preference further restricted the choices available to Islamist women. Islamist women could not find jobs and they also had difficulties in finding spouses and creating their own families. So the women faced stigmatization on two fronts (from secularists and Islamist men) and they openly criticized Islamist men. Liberal democrats heard these criticisms more than the Islamist men, and saw Islamist women's criticisms as a variety of feminism.[39]

Women saw themselves in the same terms, too, and situated themselves as fighting on two fronts, against double marginalization.[40] This helped them gain a unique strategic position, giving them access to debates and forums. Within this framework, the headscarf became the symbol of the conservative women's double fight. The argument of double marginalization seemed to prove Göle's approach that situated women as "transformative" actors within the Islamist movements. Looking at this picture, many liberals believed that if anyone could transform the Islamist movements, it would be the Islamist women with their double victimization. According to this argument, Islamist women's increasing participation in university education and their willingness to embrace modernity, albeit on their own terms, empowered these women to challenge the sexism of the Islamist men. Göle in particular saw these women as the engine of transformation from within.

The quick integration of the Islamist right-wing into capitalism was also taken as further evidence of "transformation."[41] Studies flourished on Muslim women's fashion,[42] and on Islamized consumption. Muslim women's use of brand-name fashion, their demands for gender-segregated beaches at five-star hotels, and their mixing with men in "Islamic" coffee houses were all seen as transformative—and transgressive—behavior that would eventually lead to the Islamist movements' integration into the democratic secular system.[43]

The liberals contributed greatly to the breakdown of the secularist interpretation of the headscarf during the 1990s. Although the headscarf ban in universities stayed in place until 2010, the hegemonic meaning of the headscarf as "a threat to Turkish secularism" started to break down toward the end of 1990s due to several reasons: the liberal democrats succeeded in gaining support for their arguments among a new generation of college students; the Turkish media became more diverse, with Islamic newspapers and television channels; and businesses realized that women with headscarves constituted a new group of potential consumers. Islamic fashion companies flourished, making the headscarf profitable, fancy, and fashionable. As a result, many young women started to wear the headscarf without necessarily following the religious lifestyle that was associated with the garment, complicating all the previous connotations that linked the headscarf to piety, observance, or Islamist political resistance.

Eventually, the liberal democrats paid a big price for supporting the conservative headscarf-wearing women and asking for an inclusive democracy. Kemalists today hold the liberal democrats responsible for carrying Islamism and the AKP to power. At the same time, the AKP has silenced, intimidated, and jailed many of them for their criticisms after 2011.[44] By 2017, Göle's famous thesis of "the forbidden modern" was challenged by a new generation of scholars. Feyda Sayan-Cengiz criticized her theory and the dominant literature on headscarf in Turkey for culturalizing the headscarf and neglecting its class dimension by focusing only on the experiences of middle-class women with higher education.[45]

So why did the liberal democratic thesis prove false in Turkey? Conservative women columnists, writers, and intellectuals were one of the main reasons that the liberal democrats believed an inclusive democracy was possible in Turkey. I want to understand why and how these same women, who once signified opposition to a rigid system that silenced them, have now become the proponents of a new rigid system that silenced the people who most supported their democratic rights. I will deal with this intriguing question in Chapter 4.

The limits of the liberal democratic approach to the headscarf

During the 1990s, Islamism in Turkey extensively used the postmodern criticisms of modernity in situating themselves as an oppressed group. In hindsight, taking their claim at face value turned out to be a mistake. While situating themselves as the oppressed, the Islamist right-wing resisted seeing the other oppressed groups as their equals. As of 2018, the AKP's suppression of the LGBT movement, and its policies toward the Kurds, feminist organizations, and Alevis,[46] prove that other claims for identity were not seen as being on an equal footing with the claim for "Muslim" identity. In that sense, approaching the Islamist movements as a form of identity politics was a mistake. Identity politics can be progressive or regressive.[47] The AKP's sixteen-year rule made it clear that the Islamist right-wing's claim to Muslim identity is located on the dark side of identity politics.

Second, the liberals' bias toward the democratic potential of market economy led them to assume that the Islamists' integration into capitalist consumption would accompany their democratization. Yet, although the AKP government has integrated very well into global capitalism, this was accompanied by increasing authoritarianism and the diminishment of democratic rights and individual freedoms. Turkey has become another case that exemplifies the happy cohabitation of capitalism and authoritarianism.[48]

Third, scholars from the liberal democratic camp focused on cultural practices in order to create space beyond political polarization in Turkey. They focused on change and "transformation," but not on the unchanging and enduring aspects of the Islamist political discourse.[49] When the liberal democrats focused on political struggles, they did so in order to criticize the deficiencies of Turkish democracy and Kemalism (for good reasons), yet they neglected the regressive potential of religious conservatism. This led them to disregard the sexist, nationalist, and authoritarian discourses within the Islamist movements and the AKP cadres. As I argued earlier in the Introduction to this book, their detachment of Islamism from right-wing politics was a significant reason behind this failure. They were right and justified in asking for a more inclusive democracy and the extensions of freedoms in Turkey. But their focus on Islam versus secularism, on culture, and on identity politics prevented them from framing Islamist activism as a form of right-wing politics, leading them to unintentionally legitimate the exclusionary right-wing rhetoric of Islamism.

I argue that the headscarf ban in the universities was wrong for a number of reasons: it denied the dynamism of life and the change that women are willing to embrace throughout their lives. Women explore different world views and ideologies, and they change the way they dress—just as their political views, social connections, and beliefs change over time. As many women within the Islamist movement have put the headscarf on, there is also an invisible group of women that took it off and left the Islamist circles for various reasons. The ban denied that possibility and approached women wearing the headscarf as frozen in time. Second, by supporting discrimination among women, the ban provided an important symbol of victimization to a regressive movement that could have otherwise been contained within democratic means. Third, the ban diverted attention from more serious discussions and debates on the role of religion in Turkey, conservatism, and the democratization process.

Scholarly work that remained less popular and less prominent than Göle's mentioned the limits of women's activism within the Islamist movements. Some voices within Turkey's feminist movement never gave up their skepticism about Islamism's potential for democracy and about conservative women's potential for women's empowerment.

The headscarf and Turkish feminists

In general, the feminist movement in Turkey was ambivalent toward the headscarf, and there were multiple views within the movement. On the one hand, feminists saw it as a symbol of patriarchal domination, but on the other hand, unlike the previous generation of women, such as Türkan Saylan and other Kemalist women, they did not define the headscarf as a threat to Turkish secularism and did not support exclusionary policies toward women wearing the headscarf. They were willing to see women wearing headscarves as active agents instead of the pawns of Islamist men and external enemies of the Turkish secular state (i.e., Iran). In spite of skepticism, the feminist movement saw the Islamist women's movement as another form of women's movement with different concerns, yet facing the same problems that affect all women as women. They were willing to see the Islamist women as part of a larger sisterhood, as sisters who follow a different path. Their writing during the 1990s reflects this position.[50] From this feminist perspective, the headscarf ban was another instance of discrimination against women, another attempt by the Turkish state to control women's bodies and choices. As a result, some feminist women and leftist students supported Islamist women's demonstrations outside of the universities in the 1980s and 1990s. Although they had some reservations, they approached these demonstrations as resistance to oppression by the state and sympathized with women wearing the headscarf.

Yet other leftist feminist voices questioned the relationships between patriarchy, religious conservatism, and the headscarf in a more critical manner. They pointed at the antifeminism of these conservative, right-wing Islamist movements and the limits of a women's movement defined within the parameters of a gender ideology based on religion.[51] For example, Handan Koç documented the antifeminism of Islamist male and female writers during the 1980s and criticized the liberal democrats for neglecting the misogyny and antifeminism within the Islamist movements. In her book *Muhafazakarlığa Karşı Feminizm* [*Feminism Against Conservatism*], she criticized Nilüfer Göle and her equation of leftism and Islamism as similar versions of identity politics. Koç focuses on the misogyny in the religious texts produced by contemporary Islamist writers and sees the headscarf as an expression of religious patriarchy. She is particularly concerned about the ways women who do not wear the headscarf are depicted in these texts as immoral, promiscuous, and untrustworthy.

Feminists in general wanted the headscarf to be a choice for women—one choice among other choices. Yet the AKP's policies on gender aim to socialize young girls into wearing the headscarf. Proving Handan Koç right, the AKP's time in power has created an unsafe environment, particularly for women who love to wear shorts and miniskirts,[52] pushing women to opt for more conservative dress. The AKP's conservative gender regime has led the feminists to reconsider their relationships with the conservative women and the headscarf, a point that I will focus on in Chapter 5.

The headscarf under the AKP

The AKP came to power in 2002, at a time when the ban was still in place, yet the attitudes toward the headscarf had become more relaxed, making the garment more socially acceptable and visible. The secular Kemalist establishment was still in power but was worn out under the criticisms coming from the liberal democrats. Extreme measures in the aftermath of February 28 had also generated criticism and a crisis of legitimacy for the Kemalist establishment.

With the AKP having the majority of the seats in the parliament, the majority of men in power had wives who wore the headscarf. As a result, the headscarf debate shifted from university students to the male representatives' wives, and then to Emine Erdoğan and Hayrünnisa Gül and their capacity to represent Turkey.[53] The government bureaucracy run by the secular establishment did not have room for the headscarf, and they started preparing invitations without spouses for official receptions. The initial years of the AKP were characterized by crises over official receptions.

Table 2.1 Timeline: Removal of the headscarf ban under the AKP

Date	Event
2002	The AKP comes to power
2004	Turkey wins the European Court of Human Rights case *Leyla Şahin v. Turkey*, thus strengthening the secular ban of the headscarf
2007	Hayrünnisa Gül becomes the first First Lady to wear a headscarf when Abdullah Gül becomes president
2008	The AKP attempts to change the constitution to make the headscarf a constitutional right; this attempt backfires, causing resistance among liberal democrats
2010	The Higher Education Council de facto removes the headscarf ban from universities[a]

Table 2.1 continued

Date		Event
2011		Female opinion leaders wearing the headscarf organize a campaign before the 2011 elections: No candidate with headscarf, No vote
2013	January 25	Headscarf ban is removed for women lawyers[b]
2013	October 8	Headscarf ban is removed for women working in public offices, with the exception of military personnel, judges, and policewomen[c]
2013	October 31	Four women MPs from the AKP decide to adopt the headscarf; after Merve Kavakçı in 1999, they become the first MPs to wear the headscarf[d]
2014	April 10	Ayşegül Jale Saraç becomes the Rector of Dicle University, the first woman rector of a public university to wear the headscarf[e]
2014	September 22	Mandatory school uniforms are removed, allowing schoolchildren to wear the headscarf after fourth grade[f]
2015	May 31	Headscarf ban is removed for judges and prosecutors[g]
2015	September 3	Ayşen Gürcan is sworn in as the first minister to wear the headscarf; she becomes the Minister of Family and Social Policies[h]
2016	August 27	Headscarf ban is removed for policewomen[i]
2017	February 22	Headscarf ban is removed for military personnel[j]

Notes

[a] Jonathan Head, "Quiet End to Turkey's College Headscarf Ban," *BBC News*, December 31, 2010. Available online: http://www.bbc.com/news/world-europe-11880622 (accessed December 15, 2018).

[b] *Haberler.com*, "Avukatlara Başörtüsü Yasağı Kalktı," January 25, 2013. Available online: https://www.haberler.com/avukatlara-basortusu-yasagi-kalkti-4276950-haberi/ (accessed December 15, 2018).

[c] *BBC News Türkçe*, "Kamuda Başörtüsü Yasağı Kalktı," October 8, 2013. Available online: http://www.bbc.com/turkce/haberler/2013/10/131008_basortusu (accessed December 15, 2018).

[d] Ayşe Böhürler, "Her Kadın Artık Milletvekili Olabilir," *Yeni Şafak*, November 2, 2013.

[e] *Anadolu Ajansı*, "Türkiye'nin İlk Başörtülü Rektörü Oldu," April 10, 2014. Available online: http://aa.com.tr/tr/turkiye/turkiyenin-ilk-basortulu-rektoru-oldu/168018 (accessed December 15, 2018). Ayşegül Jale Saraç was arrested following the failed coup attempt on July 15, 2016: *T24*, "Türkiye'nin İlk Başörtülü Rektörü Cemaat Soruşturmasında Tutuklandı," July 24, 2016. Available online: http://t24.com.tr/haber/turkiyenin-ilk-basortulu-rektoru-cemaat-sorusturmasinda-tutuklandi,351666 (accessed December 15, 2018).

[f] *Radikal*, "Ortaöğretimde Başörtüsü Yasağı Kalktı," September 22, 2014. Available online: http://www.radikal.com.tr/turkiye/ortaogretimde-basortusu-yasagi-kalkti-1214245/ (accessed December 15, 2018).

[g] Kemal Göktaş, "Hâkim ve Savcıya Başörtüsü İzni Çıktı," *Milliyet*, June 1, 2015. Available online: http://www.milliyet.com.tr/hakim-ve-savciya-basortusu-izni-gundem-2067366/ (accessed December 15, 2018).

[h] *Sabah*, "İlk Başörtülü Bakan Yemin Etti!" September 3, 2015. Available online: https://www.sabah.com.tr/gundem/2015/09/03/ilk-basortulu-bakan-yemin-etti (accessed December 15, 2018).

[i] *T24*, "Polislere Yönelik Başörtüsü Yasağı Kalktı," August 27, 2016. Available online: http://t24.com.tr/haber/polislere-yonelik-basortusu-yasagi-kalkti,357095 (accessed December 15, 2018).

[j] Patrick Kingsley, "Turkey Allows Women in Military to Wear Hijabs, in Cultural Shift," *New York Times*, February 22, 2017. Available online: https://www.nytimes.com/2017/02/22/world/middleeast/hijab-turkey-military.html (accessed December 15, 2018). *Hürriyet*, "Son Dakika: TSK'da Başörtüsü Yasağı Kalktı," February 22, 2017. Available online: http://www.hurriyet.com.tr/gundem/tskda-basortusu-yasagi-kalkti-40373902 (accessed December 15, 2018).

In 2004, the AKP had a significant challenge on the question of the headscarf in the case against the Turkish government, *Leyla Şahin v. Turkey* at the European Court of Human Rights (ECHR).[54] In its landmark decision, the ECHR rejected the case of Leyla Şahin, a student wearing the headscarf, against Turkey and strengthened the secular justification for the headscarf ban. For Turkey's Islamist women, the ECHR was the last legal resort (which had generated big hopes in Strasbourg) and the decision did not come in their favor, making it harder to change the legal framework in favor of the headscarf in Turkey's domestic courts. ECHR argued that the headscarf, in a Muslim-majority country, could place students who do not practice religion under pressure. Erdoğan severely criticized the European Court and has become the laughingstock of the secular establishment. This was one of the few cases that Turkey did not lose in the ECHR, and the country's prime minister was unhappy about it because the decision conflicted with his stance on the headscarf ban.

The AKP gradually removed the ban by mostly using de facto measures over the course of ten years. By October 2014, the headscarf ban was removed not only in universities but in all schools from fifth grade onward, allowing girls as young as ten years old to take it up. Extending the removal of the ban to schoolgirls made this "right" questionable. For liberals, the headscarf was an adult woman's issue, of choice. But from the AKP's conservative perspective, families have the right to socialize their children into religious practices from a very young age and there is no problem when a ten-year-old girl is socialized into the headscarf and restrictive gender roles. In other words, as opposed to what liberals had hoped, under the AKP, the gradual removal of the headscarf ban went hand in hand with gender policies that reinforced conservatism at the expense of the Kemalist and feminist gains.[55]

The Republican People's Party (CHP) had to adapt to the new situation in spite of its strong secularist stance. Seeing the power of the AKP's conservative religious discourse, the CHP also has increasingly resorted to religious arguments to oppose the changes pushed forth by the AKP. When AKP made the headscarf possible for all young schoolgirls, the CHP used a religious argument instead of a secular one to oppose the measure,[56] testifying to the narrowing down of the secular space in Turkey. The secular arguments questioning the headscarf and religion were marginalized,[57] and even the strongest defenders of Turkish secularism had to bend themselves to accommodate to the changes taking place.

Particularly after the Gezi protests, the AKP linked the headscarf to the will of the majority, and the morality of the nation. The AKP has extended the connotations of headscarf to represent "the people" who are threatened by foreign and domestic enemies. Following the failed coup attempt on July 15, 2016, the pro-government newspapers started to create the myths of a new era by using images of the headscarf. The image of a woman in full black, trying to stop the tanks, was carried in the headlines as the representative of the courageous nation who defended democracy.

The images of women in Turkish newspapers have changed in important ways in the sixteen years of AKP rule. The next chapter looks at the change in the representations of the headscarf and how the Islamist right-wing newspapers have carried it into the mainstream as a symbol of desirable womanhood. Let's look at the images of the headscarf in the Turkish press within a single decade, from 2002 to 2012.

Transformation of the Representations of the Headscarf in Religious and Secular Newspapers

Gender and visual culture of newspapers in Turkey

The representation of gender in Turkish newspapers reflects multiple historical and contemporary dynamics in Turkey. The visual depiction of women in different newspapers is tied to a history of competing political projects, lifestyle preferences, periods of censorship, male domination in the media industry, and the visual culture of newspapers. As a result, Turkish newspapers have presented a challenging and contradictory site to study the representations of gender and the headscarf.

The media in early republican Turkey was an ideological ally to the state in spreading the Kemalist project and the new gender conceptions to the wider population. In the Republic's early years, successful women made the news on the front pages. For instance, in 1928 one of the front-page stories in *Cumhuriyet* (established in 1924, a year after the declaration of the modern Turkish Republic) was about a female student who submitted her doctoral thesis in political science to her committee for review.[1] At the same time, the newspaper introduced Western fashion models to its female readers, organized beauty contests, and defined a model of ideal womanhood in line with the Kemalist Westernizing reforms. In another issue of *Cumhuriyet*, a news item appeared with the title "Fashion Models Are the Happiest Women in the World." The article introduces the term "fashion model" (*manken*) in quotes and lists the reasons why these women are the happiest in the world: they are beautiful and they are the ones wearing the most expensive clothes and jewelry. "Miss Rose Marie of London is maybe the happiest among them with her necklace that worth around a million Turkish liras."[2] Such content, praising the successful educated women on the one hand and, on the other, introducing the concept of celebrity with the ideals of beauty, affluence, and fashion, carried the germs of the later female representations in the Turkish mainstream media.

The press underwent a major shift in the aftermath of 1945, following the transition from one-party rule to multiparty democracy in Turkey. The 1950s witnessed the emergence of mass press (as opposed to more elitist party newspapers) in the tradition of yellow journalism. These newspapers introduced tabloid content with more pictures and catchy, sensational stories that aimed to attract the audiences at the center of the political spectrum.[3] *Hürriyet* (established in 1948) was the leader in the field and the newspaper defined the visual style of newspapers in Turkey for decades to come. To this day, Turkish newspapers are very visual. According to data from 2005,[4] a single newspaper issue contains an average of 120 visuals (photographs, graphics, cartoons, advertising images, etc.), excluding the sports pages and supplements.[5] The Turkish press has retained its tabloid-like character with plenty of visuals and sensational news designed to reach mass audiences. Even a "serious" newspaper like *Cumhuriyet* contains an average of seventy-four visuals in a single issue.[6]

Women's images have constituted an important part of the visual layout of the Turkish newspapers, especially in the mass-circulating press. The secular mainstream press regularly features photographs of models in bikinis on their front and back pages. Images of celebrities in sexualized poses have been a regular feature. While around 9 percent of females are depicted as nude or scantily dressed, only 2 percent of males are depicted in the same way in Turkish newspapers.[7] The visualization of women in the Turkish press has conformed to the gender stereotypes common elsewhere in the world.[8] In other words, the modernization reforms greatly improved women's status in the country yet did not make the mainstream media less sexist.

The rise of feminism in the 1980s and 1990s in Turkey led to a body of research on the representation of women, and sexism, in the Turkish media. Similar to feminist media scholars in the West, Turkish scholars and feminist activists identified sexism at work in the mainstream Turkish media on many levels.[9] Feminist research interested in the news about the headscarf followed the dominant themes in the literature that aimed to reveal sexism, the male-dominated nature of the news, and women's underrepresentation in the media.[10] While the secular press sexualized women's bodies, the Islamist publications that emerged during the 1980s defined womanly desirability in relation to modesty, domestic roles, motherhood, and Islamist activism.[11] They idealized the Muslim woman and pictured her in opposition to the Western woman.[12] When compared on the basis of a sample from 1997, Islamist newspapers contained more references to the female headscarf, and they depicted women in passive roles more often than the secular newspapers.[13] Women were seen in active roles only when they made demands for the right to wear the headscarf.[14]

Despite an ever-growing body of literature on the headscarf, few studies mentioned or paid attention to the visual aspect of the media representations of the headscarf in Turkey. Yet when women are in the news, they appear with accompanying pictures more often than men.[15] Visual rhetorics play a big role in the efforts to legitimate, or delegitimate, the headscarf. Furthermore, in textual content analysis, researchers often use keywords to retrieve articles, and those searches produce results based on the ban—where the headscarf is framed as a problem.[16] This approach has a limiting effect: the images of women in headscarves are tied to the headscarf ban only in rare instances. Therefore, an analysis of these images and accompanying news items gives a better idea of the symbolic and rhetorical uses of the headscarf, as well as how different newspapers employ such images.

News photographs are "very effective tools for framing and articulating ideological messages."[17] According to cultural theorist Stuart Hall, the newspaper "*translates* the legitimations of social order into faces, expressions, subjects, settings and legends."[18] Goodnow argues that the news photograph is positioned in the greater cultural myth and has "the power to challenge, affirm, or reconfirm that larger narrative."[19] Similarly, images of headscarves play an active role in the struggle between the competing discourses by underpinning cultural myths about the headscarf in both "Islamic" and "secular" newspapers.

Studies on the Turkish press, including my own in 2009, have taken the distinction between the secular and the Islamist press for granted. As I question this distinction in this book, I would like to suggest the term "religious right" to refer to the newspapers mentioned in the literature as "Islamist" newspapers. The Turkish Right has had three main branches: the center-right, which is secular; the religious right; and the nationalist right. As I will explain later, in this study I therefore focus on the newspapers on the center-right and religious right. Considering the secular nature of the Turkish center-right, I sometimes use the terms "secular" and "religious" to avoid excessive repetition of the designation "right."

In 2005, noticing the absence of studies on images of gender, I analyzed a sample of six Turkish newspapers as part of my dissertation project.[20] The AKP government was still in its first term when I selected my sample in 2005. I had two newspapers from the secular center-right (*Posta* and *Sabah*), two arguably secular left (*Cumhuriyet* and *Radikal*), two on the religious right: one moderate (*Zaman*) and the other radical (*Anadolu'da Vakit*). My results showed that women constituted 30 percent of figures in all types of images (news photographs, advertisements, and other types), while males constituted the rest.[21] Women without the headscarf were the norm in pictures. Only 16 percent of women were seen with the headscarf in the totality of these newspapers, secular and Islamist combined.[22] Based on Çarkoğlu and Toprak's study published in 2006, it is safe to say that the percentage of women wearing some form of headscarf in the population was much higher at the time: 63.5 percent.[23] Overall, the newspapers clearly reflected the dominant ideology of Kemalism three years into the AKP's rule. My visual analysis also showed that the "Islamic" headscarf had become the dominant way of covering, at least in newspapers' images. Some 65 percent of women seen with the headscarf in the newspapers had an Islamic headscarf, as opposed to 35 percent wearing traditional styles that were lenient in terms of showing part of the hair and the neck.[24]

My study produced very interesting qualitative results showing how the images of the headscarf are used in different newspapers. For instance, victims of domestic violence wearing the headscarf were seen rarely (if at all) in Islamist newspapers. These newspapers, rather, presented stories about the headscarf ban and success stories of women wearing the headscarf. The secular-right newspapers, on the other hand, included stories that would not show up in religious newspapers: for example, tabloid stories about women wearing the headscarf who left their husbands for lovers. These stories normalized the headscarf by detaching religious ideology from the garment and could be read in multitude of ways, as for or against the headscarf. The left-wing newspapers *Radikal* and *Cumhuriyet* contained only a very few images of headscarf.

By 2013, four years after completing this initial project, it became clear, without a doubt, that the AKP had adopted an authoritarian path and was on the way to create a new hegemony based on religious conservatism. Seeing the political changes that had taken place since 2005, I grew an interest in analyzing the visuals of the headscarf in newspapers within a ten-year time frame, starting with the AKP's rise to power (between 2002 and 2012). I developed a new research project with the aim of answering the following questions:

1. Has there been an increase in the images of women with headscarves between 2002 and 2012?
2. If so, what changes have been taking place in religious and secular newspapers?
3. In what ways are the women with headscarves represented in stories where they are the primary focus? What are the differences between the religious and secular newspapers?

To answer these questions, I used qualitative content analysis[25] as a springboard for qualitative discussion.[26] This approach helped me to gain familiarity with various types of headscarf images in the newspapers and the multiple ways they are used, and to determine whether there was an increase in numbers over time. Then, in an in-depth qualitative analysis, I focused on the stories where the women in the pictures were the primary focus.

In 2013, I selected a new set of newspapers on the basis of their longevity. Because of Turkey's tumultuous political history, few titles have survived longer than fifteen or twenty years. I focused on newspapers that, in spite of changes in ownership, had been published without interruption since the 1980s. Out of these newspapers, I selected two secular (*Hürriyet* and *Sabah*) and two religious newspapers (*Yeni Şafak* and *Zaman*), which had been on the market at least for the previous ten years. All these newspapers are on the Right of the political spectrum. *Hürriyet* and *Sabah* are on the secular right,[27] and *Yeni Şafak* and *Zaman* are on the religious right. I decided against including the newspapers on the Left because my earlier study had indicated that they contained very few images of headscarves. I explain the rationale behind selecting each newspaper in more detail below.

The largest newspaper archive in Turkey is in Atatürk Library in Istanbul. Because of the feasibility issues in their retrieval system, I sampled three significant election periods using consecutive day sampling: November 3, 2002, July 22, 2007, and June 12, 2011 (all elections won by the Justice and Development Party—AKP). I collected all the images of headscarves on election day as well as the weeks before and after (fifteen days of coverage during the peak of each election season). I then selected two weeks outside of the election period: one week in August 2002 and another in August 2012.[28] The result was a sample of a total of 236 newspaper issues over a ten-year time frame.

Hürriyet

Hürriyet, one of the oldest Turkish newspapers on the market, published its first issue on May 1, 1948 in the aftermath of the Second World War, during the transition from the one-party to the multiparty regime in Turkey. According to Ali Gevgilili, *Hürriyet* is the first mass newspaper in Turkey[29] and it represents the shift from the elitist to the mass press.[30] By the mid-1960s, *Hürriyet* had succeeded in selling more than a million copies,[31] which was unprecedented for the Turkish press. I consider *Hürriyet*'s founder Sedat Simavi (1896–1953), a journalist himself, as Turkey's Joseph Pulitzer. The Simavi family became very influential in establishing the characteristics of mass popular press in Turkey. *Hürriyet* changed the visual conventions of the press and put more emphasis on catchy images and photographs by using the novel printing technologies of the time.[32] Aydın Doğan, Turkey's then-emerging media mogul, bought *Hürriyet* in 1994, representing the shift in media ownership from journalism families to entrepreneurs interested in the media sector.

The Doğan group had shaky relationships with the AKP government. *Hürriyet* became the target of criticisms in 2008 when the newspaper opposed the government's attempts to remove the headscarf ban by changing the constitution. Religious conservatives used the newspaper's long-time editor in chief Ertuğrul Özkök's catchy headline "411 Hands for Chaos" to attack the newspaper and frame it as hostile to the parliament and the people's vote. The headline referred to the yes vote in the parliament in favor of incorporating the right to wear the headscarf into the constitution. Religious conservatives framed the headline as a call for military to take action. The next year, in 2009, Aydın Doğan's media group received tax fines in record numbers as part of the AKP's attempts to restructure media ownership and silence unfriendly media. Ertuğrul Özkök, *Hürriyet*'s editor in chief, whose piece on the headscarf yields the epigraph to this volume's Introduction, shaped the agenda in the Turkish media, for good and bad, until he left his position at the end of the same year (December 29).[33] He was regularly called "the captain of the admiral's flagship." His critiques emphasized his contribution to the corporatization of the Turkish press at the expense of independent journalism throughout his twenty-year tenure as editor in chief. Özkök remained at the newspaper as a columnist and board member after his resignation. Over time, the newspaper significantly toned down its criticism of the government and managed to survive until 2018. On March 21, 2018, Aydın Doğan sold all his remaining media assets, including *Hürriyet*, to Demirören Holding,[34] a pro-Erdoğan media group who had already bought two newspapers from Doğan in 2011.[35] *Hürriyet*'s change of hands signifies the closure of a significant chapter in the history of the Turkish media.

Sabah

Sabah was founded on April 22, 1985 as a competitor to *Hürriyet*. Its founder, Dinç Bilgin, came from a journalism family who published an influential regional newspaper in İzmir.[36] During the 1980s, *Sabah* provided a new liberal alternative in the Turkish press. By the end of the 1990s, Bilgin's investments in the media had evolved into a new media group, Merkez Media, with television channels, radio stations, magazines, and advertising companies—it had become a significant competitor to Aydın Doğan's media group. The two media groups entered into cutthroat competition and became involved in financial and political scandals because of their investments in banking and other non-media sectors.

Dinç Bilgin's media companies became the first secular media group that was transferred into pro-AKP hands. On April 1, 2007 the Government Agency for Public Funds (Tasarruf Mevduatı Sigorta Fonu—TMSF) took over the management of Bilgin's Media Group due to its unpaid debts to the public sector that amounted to $880 million.[37] Dinç Bilgin had deals with another well-known media owner, Turgay Ciner, and the TMSF argued that these deals were part of a fraud to mislead the agency. On December 5, 2007, the government-friendly Turkuvaz Media group, with Erdoğan's son-in-law Berat Albayrak occupying one of the top positions at the corporation to which Turkuvaz belongs (Çalık Holding), bought *Sabah* along with the television station ATV, which once constituted the major holdings of Merkez Media. Journalists working at *Sabah* did not report intervention by the new owners at the beginning, but voices critical of the government were gradually eliminated from the newspaper throughout the subsequent decade. In 2013, another government-friendly business group (Kalyon Group) bought Turkuvaz Media.[38] By 2017, *Sabah* has become the mouthpiece of the AKP government and the flagship of pro-AKP media. Erdoğan's advisor and son-in-law Berat Albayrak wrote a column in the newspaper that ran between February 10, 2014 and September 28, 2015. Albayrak stopped writing shortly before he became the Minister of Energy and Natural Resources in November 2015. He became the Minister of Finance and Treasury following the elections on June 24, 2018.

In line with its owners' gender conservatism, *Sabah* stopped publishing pictures of scantily clad women in December 2011, following the AKP's third victory. In February 2015, the newspaper transferred the famous pro-AKP conservative female columnist Hilâl Kaplan from the pro-AKP newspaper *Yeni Şafak*.

Yeni Şafak

Yeni Şafak was founded in 1995 by a religiously conservative businessman and was bought by the Albayrak family in 1997.[39] During its first decade, *Yeni Şafak* made a reputation for being an "intellectual" Islamist newspaper. Following the February 28 directives in 1997, the newspaper employed a number of well-known liberal democrats and center-right journalists (Cengiz Çandar, Kürşat

Bumin, Nazlı Ilıcak, Murat Aksoy) who got into trouble with the Kemalists for their critical attitude.[40] The last liberal democrat, Ali Bayramoğlu, left the newspaper in September 2016, following the failed coup attempt.[41] His departure can be seen as a full stop marking the closure of a two-decade period during which Turkey's liberal democrats allied with the religious right to establish a bridge between opposing political views.

Yeni Şafak's owners, five brothers, have had very close relationships with AKP's leader Recep Tayyip Erdoğan throughout his political career, dating to long before the establishment of the party in 2001. One of the owners, Nuri Albayrak, attended Imam Hatip High School together with Erdoğan in the 1970s.[42] Under the AKP governments, the Albayrak Group, which also owns the Albayrak Media Group that includes the television stations TVNET and Tempo Türk TV, grew tremendously. According to Bianet and RSF's Media Ownership Monitor, the group "has taken many large public tenders ranging from construction of the Istanbul metro to producing tanks for the Turkish army, many of which were subject to controversy and investigations of corruption.... The group's revenue in 2000 was USD150 million, whereas in 2008 it was up to approximately USD1 billion."[43]

Yeni Şafak is a prime example of partisan press. In August 2002, the newspaper proudly announced that its CEO, Mehmet Atalay, was one of the candidates for the AKP's list of representatives.[44] Gürcan characterized *Yeni Şafak* as an "ultra pro-government" newspaper.[45] The newspaper has been an unconditional and loyal supporter of Erdoğan.

Zaman

Owned by Feza Media Group until its take-over by the AKP government, *Zaman* was the newspaper of the Fethullah Gülen community.[46] The Gülen community had long been known as a secretive and shadowy organization on the religious right, encouraging its members to get into positions of power in the military and judiciary by hiding their Islamist identity. Thanks to their extremely successful PR, the Gülenists made a reputation for their "moderate" Islamist stance and searched for dialogue between cultures. Because of its famous investments in schooling and education all around the world, many observers saw the movement as an alternative to political Islam, representing a bottom-up strategy for spreading Islamist ideology.

Erdoğan allied with the Gülenists in the aftermath of 2007 to defeat the secular establishment and diminish the power of the military through the

Ergenekon and Balyoz trials. The community gained enormous political power between 2007 and 2012, until its relationship with the AKP government was severed as a result of a series of crises starting with a disagreement over reshaping the education system. *Zaman* changed its pro-AKP position in 2012, signifying a major fissure within the religious right. The newspaper stayed in opposition until its take-over by the AKP government on March 4, 2016. Friends turned into enemies and the tension between the Gülenists and the AKP gradually escalated to the coup attempt on July 15, 2016, the details of which have remained in shadow. Erdoğan blamed Fethullah Gülen and his followers for the coup attempt and for constructing a "parallel state" which the government abbreviated to PDY (Parallel State Organization), creating a perceptual affinity with the Syrian Kurdish party PYD (Partiya Yekîtiya Demokrat—Democratic Union Party). Erdoğan used the occasion to silence and eliminate critical voices on all fronts: Kurdish, liberal, leftist, secular, and religious (Gülenist or not). AKP rebranded the Fethullah Gülen Movement the FETÖ, the Fethullahist Terrorist Organization (Fethullahçı Terör Örgütü).

Zaman's first issue appeared on November 3, 1986.[47] Following its rather independent first year, the newspaper came under the control of the Gülen movement. *Zaman* avoided direct confrontation with Turkey's secular establishment throughout the publication's lifetime.[48] Yet in its struggle for legitimacy, the newspaper consistently framed religious issues in modern terms that sounded scientific and prestigious. The best example for this was the newspaper's "Akademi" page that was devoted to Fethullah Gülen's writings on Islam, the Qur'an, and good and evil.[49] Within its framework of "dialogue," *Zaman* frequently invited or employed leading liberal democrats as columnists including Turkey's best-selling author Elif Shafak.[50] The newspaper's inclusive stance was one of the reasons that convinced Turkey's liberal democrats on the democratic potential of Islamism.

Over the course of two decades (1986–2006) *Zaman*'s circulation increased from around thirty thousand to five hundred thousand readers. The newspaper went through a visual makeover in 2001 that gave the newspaper a serious and prestigious look with fewer, but higher-quality, pictures, and had its golden years in the following decade. Although *Zaman* claimed to have sold a million copies by 2012, its figures remained controversial because of the community support behind the newspaper and its subscription system, which was unusual in the Turkish press.[51] The time frame of my research project coincided with *Zaman*'s golden years, and the period in which the newspaper supported the AKP governments.

Table 3.1 Sampled newspapers according to political orientation and circulation

Newspaper	Political orientation	December 2002	July 2005	March 2010	June 2012	May 2014	September 2018
			Circulation				
Hürriyet	Secular right	461,504	527,301	501,422	405,978	375,876	282,979
Sabah	Secular right	384,000	451,346	389,335	325,483	326,138	297,129
Yeni Şafak	Religious right	n/a	105,473	102,205	103,379	110,343	112,834
Zaman	Religious right	301,694	464,572	794,102	973,087	1,035,305	Defunct

Note: Circulation figures for 2005–14 were obtained from Dördüncü Kuvvet Media (Media as the Fourth Estate), the watchdog website. Available online: http://www.dorduncukuvvetmedya.com/tiraj-raporu/6097-gectigimiz-haftanin-tirajlari-.html (accessed regularly 2005–14, last accessed December 18, 2018). Circulation figures for 2002 were obtained from http://serbestsiyasa.com/?p=1074 (accessed December 18, 2018). Circulation figures for September 2018 were obtained from http://gazetetirajlari.com/HaftalikTirajlar.aspx (accessed September 25, 2018).

Zaman was shut down by executive order following the July 2016 coup attempt, and many of its former journalists were either jailed under charges of plotting a coup against the government or they fled the country. At the moment of this writing in 2018, all of the remaining newspapers in my sample (*Hürriyet, Sabah, Yeni Şafak*) are owned by pro-AKP groups.

For this study, I coded all the images that showed women wearing headscarves in the newspapers and their supplements. I counted any image that included more than one woman wearing a headscarf as still one image. I developed a coding scheme that included the categories listed in Table 3.2.

I coded 983 images in total. On average, a newspaper issue contained four images of women with headscarves. Some 10 percent of the images are photographs of female columnists wearing headscarves—overwhelmingly in religiously conservative newspapers; 14 percent are pictures of the wives and close relatives of AKP leaders and MPs; and another 14 percent are the pictures of non-Turkish Muslim women from around the world. The remaining 62 percent cover all types of images of the headscarf. Only 10 percent of the images included reference to the headscarf in the story, and out of those images 36 percent included reference to the headscarf ban. Overall, 4 percent of images made reference to the ban, and 90 percent of these references were in Islamic newspapers. As Table 3.3 illustrates, the number of women with the headscarf has increased over time in all newspapers with some periodic fluctuations.[52] In

Table 3.2 Coding categories for content analysis

Coding categories	Responses
Is the image in the main body of the newspaper? (If in a supplement, select No.)	Yes or No
Is the image part of a news item, an entertainment (i.e., TV pages) piece, or an advertisement?	News Entertainment Ads
Is the woman in the image at the center of the story?	Yes or No
(Yes, if the whole story is about her and/or her name is cited in the report and she is quoted)	
Is there any reference to the headscarf in the text?	Yes or No
If there is any reference, is it about the headscarf ban?	Yes or No
Is the woman in the picture the spouse or a close relative of a prominent AKP politician?	Yes or No
Is the woman in the picture an author or journalist writing for the newspaper?	Yes or No
Is the woman in the picture from Turkey or is she a Muslim woman from elsewhere?	Yes or No

Table 3.3 Average number of women with headscarf per newspaper issue (2002–12)

	Secular right		Religious right	
	Hürriyet	*Sabah**	*Zaman*	*Yeni Şafak*
August 2002	2.0	1.6	1.7	1.9
Election 2002	2.0	3.9	2.4	3.4
Election 2007	3.3	2.7	3.5	6.3
Election 2011	4.3	4.7	6.7	8.6
August 2012	4.3	6.6	5.1	6.1

* Note that *Sabah* was in the hands of the Government Agency for Public Funds (TMSF) during the 2007 election. It was sold to a pro-AKP corporation in December 2007.

2002, all the newspapers, secular or religious had about the same number of images of women with headscarf. By 2012, the numbers had doubled or tripled depending on the newspaper.

For qualitative analysis, I focused on those stories that placed women wearing headscarves at the center. In these stories, the image of the headscarf stood out because of the size of the image or because I noticed a pattern. In some cases, articles focused on the stories of women seen in the accompanying images; in others, the text did not mention at all who the women were but the images clearly were part of a representation-work, connecting the headscarf to abstract concepts such as democracy and freedom. I did textual analysis of these stories to map out the major themes, looking closely at how the images were used, what the relationships between the text and the images were, and how the images were connected to larger narratives.[53] What are the most common visual rhetorical strategies employed in the Turkish media to defend or question the headscarf? I answer this question below.

The headscarf representing "the people"

A close analysis of visuals during the election periods shows that the image of what is understood to be the traditional headscarf, as worn by senior women mostly with a knot in the front, represented "ordinary" citizens in Turkish newspapers. Politicians across the board, from the Right to the Left, were depicted with senior women wearing traditional, rural forms of the headscarf to convey the message that they care about "the people." For example, in 2002, İsmail Cem, a leftist politician and the leader of the defunct New Turkey Party (Yeni Türkiye Partisi) was depicted while talking to a senior woman wearing a traditional headscarf.[54] In this case, the image of the lady with the traditional headscarf clearly stands for "the people" as the title says: "Cem: 'The people will cast their votes with their good judgment.'" Similarly, AKP's Minister of Finance was depicted while talking to a senior woman from the provincial city Batman,[55] and Kemal Kılıçdaroğlu, the leader of the opposition party CHP (Republican People's Party) was depicted at a visit of condolence, kissing the hand of a senior woman with a traditional headscarf.[56] Kissing the hand of a senior is a traditional gesture, and the image depicts Kılıçdaroğlu in touch with the people's pain and traditions.

The most outstanding example connecting the image of traditional headscarf not just to the people but to democracy and freedom appeared in *Zaman* two days in a row, before and on election day in 2011. The image showed a senior woman wearing a traditional headscarf with a knot in the front, casting her vote while directly looking at the camera. Before the election day, the image appeared in a huge size on a two-page spread analyzing the elections, placed right under the title "What kind of Turkey do we want on June 13?" and above an article titled "Long live democracy."[57] On election day, the image appeared on the front page under the title: "Celebration of (or victory of) democracy," in an article giving the details on the number of candidates and number of voters.[58]

Even though that was a huge picture for newspaper standards, the stories did not give any information at all about who she was. Her image simply stood for the electorate, "the people" who would determine the country's future by their votes.

These images are part of a pattern in the sample starting in August 2002, before the AKP came to power. In other words, the representations that connected the headscarf to "the people" were already there as part of the broader culture independent of political ideologies. This was also apparent in the papers' TV schedules. For example, in 2002, *Hürriyet* included numerous images from Turkish soap operas showing women with folkloric or traditional headscarves, exposing some hair and neck. Apparently, secular television producers saw traditional, lenient forms of the headscarf as part of ordinary life in Turkey.

In 2002, the headscarf also appeared in the newspapers to stand for Turkey's cultural richness and ethnic diversity at a time the country strived to join the European Union. News about a concert in Brussels by the famous Turkish singer Sezen Aksu was the perfect case in point. The story appeared in *Sabah*, *Zaman*, and *Hürriyet*. The news stories in *Sabah* and *Zaman* accompanied an image of Sezen Aksu on the stage with a chorus of young girls, all wearing the folkloric style of headscarf.[59] The stories emphasized that the concert brought songs from "Turkey's mosaic"[60] and aimed to show Turkey's multicultural richness. In other words, the traditional and folkloric images of the headscarf were utilized to promote Turkey's image in Europe as a place of ethnic and cultural treasures. Yet the stories did not make it clear who stood for Turkey's ethnic and cultural diversity. *Zaman* mentioned that the girls were from Diyarbakır, without mentioning the Kurds who constitute the majority in the region.[61] The newspaper, though, did mention Greeks, Armenians, and Jews, groups who are officially recognized as minorities in Turkey.

The news that appeared in secular-right newspapers after the elections in 2002 show that at that time the Erdoğan family was engaged in a discursive struggle to be seen as part of "the people," and normalize their distinct form of headscarf based on a particular interpretation of religion. The secular-right newspapers had approached Erdoğan with suspicion before the elections. For example, in August, *Sabah* had questioned Erdoğan's financial arrangements, particularly the donations he accepted from wealthy conservative businessmen to send his daughters to colleges in the United States. The same newspaper published a series of stories to "normalize" the family after Erdoğan won the elections.[62] *Sabah* presented Emine Erdoğan as an ideal wife, a woman engaged in politics yet who always supported her husband. Erdoğan's daughters, all wearing an Islamist headscarf, were portrayed as regular teenagers who listened to Shakira.[63] In his interview with *Sabah*'s journalist, Erdoğan's son Bilal underlined that they were not "apart from the people," and the newspaper used his phrase as a subtitle in the article.[64] The story had even a populist feel to it: while the other leaders' children were having fun at posh night clubs, Erdoğan's children were studying the Copenhagen criteria to join the European Union.[65] As part of this normalizing work, differences were de-emphasized. As part of these series, *Sabah* reprinted an interview with Emine Erdoğan and highlighted the parts where she mentioned that she was once a woman without the headscarf and the women not wearing it need not to feel afraid of women like her in the party.[66]

Sabah and *Hürriyet* devoted large amounts of space to Emine Erdoğan, particularly in 2002, a point that differentiated them from the religious newspapers. Her fashion choices became the focus of two-page spreads and interviews. Emine Erdoğan stopped talking to the press after a journalist published her off-the-record story about how her brother put pressure on her to cover her hair when she was fifteen, even making her consider suicide. She resisted her brother, yet eventually covered her hair by her own decision after a period of questioning.[67] She was strongly offended by the publication of this story that, according to her, made it look as if covering was not her own decision.[68] Indeed, her story provides a great case for discussing the structural and relational influences on a woman's decision to adopt the headscarf, a case for discussing the tension between structure and agency. Her ensuing silence on the matter might be interpreted as an effort to protect the argument for the headscarf as a woman's independent choice from further harm.

In short, before the AKP redefined the meaning of the religious headscarf as representing "the people," other forms of headscarf were available in secular newspapers and television depicting "ordinary" people in news or in works of fiction. Eventually the AKP reworked the meanings of the traditional headscarf in favor of religious conservatism and in favor of women wearing the headscarf as part of their Muslim identity. As I will explain in detail in the next chapter, since the Gezi protests in 2013 the headscarf has become strongly attached to the "nation" in an exclusive manner, pushing critiques of the AKP outside of the "nation."

Narratives and counter-narratives

I would like to emphasize that the meaning is always in the making, and whenever there is a narrative, there is always a counter-narrative. The visuals of the headscarf should be interpreted within that interplay of contesting narratives.

The ways the secular-right newspapers depicted women from other Muslim-majority societies is a clear example of this. While the religious newspapers regularly depicted women wearing headscarf as acting on their independent choice to fulfill a religious obligation, secular newspapers regularly featured stories about women covering their heads and suffering under religious oppression in other Muslim societies. *Hürriyet*, more than *Sabah*, published news stories with pictures showing women from Iran, Iraq, Afghanistan, Malaysia, and Nigeria. Iranian women facing restricted access to higher education,[69] a Nigerian woman facing stoning as punishment,[70] and the Malaysian "Club of Submissive Wives"[71] are among the examples. These stories are often sensationalized with an orientalist tone, as a story about the opening of Victoria's Secret store in Tehran started with the sentence "Iranians are running after freedom" and emphasized how strange it was to see so many women with limited freedom waiting in line.[72] These types of sensationalized stories provide counter-narratives to claims based on religion and work to reinforce and justify Turkish secularism. Except for rare instances, stories about women from other Muslim countries facing religious oppression were not part of the coverage in religious newspapers. A story about Saudi women's protests for driving privileges could not escape even the religious newspapers.[73]

Within the framework of depicting religion in positive terms, *Yeni Şafak* and *Zaman* showed images of young girls wearing headscarves, praying, or learning to read the Qur'an. The newspapers used such pictures to encourage their readers to send their children to Qur'an courses during the summer. On July 22, 2007, *Zaman* featured a typical example of that genre: a picture showing a little girl, blonde with blue eyes and aged four or five, wearing a pink headscarf in traditional style and praying with her hands held up.[74] The innocence represented by a small young girl is coupled with piety and devotion and used to convey a positive meaning about religion. Her facial expression, focused on an unknown point, connotes a connection between childhood purity and divine power. The image of a small young girl wearing the headscarf and asking something from God, aims to arouse sympathy in the reader. While the religious newspapers used such images, secular newspapers had a repertoire of counter-narratives. *Hürriyet* showed an image of a young girl with a broken arm and wearing a headscarf. The title of the story read "Faced the imam's rage when she recited the prayer wrong."[75] According to the story, the girl who attended a Qur'an course misread a prayer that she was asked to memorize. The imam grew angry and pushed her; the girl fell onto an arm with a previous injury. In other words, while the religious newspapers designated these courses an ideal summer pastime for kids, secular newspapers circulated counter-narratives and linked religion not to peace and innocence but to aggression.

Images of success

Secular newspapers depicted the headscarf as something that could be easily taken off when conditions required; it was not an indispensable part of the wearer's sense of identity. They depicted success as part of a larger narrative on modernization, Westernization, and urbanization.[76] The typical story in a secular newspaper piece would involve a young woman (or a young man) from a small rural town or village who overcame the odds to receive education and excel in their field. Stories of modernized women helping young girls to receive education accompany these narratives.[77]

On July 21, 2007 *Hürriyet* published a story about Leyla Uyan with the title, "Went to school for two years, came as the 839th in the university entry exam." Leyla Uyan attended elementary school only until the second grade but succeeded in becoming one of the top thousand scorers among students who took the university entrance test. Leyla lived in a village in Bingöl, a city in eastern Turkey. According to the story, Leyla's elementary school was shut down because of terrorism. Her mother did not speak Turkish (the text does not mention her native language), and her father was not educated enough to help her in her studies. Leyla regularly read books and educated herself while working on the farm, doing animal husbandry, gardening, and cleaning the house. Even though she could read, she learned how to write only after she enrolled at a Public Education Center (Halk Eğitim Merkezi) aimed at adults like her. Following a series of other hardships, she managed to earn her high school diploma. She received support from her brother and teachers during the process. She worked day and night and became one of the top students. At the time of the story's publication, Leyla aimed to become a Turkish teacher.

Leyla's story, as narrated by the newspaper, clearly has a nationalist subtext. Especially from the lack of education in her mother's tongue, it is not hard to guess that she was Kurdish on her maternal side, and suffered from the government's policies in the region. The text does not mention who closed her school, either. The newspaper's narration erases her ethnic identity and, at the end, positions her within the nationalist project of Turkifying the region by teaching Turkish to other children. In her photograph, Leyla looks at the camera while gardening. The caption says, "In everyday life Leyla covers her hair with a yemeni [a traditional scarf made out of embroidered cotton]. Leyla Uyan had her picture taken without the headscarf for the university and said, 'I will go to university without the headscarf anyway.'"[78] In this quintessentially modernist narrative, Leyla willingly leaves the headscarf and her ethnic identity behind. This is also a story of upward social mobility from a village that has no school or university.

The stories of success featured in religious newspapers did not have a narrative of upward social mobility. They were exclusively stories of middle-class, educated women who overcame the restrictions imposed on them by the headscarf ban at universities. The headscarf was an indispensable part of their identity. The stories sometimes mentioned their family background, indicating that they were brought up with access to networks as well as financial and intellectual resources. In these stories, victimhood stems only from the headscarf ban, not from poverty, violence, or lack of schools. A typical success story from a religious newspaper would involve a woman who had to go abroad to get her college degree because of the headscarf ban at Turkish universities. These stories describe how Turkey lost these young women (mostly) to Western countries, where women found the environment of religious tolerance that they missed in their own country.

Stories that appeared in 2002 and 2007 in religious newspapers in my sample directly referred to the headscarf ban. Newspapers particularly deemed top students wearing headscarf newsworthy. Tuğba Yumak's story is one focusing on a high-achieving student. The story appeared in both *Zaman* and *Yeni Şafak* in 2007. *Yeni Şafak* gave the news both on the front page and on page 10. The title reads, "Could not get education in Turkey, graduated with honors in England."[79] The caption accompanying the image says "Tuğba, the pride of Liverpool University, is now considering the academic offers she has received." Overall, the text mentioned five times that she completed her studies at the top of her class. Tuğba studied genetic engineering and she wished to continue her academic career in Turkey. The story underlined the tolerant environment that she found in England: they even reserved a "special room" for her so that she could practice her religious duties. The story mentioned that her father once acted as the chair of the Islamic Cultural Centre in England.

The stories of women who overcame the restrictions imposed on them by the headscarf ban yielded to another genre in 2011: stories that presented successful role models wearing headscarves, but without making strong reference to the headscarf. The main characters were lifecycle-event organizers, fashion designers, painters, writers, artists, and housewives who organized charity benefit events. These are invariably the stories of middle- or upper-class women wearing the headscarf. I focus on two examples where the religious practice of headscarf has become part of upper-class "taste."

Nesrin Çaylı's image appeared in *Zaman*'s Friday supplement, both on the front page and on page 4.[80] She is a painter, writer, and poet. The picture shows a confident, fashionable, and stylish woman in her ruffled dress with a bow on the sleeve. She wrote stories to accompany another artist's paintings on Muslim ritual prayer. Introducing her book *Stories of Prayer with Paintings*, the news story emphasizes the importance of the ritual prayer and her commitment to the subject. The story mentions that Çaylı aimed to experience the prayer as a "gourmet taste." This is a truly interesting and telling metaphor. It gives a contemporary upper-class twist to the centuries-old Muslim religious practice, originally seen as an equalizer between the rich and the poor. The metaphor implies her search to create distinction in prayer, expressed in the language of upper-class taste with a term borrowed from French.

The story of another artist is expressed in similar terms. Fatma Zeynep Çilek's picture and story stand for another typical success story from 2011. *Zaman*'s Sunday supplement devoted almost a whole page to her story. According to the piece, Fatma Zeynep studied psychology and was a young artist. A devotee of traditional art, she combined traditional Islamic art with graffiti and experimented with novel methods. In the picture, she looks confidently into the eye of the beholder. The color of her eye makeup emphasizes her blue eyes and matches the color of her headscarf, her outfit complemented by a necklace and an eye-catching ring. Although she also suffered from the headscarf ban during her Imam Hatip School years, that's not the focus of the story but mentioned in passing as a restriction that introduced her to arts. The newspaper picked up her story after she had an appearance on a popular television series, *The Valley of the Wolves*, which featured ultranationalist themes. According to the story, her father was a historian, and that distinguished her: unlike her peers, she had encountered traditional Islamic arts early on. Fatma Zeynep Çilek later moved to the posh secular neighborhood of Nişantaşı and made a reputation for herself as a conservative artist. She went through a make over and switched to a new style of head-covering that exposes her neck and emphasizes her identity as an artist. Another interview with her, in 2014, emphasized that she enjoyed taking breakfast at House Café, a pricy, upper-class café, and that she distinguished her lifestyle from the lifestyle in Fatih, Istanbul's neighborhood famous for lower-class religious conservatism.[81] In other words, middle-class, educated women with the headscarf, like Fatma Zeynep, play the role of ambassadors for conservatism, carrying the headscarf to upper-class secular neighborhoods where they feel more comfortable than in lower-class conservative neighborhoods. Her story testifies that upper-class secular life style as exemplified by Nişantaşı, Istanbul's iconic neighborhood that constituted the focus of a number of studies,[82] remains as the main location that defines the horizons and aspirations of conservative professionals.

In its first term, the AKP had already clearly given women wearing the headscarf more confidence. When success stories from 2002 are compared with the stories from 2007 and 2011, differences become clearly visible. In August 2002, *Zaman* ran a story about fifteen young women who had to go abroad to complete their education following the February 28, 1997 directives. These women, mostly students of medicine, had started at university when the headscarf ban was not in effect, yet they could not complete their studies following the enforcement of the ban in 1997. In August 2002, they organized a symbolic graduation ceremony. *Zaman* talked to three of them two days before the event.[83] Unlike the women pictured in 2007 and 2011, these successful women who overcame great hardships did not look directly into the camera. It appears as if they were not comfortable with the camera's presence. They were photographed in long shots, showing them as a group, rather than individuals. As a group, they had a calm demeanor without a smile. Compared to the stylish coverings of the women who appeared on the news in 2011, the women with headscarves in 2002 had just very simple long gowns, understated headscarves, and no visible accessories. The image that was published two days later from the ceremony depicted the women in similar terms. Their style is reminiscent of the 1980s when religious movements in Turkey had an anti-capitalist, anti-consumerist stance. Within ten years, the images of the headscarf had a whole makeover, and moved from depicting victimhood to depicting confidence, distinction, style, and wealth. Women also looked far more comfortable in front of the camera.

An apparent contradiction is visible in the narratives of success in religious newspapers. A top student of genetic engineering is praised for her success upon her graduation, yet another female engineer proudly says: "I discovered how good I am in the kitchen when I left engineering." In a full-page story, *Zaman* proposed a route to happiness for women: working in a home office.[84] The article included stories of women both with and without the headscarf and explained how they switched to home offices and found fulfillment by prioritizing motherhood over their careers. By using women's own words, the story praised home as the source of peace, productivity, creativity, success, and happiness. The story closed with the following quote from one of the women: "Why would I need a career if I am not happy and peaceful?" While praising flexibility, the story did not mention the insecure nature of freelance jobs done from the home. Instead of pointing to the structural conditions at work and home that burdened the women with a double shift, the article offered a solution within the boundaries of traditional gender roles. Also, men's responsibility for parenting was never mentioned.

Women were also praised for their social, philanthropic, and fundraising activities in religious newspapers. In these stories, women find "peace" by helping others and embracing their stereotypically feminine caretaker roles.[85] These stories are in sync with the larger political narrative that the AKP supports for women. In her study of conservative NGOs in Turkey, Zehra Yılmaz emphasized how global Islamism has incorporated into the global neoliberal economy, reorganizing the division of labor between men and women along gendered lines in response to the demands of neoliberalism.[86] According to her, the neoliberal economy eliminates the social security and safety nets, and NGOs fill in this space by mobilizing women's "voluntary" work, carrying their traditional caretaking roles outside the home.[87] Sibel Özbudun also emphasized the overlap between the AKP's policies on women and the global neoliberal project. She pointed out that as part of their policies to integrate into the global neoliberal economy, the AKP governments have encouraged women to work in project-based, part-time, and insecure jobs, praising them as "flexible."[88] In other words, the demands of the neoliberal economy are in tune with the religious conservatives' approach to gender roles. This economic system requires slight modifications that do not threaten the gendered order, and these modifications are presented as improvements. The religious newspapers' typical image of the successful woman—educated, working in flexible jobs, and finding peace at home—might be seen as part of this larger narrative, legitimating the structural reorganization of society to meet the demands of both religious conservatism and the neoliberal economy at the same time. June 2011 in fact witnessed another development, the publication of the first fashion magazine for women wearing the headscarf, underlining the integration of Muslim women into consumerist culture.[89]

To sum up this section, I see the images of middle-class successful women wearing the headscarf as an active attempt to undo the negative secularist connotations of the headscarf. The images of middle-class women reshape the meanings of the covering by linking it to success, wealth, and status, making it more stylish and desirable. These stories include narratives of distinction, marking the wearer as middle- or upper-middle-class. While making the headscarf desirable, the images have also an unsettling effect for the religious conservatives' ideological narrative: these images contradict the ideological narrative that support the idea that women wearing the headscarf are part of a larger sisterhood based on religious belief and practice. The images show middle- or upper-class women with headscarves making every effort to distinguish themselves in style, taste, and appearance from their lower-class "sisters" wearing the headscarf.

Images of poverty

The complex relationship between the headscarf and class, and how lower-class women navigate the meanings attached to the garment, remains understudied.[90] Stories about the lower classes have been a staple of Turkish newspapers, and the headscarf is inseparable from representations of poverty. The type of headscarf a woman wears bears strong marks of distinction and class: fabric (silk vs. cotton or nylon), color, pattern, design, brand name, and embellishment all point at the class status of the wearer. Cotton, flower-patterned, and embroidered headscarves mark the wearers as lower class (Figure 3.1). It is safe to say that when poverty is covered in Turkish newspapers, it mostly appears along with imagery of lower-class women wearing headscarves. When the elite conservative women with headscarves complain about their lack of representations in the media, they mostly refer to the lack of representations of middle-class, educated women wearing the headscarf in their own style.

Figure 3.1   Embroidered cotton headscarves in a neighborhood market. They are mostly worn by lower-class women. Photograph by the author.

When success stories are compared to stories on women and poverty, an interesting difference becomes visible. In 2002 almost all the images of women with the headscarf in *Yeni Şafak*, the pro-Erdoğan newspaper, were poor women, and they appeared in stories about poverty. Women farmers struggling because of the economy and women textile workers appeared on the news.[91] Almost every day before the election, the newspaper published stories about poverty always accompanied by images of women with headscarves. The story titled "On the poor's table, the cheese is broken, bread is old" focused on the consumption patterns of the poor and how they survived. The story showed a poor woman with a child, picking up broken watermelons from the street, probably leftovers from a market place.[92] Women waiting inline to receive aid for food was part of the coverage in *Yeni Şafak* before the 2002 elections.[93]

An iconic image depicting the AKP in the service of the poor appeared right after the elections in 2002. As part of the election campaign that year, Erdoğan had frequent visits to the poor in shantytowns.[94] A couple of days into the aftermath of elections, Ramazan, the holy month of fasting, started. On the first of day of Ramazan, Erdoğan and his wife had separate visits to shantytowns to have the *iftar* meal[95] together with the poor, continuing the "tradition" that they set before the 2002 elections. These visits, widely covered in the media, conveyed the message that Erdoğans would remain connected to the poor during their time in power. An image from *Yeni Şafak*, which appeared also in *Zaman*, depicts Erdoğan when he is leaving a poor family's house (Figure 3.2). The image

Figure 3.2 "İlk İftar Gecekonduda," *Yeni Şafak*, November 7, 2002, 13. Photographer unknown, image source not mentioned.

appeared both on the front page and inside of the newspaper. The caption reads, "First iftar meal is in a shantytown house."[96]

I find this image iconic because of the way it captured highly dense power relations in a single frame. Erdoğan is positioned as the "protector" of the poor with his powerful hand gesture that dominates the frame. He makes assuring eye contact with the senior woman wearing an embroidered headscarf. The other woman with a headscarf looks admirably at the blonde CNN Türk reporter; the reporter does not reciprocate her attention. The two women's embroidered and flower-patterned headscarves signify their social position as lower class. As can be seen from the number of reporters, the visit was highly publicized, yet it was staged as a surprise to the family. The text mentioned that the family served Erdoğan beans and rice, the staple of the poor.

In sharp contrast to 2002, the discourse of poverty disappeared in *Yeni Şafak* following the national elections in 2007. When poor women were shown, their images were not connected to poverty in the text, but were displayed as an accomplishment by the AKP or to Erdoğan's benevolence in helping the poor.[97] By looking at the images, one could get the impression that poverty had disappeared during the AKP's first term. This indicates the extent to which the newspaper heavily politicized the images of poverty in favor of Erdoğan during the election seasons. Depictions of middle- and upper-class Muslims in growing numbers accompanied the disappearance of the images of the poor, rendering the growing gap between wealthy conservative Muslims and the poor invisible.

The stories of poverty in *Yeni Şafak* took an interesting turn during the elections in 2011. The only poverty story that *Yeni Şafak* picked up was a poor family who lost their two-and-a-half-month-old baby girl named Kübra. The story reported that the little girl "allegedly" died of malnutrition. According to *Yeni Şafak*'s report, these allegations were not true because the forensic medicine report gave the cause of the baby's death as unknown. The newspaper picked up the story, titled on the front page "Take your hands off Kübra," not to talk about the family or the baby but to criticize the Republican People's Party on the opposition.[98] The Republican People's Party had based its campaign on poverty that year and, according to *Yeni Şafak*'s story, Kemal Kılıçdaroğlu, the party's leader, referred to the family's loss in a number of campaign rallies to criticize the AKP. Using the words of the baby's parents, "Don't exploit the name of our children for politics,"[99] the story accused Kılıçdaroğlu of using the family's loss for political gain. The newspaper utilized the story to attack Erdoğan's opponents and deny them their claim of supporting the poor.

In its narratives of poverty over a period of ten years, *Yeni Şafak* never established a link between poverty and politics (in the negative sense) as long as the stories involved Erdoğan. The newspaper did not use the framework of political gain when Erdoğan sent presents to the family of a poor toilet cleaner who named their newborn son after him.[100] I propose that the visual rhetorics of poverty in *Yeni Şafak* are part of a larger discursive struggle to establish the AKP as the new hegemonic power in Turkey. As I will explain in the next chapter, depicting Erdoğan as a politician without "politics" or "ideology," whose only purpose is to serve the people, is a common strategy of legitimation that frequently appeared in pro-AKP conservative women's columns as well.

Images of conservative female journalists

The most significant change in religious newspapers between 2002 and 2012 was the rise of the female columnists with headscarves, around nine times more of whom were published in *Yeni Şafak* than in *Zaman*. In this section, I will focus mostly on the images from *Yeni Şafak* because of its consistent pro-AKP stance and because the newspaper carried conservative female columnists to the mainstream more than *Zaman* did. *Zaman* played an important role in carrying images of middle-class conservative women to the center and also employed female journalists and reporters who sometimes appeared in the pictures. Yet the newspaper had only one lead female columnist, Nihal Bengisu Karaca, who became very well known during her time at *Zaman*. She regularly wrote in the "Commentary" and "Culture and Art" pages, and moved to the center-right newspaper *Habertürk* when it was established in 2009. After her departure, *Zaman* was left without an influential conservative woman writer.

Between 2002 and 2012, *Yeni Şafak* opened its pages to women columnists and journalists to a great extent and made them visible to an unprecedented degree. In 2002, Özlem Albayrak was the only female columnist wearing a headscarf whose column had appeared with her photograph next to her byline in *Yeni Şafak*. Her column appeared on the TV schedule page, not a very prestigious location in the symbolic space of the newspaper. Fatma Barbarosoğlu, a veteran headscarf-wearing female columnist at *Yeni Şafak*, did not have her picture next to her byline.[101] By 2012, they had columns—as men did—on the "Commentary" and "Today's Agenda" pages, and the space allotted to them became larger.[102]

In addition to moving the existing authors to new pages, *Yeni Şafak* invited influential conservative women active in politics and media to write columns in the newspaper. Two of the most well known among them were Ayşe Böhürler and Hilâl Kaplan, who wrote columns in the main body of the newspaper. In addition to them, photographs of young conservative female journalists wearing the headscarf regularly appeared in the supplements. For example, in a Sunday supplement in 2011, the journalist Merve Sena Kılıç was shown while interviewing one of the conservative board members of a private university. She has her photograph placed over her byline; she is smiling and wearing a fashionable style of covering. She has also appeared in a picture together with her interviewee in a very stylish dress and headscarf.[103] Two other journalists who are twin sisters, Kübra Sönmezışık and Büşra Sönmezışık were also frequently seen with their interviewees.[104] The depiction of conservative journalists in fact followed a convention set earlier by secular newspapers in depicting female interviewers with their interviewees.[105]

During this decade, the conservative female journalists also became much more visible on television. They started to produce their own discussion shows, giving them more access to the key people in conservative networks. By 2011, their newspapers had started to advertise their television shows, broadcast by the stations owned by the newspapers' parent media company. For example, the twin journalists Kübra and Büşra Sönmezışık had also their own television show called *Twin Mirror*. Their show on TVNET was largely advertised in *Yeni Şafak*,[106] whose owners also own the television station. Two other female journalists with large advertising space (one is Hilâl Kaplan) have produced programs for this television station.[107] While conservative female journalists in *Yeni Şafak* gained more access to broadcasting, the media group that owned *Zaman* also employed its first female news presenter wearing a headscarf.[108] In two years, the state television TRT Türk, under the control of the AKP, employed its first headscarf-wearing anchorwoman in November 2013.

The newspapers on the religious right provided a space for conservative women wearing the headscarf and gave them opportunities as the AKP worked to consolidate its power. The images of female journalists conformed to the visual patterns seen in the images of successful, middle-class conservative women wearing a headscarf. Their style, fashion, and makeup distinguished them, and they were all thin, able, young, and conventionally good-looking. As they become more visible in their own newspapers with their success and fashionable headscarves, they received more and more attention from the secular press, mainly the center-right and the liberal left-leaning sectors who were sympathetic toward the conservative women's struggle against the headscarf ban.

Conservative women columnists in the center-right and the left-leaning media

Toward the end of the 2000s, paralleling their move to the center of the newspaper, conservative women columnists were discovered by the secular mainstream press on the center-right and the liberal-left.[109] *Hürriyet*'s star journalist, Ayşe Arman, who made a name for herself by asking unexpected and tough questions of her guests, held an interview with Ayşe Böhürler of *Yeni Şafak* in 2006.[110] The interview was accompanied by photographs that depicted Böhürler as a successful, beautiful, well dressed, and sophisticated actor of Turkish media. In 2007, *Hürriyet*'s editor in chief, Ertuğrul Özkök, praised conservative women's writing in his column.[111]

One well-remembered yardstick during this process was a 2007 article by Nihal Bengisu Karaca, published soon after Özkök's piece. Karaca was the lead female columnist at *Zaman* at the time and she wrote a guest article for the left-leaning newspaper *Radikal* about her experience at the beach.[112] Karaca loved swimming, and as a practicing religious woman she looked for women-only beaches. Since they had started to appear, at the end of 1990s, beaches catering to conservative women had been an interesting topic for the media and for academia.[113] Karaca had to seek those unfrequented areas to be able to swim without being seen by a man. In Karaca's experience, the available gender-segregated beaches were mostly located in remote corners; their rough sea and bad service made the experience unenjoyable. She humorously wrote about how her search to find a suitable place to swim as a religious woman turned into an ordeal for her and for her family. Karaca's article was widely discussed by other journalists in the secular media.[114] The article could not escape the notice of *Hürriyet*'s Ayşe Arman, who soon had an interview with Karaca. The guest piece introduced Karaca to audiences outside conservative circles.

In the following two years, *Taraf*, the newspaper of anti-Kemalist liberals supported by the Gülenists,[115] employed a number of conservative female columnists wearing the headscarf, Hilâl Kaplan among them, before she started writing for *Yeni Şafak*. Many liberal democrats interpreted such crossovers as important steps for going beyond the Islam-versus-secularism divide, testifying to the democratic potential of political Islam in Turkey. The conservative female authors received a lot of sympathy from liberal democrats because of the way they situated themselves as fighting on two fronts. The women were critical of secularism and the deficiencies of democracy in Turkey, but they also regularly criticized conservative men. Because of their positioning as individuals suffering from double marginalization, the liberal democrats came to see conservative women columnists as bridge-builders between the secular and Islamist camps.

In January 2010, soon after he resigned from his position as *Hürriyet*'s editor in chief, Özkök wrote a piece about women columnists wearing the headscarf and lamented that he had not discovered a conservative female writer like them. He praised their style, mentioned four columnists, and named them as "pioneers of change."[116] Whether he truly discovered conservative women anew or this was part of an attempt to mend the newspaper's strained relations with the government because of huge tax fines is open to speculation. In November 2012, in three successive articles, Öztürk named "the most influential ten women wearing headscarf" since 1950s.[117] By 2013, it was Özkök who was interviewed by a conservative woman journalist from a small Islamist newspaper, *Milat*. Özkök published parts of the interview in his column for two days,[118] argued that conservative women were more democratic than conservative men and he could relate to them much more.[119] He found them in a "revolt" (*isyan*) against conservative men. He identified their revolt as one of the defining developments that would lead to Turkey's democratization.[120]

I opened the first chapter with Özkök's predictions about headscarf made in 2005—they proved wrong. As of 2018, his predictions about the role of conservative women in Turkish politics made in 2013 have likewise been proven wrong. While Turkey has moved to authoritarianism since 2010, conservative women did not revolt against conservative men, as Özkök had foreseen. Instead, they became strong defenders of a new hegemony established by an authoritarian conservative man. Ironically, as I will show in the following chapter, Özkök's celebration of conservative women as Turkey's defining democratizing force coincides with the surfacing of major disagreements between conservative women and the liberal democrats in terms of the performance of the AKP government.[121]

In the subsequent eight years, conservative women columnists started to be regularly quoted in secular, liberal, and leftist media. They not only gained more power in the conservative newspapers they had been writing in, but they also moved into the mainstream as columnists whose opinions mattered to understand the AKP government and its domestic and foreign policies.[122] They became regular guests of television discussion shows and had more opportunities to insert their perspective into the public discourse within an environment of increased government propaganda and decreased media diversity. Conservative women columnists' rise to positions of power in the media did not accompany democratization. On the contrary, this period witnessed unprecedented authoritarianism under a civil government in the history of modern Turkey.

Ertuğrul Özkök was not the only one in Turkey who saw conservative women wearing the headscarf as democratizing, transformative agents. He based his predictions on Nilüfer Göle's influential book *The Forbidden Modern*. Yet, instead of being democratizing agents, conservative women have opted to support an authoritarian leader who practically abolished democracy. Why did the liberal democrats' thesis fail so badly? What does the mainstreaming of conservative women journalists mean within a climate of increasing religious conservatism, authoritarianism, and media repression? I address these questions in the next two chapters by analyzing the columns of three prominent conservative women, Ayşe Böhürler, Hilâl Kaplan, and Nihal Bengisu Karaca, who stood out in the press and in broadcast media between 2002 and 2012.[123] I would like to introduce them before I move to the next chapter.

Conservative women columnists: The stars of a new hegemony

Ayşe Böhürler (born in 1963), Nihal Bengisu Karaca (born in 1972), and Hilâl Kaplan (born in 1982) are three stars of this new hegemony. I selected them because they are present in print, online, and on broadcast media. In addition to writing regular columns, they all produced their own television programs in conservative and secular channels and have been active on Twitter. All of them frequently appear in media as discussants. All three women were once seen as bridge-builders between Turkey's hostile neighborhoods. As of this writing in 2018, they continue to support Erdoğan and the AKP in spite of the authoritarianism and heavy repression.

Nihal Bengisu Karaca started to write in *Zaman* in 2002, the year that the AKP came to power. In 2009, she started writing in *Habertürk*, a secular center-right newspaper. She made the discussion program *İkide Bir* [*Two in One*] together with Serdar Turgut, another journalist from *Habertürk*.[124] Karaca became part of the AKP's publicity initiative of "sensible people" (*akil insanlar*) for democratization in 2013, and traveled Turkey to convince local opinion leaders and residents of the significance of the AKP's Kurdish peace process. In spite of her occasional criticisms, Karaca has remained supportive of the AKP government. She became one of the journalists who were invited to join Erdoğan and other AKP ministers in their trips to foreign countries.[125] She positions herself as an open-minded, objective, democratic, and fair journalist. She can at moments be aggressive, defiant, sarcastic, and scornful toward the opposition. Writing in a colloquial and vivid style, she likes to show her mastery of culture, film, and literature. Following the failed coup attempt of July 15, 2016, Nihal

Bengisu Karaca was one of the star journalists invited to CNN Türk to comment about the Yenikapı Rally that brought Erdoğan and opposition leaders together and was broadcast live for hours. She discussed the rally with İsmail Saymaz, a star journalist from the Left.

Hilâl Kaplan, the youngest of conservative women in this study, has a career as an activist. She was a member of the group Genç Siviller (Young Civils), who organized protests against the military's "e-coup" in 2007.[126] She started writing in *Taraf* in 2009 and moved to the pro-AKP newspaper *Yeni Şafak* in 2011. While writing for *Yeni Şafak*, she prepared the television program *Muhalif* (Dissident) for TVNET. Hilâl Kaplan defines herself as an advocate for rights and justice.[127] Throughout her years in *Yeni Şafak*, justice for all, irrespective of belief or political standing, was the main theme of her columns. Like Nihal Bengisu Karaca, she became one of the "sensible" (*akil*) people to promote the Kurdish peace process in 2013. She was transferred to the now-flagship pro-AKP newspaper *Sabah* in 2015. The oppositional media interpreted this transfer as a promotion, rewarding her commitment to supporting the AKP government. By 2016, she had become one of the journalists who would have the privilege of interviewing Erdoğan following key events and turning points. Erdoğan gave her and a male journalist his first exclusive interview after the failed coup attempt on July 15, 2016.[128] The interview was broadcast by ATV, whose owners also own *Sabah*. Because of her polemics over Twitter posts, Kaplan earned the title "queen of trolls" (*trolliçe*).[129]

Ayşe Böhürler, a columnist from *Yeni Şafak*, is one of the founders of the AKP. She is a well-respected conservative woman who also was seen as a bridge between the AKP and the liberals. She started to write in *Yeni Şafak* in 2006. Before *Yeni Şafak*, she produced a television program for Kanal 7, a religiously conservative television channel. She traveled to a number of Muslim countries to produce a documentary about Muslim women in the world. This documentary and her other work in women's rights led liberals to think of her as an Islamic feminist. In 2009 she made a television program with two secular women on the secular television channel Kanal 1. She described her appearance, a woman wearing a headscarf on a secular channel, as the disappearance of a taboo.[130] Böhürler stopped her active engagement in the party's highest decision-making organ, known as the Central Decision and Executive Committee, in 2012 but continued to write for *Yeni Şafak* and support the AKP. She ran as a candidate from the AKP during the June 24, 2018 national elections, but could not win a seat in the parliament.

I collected and read all the columns that these female writers published through the end of 2014. The start dates differed, as I started reading from the

Table 3.4 Distribution by author of articles analyzed

Author	Newspaper	Time frame	# of articles
Ayşe Böhürler	*Yeni Şafak*	2006–14	421
Hilâl Kaplan	*Yeni Şafak*	2011–14	692
Nihal Bengisu Karaca	*Habertürk*	2009–14	856
TOTAL:			1,969

first day each columnist started writing for the newspaper. I read from the very beginning to be able to see how these women developed their voices and narratives and to see how they positioned themselves in relation to the other actors in Turkish politics over time. I analyzed 1,969 articles in total by using open coding and discourse analysis. I grouped their articles according to the themes and subject areas and the ways in which they mobilized arguments in defense of the AKP. I first read Nihal Bengisu Karaca's articles and summarized each article in memos. I coded the articles of other columnists in PDF files line by line.

Aside from analyzing the collected data, I checked for changes in women's position around the national elections of June 7, 2015 and November 1, 2015. I read women's columns on the presidential referendum that took place on April 16, 2017. This constitutional referendum changed the political structure in Turkey from a parliamentary to a presidential system and opened the way for Erdoğan to control the legislative, executive, and judicial branches of the government.[131] I read their columns before and after the elections on June 24, 2018. In short, I followed these women's columns beyond 2014 to see whether any significant departures from the AKP had appeared in their writing. As of late 2018, no such departures were in evidence.[132]

The Rise of the Conservative Female Journalist and the Mainstreaming of the Headscarf

In a series of articles in 2011, Hilâl Kaplan, one of the conservative women columnists at *Yeni Şafak*, analyzed the workings of power from the Ottoman period until the Turkish Republic. She pointed out how the power holders ordering the Armenian genocide and later those who banned the headscarf used the same exclusionary language.[1] She wrote about how the system created an idea of "threat" that pitted marginalized groups against one another and spread fear. She supported pluralism by defending the rights of all marginalized groups in Turkey: Kurds, Jews, gypsies, Christian minorities, and practicing Muslims.[2] In another article she deconstructed the governments' use of the term *terrorism* and criticized the process by which Muslims are made into an enemy.[3] She criticized the binary politics of "either you are with us or against us."[4] In 2011, any left-wing intellectual could easily agree with her on all these points.

Yet, in 2017, at a time when Erdoğan was concentrating power in his hands to an unprecedented degree, Kaplan went on to declare any categorical rejection of Erdoğan as anti-Turkey—as collaborating with Turkey's enemies in and outside.[5] "Turkey" became synonymous with Erdoğan in Kaplan's and other conservative women's writings. In the April 2017 presidential referendum where Erdoğan was given tremendous powers at the expense of the parliament, Kaplan supported Erdoğan in her article "248 times YES."[6] Similarly, Nihal Bengisu Karaca, who criticized the government's populist policies in 2010,[7] embraced and praised Erdoğan in 2014 as an exceptional leader who used even populism to solve problems.[8] How did women who passionately argued for the expansion of democratic rights, participation, justice, inclusion, and openness end up supporting authoritarianism and the concentration of power in the hands of one man? As Kemalists have argued, were they faking it (*takiyye*) from the beginning to deceive the system? What happened within a decade? This chapter aims to provide answers to these questions by analyzing women's columns and telling the story of how these women moved from being "bridges" to acting as strong defenders of Erdoğan's New Turkey.

Conservative women's narratives have regularly received scholarly attention since the 1980s. The first generation of conservative women communicated their ideas through book publishing. Novels were the first medium they embraced. As a result, we have a large body of scholarly research on conservative women's novels and books in other genres.[9] The earlier generation was on the defensive and wrote for rather limited audiences in their own circles. But the generation of younger conservative women whose columns I am analyzing here are on the offensive and can reach far wider audiences thanks to their skillful media management. Their presence in journalism, TV production, and social media distinguish them from their senior sisters.

There are only a few systematic studies analyzing Islamist female journalists' columns, in spite of these columnists' growing presence and influence in the media.[10] Yet, these existing studies focus on the headscarf ban, women's issues and Islamist women's struggles with the Islamist men. For example, Arat focused on how Islamist women covered a number of women's issues in their columns.[11] In this chapter, I argue that looking at conservative women's writing mainly on women's issues has misled scholars into situating them as progressive actors or feminists. When we analyze these women's writing over a variety of issues, and take changing political contexts into account, we end up with a different, far more complicated picture. I share some observations with Arat, particularly on women's positions on women's issues. Yet my theoretical framework and additional findings have led me to totally different conclusions.

The position of conservative Turkish women has changed and shifted through time on numerous issues: what constitutes democracy; Turkey's involvement in Syria; the transition from the parliamentary to the presidential system; solutions for the Kurdish problem; the role of secularism, and, finally, Turkey's shift to authoritarianism under Erdoğan. For example, Nihal Bengisu Karaca's approach to democracy has changed over time from an emphasis on pluralism[12] to an emphasis on the ballot box.[13] She criticized gender essentialism in one of her columns within the context of supporting women's employment outside of home,[14] yet in other instances adopted a language that essentialized men and women.[15] As I argued in the Introduction to this book, such contradictions cannot be explained with reference to the "feminist voice"[16] in women's columns.

To give another example, Ayşe Böhürler regularly criticized secularism between 2006 and 2011. Yet when the conflict between the AKP and the Gülenists emerged in 2013 and both sides accused each other of being un-Islamic, she called on them both to adopt a secular language in discussing "worldly issues," hoping that this could alleviate the conflict.[17] In 2016, Böhürler went back to her critical position, arguing that secularism, a concept developed out of resistance to the church in Christian societies, has lost its function in the twenty-first century.[18] She made this argument within the context of defending an AKP parliamentarian who had asked for the removal of the secularism clause from the Turkish constitution. Böhürler argued that the removal of this clause would not jeopardize the lifestyles of nonreligious citizens. She did not clarify how exactly this would be so.

To understand such shifts, it is crucial to locate women's writing within the changing political context and to identify the strategies they employed to redefine the mainstream in their own religiously conservative terms. Kandiyoti cautioned against overlooking "important conjunctural and tactical elements in the self-presentation of Islamic actors whose positions may respond to changing external circumstances."[19] In my analysis of women's columns, I aim to highlight such "tactical elements" and "external circumstances" by paying attention to the issues they are responding to and the rhetorical-argumentative strategies that they use in their response. Such contradictions in women's discourse cannot be explained without looking at to whom they are talking, the timing, the specific struggle taking place, and the stakes.

In this chapter, I argue that women as media figures have struggled to establish themselves as a new intellectual class by aggressively working to delegitimate liberal democrats and academics on the Left, even in some periods by using the language of the Left, as Hilâl Kaplan's example at the beginning of the chapter indicates. The struggle to gain control of the intellectual realm has reached new heights during the AKP's time in power, and women actively took part in this struggle. Women attacked even secular intellectuals who strongly argued against the headscarf ban in universities—like Nilüfer Göle, Binnaz Toprak, and Nuray Mert. The purge against the media and academia in Turkey can be seen as part of the process of delegitimating leftist academics and liberal democrats, a process that conservative women sanctioned in their columns by casting liberal and leftist intellectuals as "foreign" to the "nation."

Second, women have regularly provided insider critiques of conservatism and the AKP government. Yet, contrary to Ertuğrul Özkök's interpretation, these criticisms never took the form of a "revolt." On the contrary, women's insider criticisms aimed to protect the party from the criticisms coming from the liberal democrats, feminists, Kemalists, and Kurds. As a result, their criticisms of conservatism, conservative men, or the government never posed a significant threat or challenge to the conservative men in power. Along with other modernist intellectuals, Özkök departed from the modernist bias that assumes religious conservative women are submissive and interpreted any criticism of men coming from conservative women as a sign of "revolt," or as something transformative. The history of conservative women's movements in Turkey and elsewhere disproves the modernist, orientalist assumption that sees religious conservative women as passive recipients of power. They are as committed and as passionate as any other women in defending their point of view. They can be strong defenders of misogynist men in power at times of heightened conflict and polarization.

I also argue that Gezi protests became a turning point for conservative women. A clear shift in language occurred following the Gezi protests with a strong populist turn. Women returned to right-wing arguments and conspiracy theories to understand the resistance to the so-called New Turkey. In conservative women's columns, "Turkey" became synonymous with Erdoğan and the AKP, and "nation" became equal to AKP voters.

Justifying and legitimating authoritarianism: the AKP, Erdoğan, and conservative female journalists

Conservative female journalists have clearly sympathized with the Justice and Development Party and supported Erdoğan from the beginning. They described Erdoğan as "our" prime minister.[20] Erdoğan is the prime minister who has won the people's hearts again and again.[21] Erdoğan is a charismatic leader,[22] a problem solver—and women trust him unconditionally. The AKP is regularly framed as a revolutionary party that stands for confidence and reason, as the party replaced unreasonable policies with reasonable ones.[23]

For conservative women writers, the AKP is a success story. They frequently list the successes of the party,[24] and "success" is defined from the conservative point of view—economy, education, foreign policy, and women's rights, among other issues. As women have easy access to AKP members, representatives, and ministers, they regularly use them as sources and accept the information coming from them as the final truth.[25] Consequently, they define success through the party's lens, by using the party's PR terminology. For example, Ayşe Böhürler described the process following the investigations of corruption started on December 17, 2013 as a "War of Independence" replicating the party's framing of the events.[26] Terms like "Big Turkey" or *Dik Duruş* ("strong stance," a term that described Erdoğan as a strong leader in party posters) appeared in Hilâl Kaplan's and Nihal Bengisu Karaca's columns.[27] Women actively propagated the party's narrative without questioning any potential for manipulation or distortion on the party's side. They clearly named the AKP while talking about its successes, yet when it came to blaming someone for the failures, the journalists created a "terminological fog"[28] by talking not about the actions and policies of the party but of the "state."[29] Failures were waved aside in a number of ways: by blaming the "republic" (representing the "old Turkey") for the party's present actions,[30] by pointing at factors outside the party, and by impugning a vague group of overzealous party supporters and/or opportunists.

I will talk more about women's approach to gender issues in the next chapter. Here, I would like just to mention that women justified the AKP's gender policies in a similar manner. Conservative women regularly criticize the ultra-sexist remarks coming from AKP ideologues and members, yet they do that carefully, without blaming the party for its policies on gender. When sexist and controversial comments come from the men in the party, women tend to cast them as exceptions not representing the values and philosophy of the party.[31]

Pro-AKP conservative women journalists use a number of argumentative strategies to defend Erdoğan and the AKP. Next, I highlight two recurring ways that they justify Erdoğan's authoritarianism.

Erdoğan: Democrat or dictator?

Conservative women have been troubled by the criticisms that point at the resemblances between the rise of Nazism and Erdoğan's increasing authoritarian policies. Calling Erdoğan a dictator directly attacks him, and delegitimates his claim to be a democratic leader. The extent to which Erdoğan can be described as a dictator at different moments of his political tenure, and whether or not his methods for suppressing dissent are the same as those used by the fascist regimes, is open to debate. Yet the arguments presented by women for Erdoğan's defense rather endorse a totalitarian social engineering project and justify the fears of those who argue that there are resemblances between Erdoğan's Turkey and the Nazi era.

In 2010, Nihal Bengisu Karaca wrote an article arguing against such resemblances.[32] She found the Hitler analogy totally wrong and disgusting (*iç bulandırıcı*) as nobody is talking about eliminating the members of a religion or race. She found the analogy disrespectful toward Jews. She argued instead that, unlike Hitler, the AKP does not imagine an external mechanism of control imposed from the outside. For her, the movement that created the AKP imagines a spiritual recipe that controls and monitors human beings from the inside. That's an inner mechanism of insight that keeps itself accountable to the creator. This movement offers a collection of spiritual values that aims to keep the destructive side of human nature and its dangerous desires under control. For her, this existential perspective is the safety valve of society. Nihal Bengisu Karaca does not seem to notice that defining what constitutes "human nature," and imposing it through the creation of an "inner mechanism of control," is an essential part of totalitarian engineering projects that can be made possible under dictatorships. Karaca's narrative leaves unexamined the oppressive mechanisms that the AKP has employed toward creating an "inner mechanism of control," a vision where individuals internalize the mechanisms of control or obey the system because of the fear of violence.

Women also defend Erdoğan's sharp and divisive language, seen as authoritarian and dictatorial by his opponents. These conservative voices see Erdoğan as a charismatic leader and are not happy about showing him as an uncompromising figure. For example, in one of her articles Karaca commented on Erdoğan's statements on private lifestyle issues: he asked women to have at least three children and criticized the consumption of alcohol, among other things. She pointed out that previous prime ministers in Turkey were cautious about their public statements for fear that words coming from a prime minister could be perceived as law and might be used to oppress others.[33] Karaca defended Erdoğan's divergence from his predecessors' practices by using two strategies: she framed him as a familial elder and emphasized his authenticity. For Karaca, Erdoğan, as a prime minister, frequently gives advice (*nasihat*) to "his citizens" on a wide range of issues. *Nasihat* refers to "friendly advice" mostly given by an elder to a younger person in the family. The word has positive and intimate connotations in Turkish and entails a power dynamic, endorsing the elders' wisdom and guidance. Applying this term to the relationship between a prime minister and "his citizens," Karaca portrays Erdoğan in familial terms, like an elder who cares about the well-being of the young people in the family. Citizens, in return, are placed in the position of receiving advice, like children, not as full-grown adults with rights and responsibilities who can make their own decisions about what to drink and how many children to have. Patronizing interventions in lifestyle choices are given legitimacy through recourse to intimate family relations.[34]

Karaca acknowledges that Erdoğan's statements on lifestyle preferences keep cultural fractures alive and are therefore problematic. But she sees a positive side to it: we know where Erdoğan stands, we know who he really is. She argued that following the "Blue Marmara"[35] incident he terrified some, but he stood "where his heart pulled him."[36] Depicting Erdoğan as a genuine leader who follows his heart is another justification strategy common in women's writing.

If Erdoğan is not behaving like a dictator, what does a dictator look like? In a number of articles, these women journalists defined dictatorial behavior as exhibited by other leaders. For example, in her criticism of the extrajudicial killing of Anwar al-Awlaki who was a Yemeni-American preacher and alleged al-Qaeda militant, Hilâl Kaplan blamed US president Barack Obama for suspending democracy and acting like Hitler.[37] For her, Atatürk was a dictator.[38] Even though her definition of a dictator perfectly applies to Erdoğan as well, she did not see him through the same lens. In 2016, she compared Erdoğan with the Ottoman Sultan Abdülhamid II, and explained how, like Erdoğan, Abdülhamid II was unfairly accused of being a dictator.[39] Strangely enough, in 2012, Kaplan had criticized another Islamist author for neglecting the repression that took place under Abdülhamid II.[40]

Authenticity and sincerity: Erdoğan as a charismatic leader

As Erdoğan's interventions in the media are very clear proof of his increasing authoritarianism, his women supporters usually downplayed the power he exercised to silence the media and emphasized instead his "authenticity" and "vulnerability" as a human being. For example, Karaca was not happy about Erdoğan's tough attitude toward the media in 2009,[41] yet she justified his behavior with reference to his genuineness. She was aware of the fact that the words of those in power carry more weight.[42] But she made an exception for Erdoğan for his sincerity. To her, Erdoğan does not need the politician's persona ("diplomatik ara yüz") to communicate with his people.[43] His politician's mask is so thin that the human behind that mask quickly becomes visible with his love, sensitivity, anger, and vulnerability.[44] He feels truly upset and hurt when he is mocked in a cartoon[45] or when a newspaper publishes documents about him from Wikileaks.[46] For Karaca, Erdoğan's critics have missed the point that he reacts in an authoritarian and arrogant style mainly when his sincerity and commitment to democracy is questioned.[47] Similarly, Böhürler praised Erdoğan because of his internal consistency.[48] She praised him for his authenticity when he moved to the highly controversial White Palace upon getting elected as president.[49] Erdoğan never changed in his essence, she said, and he remained true to his original Islamist perspective that regarded the former president's house in Çankaya as a symbolic monument of Westernization and Kemalism.

Authenticity as a justification mechanism is also extended to the party. As I mentioned earlier, this is done, first of all, by taking Erdoğan's and AKP politicians' statements as patently truthful and not questioning the validity of these statements. At times of controversy, women simply call the AKP ministers and present the official perspective the final "truth."[50] The AKP is not construed as a party in power who should be held accountable. In addition, across a variety of issues, the AKP is portrayed as always having moral superiority over other actors. This rhetorical strategy is most prominently used to defend the AKP's foreign policy in Syria.

Second, the women's writing situates the AKP as a political actor above and beyond parochial interests, as an apolitical and non-ideological actor. It is the others who are motivated by self-interest and opportunism, which is never the case for the AKP. In that sense, their writing conceals the ways the party's power has marginalized other actors, transformed the institutions in Turkish politics, and eliminated democratic oversight and accountability as well as checks and balances. In 2009, in her article about the Ergenekon case, Karaca described the AKP as if it were a neutral actor without influence and power over the judiciary.[51] She described the AKP's role as "shielding" the judiciary from others' influence as if the AKP's "shielding" did not constitute an intervention into the judicial process. The AKP also appears as a party without an ideology through an emphasis on its role as the "executive power" in the parliament. In other words, Turkey's "official ideology" is not challenged by another ideology but by the "executive power" that represents the people.[52] The AKP's religiously conservative ideological standpoint was also made invisible by underlining "serving the people" as the sole purpose of the party, with Böhürler mentioning the hospitals and the roads the party has built and situating the AKP as a party without a political ideology.[53]

Conservative women columnists defend Erdoğan as an authentic leader and they also situate themselves as sincere and authentic. They react very strongly when their own sincerity and motives in wearing the headscarf are questioned.[54] Yet, at the same time, they frequently question others' sincerity and authenticity. The group who is most often the subject of sincerity test in women's writings are the Kurds, and Kurdish politicians who are members of the Kurdish party on the opposition (HDP and its predecessors). They are constantly blamed for being insincere about what they want or abusing the sincerity and good intentions of the government to solve the problems of the Kurds.[55]

Dilemma between objectivity and partisanship: women as critical voices from inside the AKP

Conservative women columnists had to sustain a difficult position: On the one hand, they located themselves as part of the "conservative neighborhood" and supported Erdoğan, but on the other hand—partly due to their positioning as "bridges" by the liberal democrats—they claimed to have objective voices and nonpartisan personas. This created a dilemma for women. As one of the founders of the AKP, Ayşe Böhürler has experienced it most strongly and tackled it in a number of articles. She talked about the difficulties of being a journalist and a political party member at the same time and attacked her critics for being unfair to her.[56] Böhürler insistently claimed objectivity and independence even though she actively worked for the AKP and wrote for a pro-government newspaper.[57] This presented an unresolvable tension in her writing. On numerous occasions, she has written from the position of a party member who witnessed insider debates in the party, and on other occasions she has positioned herself as a journalist and spoken from the authority of that position. Contradictions became unavoidable during that interplay between objectivity and partisanship.

Nihal Bengisu Karaca's writing style is emblematic of the tension between belonging and criticism. Over the years she regularly used the rhetorical style "it is OK but..." (*tamam ama...*) in her criticisms of the AKP.[58] This rhetorical style has become the means through which she constructed an "objective" voice. "It's OK but..." made it possible for her to criticize the party and endorse her support simultaneously. For example, in January 2016, when 1,128 Turkish academics signed a document criticizing the government's policies in Kurdish regions, Karaca argued that she did not believe these academics could properly educate students. She characterized them as people who could not "distinguish even between a saltshaker and vinegar in their own kitchen." She then continued: "But we cannot conclude that they are big traitors with dirty and secret agendas." She argued that she finds it wrong to "crown" these academics with detentions and trials following their call to the government.[59] In this typical example, Karaca endorsed the government's position on academics first, and then went on to criticize what she found as excesses of the policy.

Pre-2011, these women's writing is characterized by the search for common ground, figuring out and defining the shared spaces and values, and finding out the middle ground by defining the "reasonable."[60] A manifestation of the search for the common ground was reflected in Ayşe Böhürler's columns, with her frequent emphasis on issues that concern us all as "humans."[61] She frequently emphasized rationality as an objective criteria, condemned emotional reactions,[62] and situated her "values" and "friendships" as her ultimate priority.[63] She emphasized the common ground with the Left with reference to a shared concern for human rights, equality, and democracy.[64] She frequently mentioned the inclusion of difference, and supporting the rights of those who are different from "us," as a fundamental principle and value.[65] She often criticized Turkish secular people for not following through on this fundamental principle.

The discourse of shared values and commonalities with the Left eventually disappeared in conservative women's writing, starting in 2011. The break with the liberals is a crucial turning point in this shift, and the women openly commented on this break in their columns. By 2013, the women started talking about the liberal intellectuals on the Left in a negative tone, particularly in relation to the Kurdish issue, and defined those on the Left as people who provoke divisions, and "base their careers on the Kurdish question."[66]

The close analysis of women's columns shows that 2011 and 2012 were the most extraordinary years in terms of women's criticisms of the AKP. This period is distinct because on the one hand, the women journalists break with the liberals and stop searching for common ground, but on the other hand, they also direct their sharpest insider criticisms toward the AKP in 2011 and 2012. Their criticisms should be read within the political context of these years. A number of studies, looking only at this extraordinary period of criticism of the government, have concluded that conservative women are significant oppositional actors. Yet, when we extend the time frame beyond these years, we end up with a more comprehensive and a different picture about how the conservative women writers navigated their closeness to the AKP and eventually opted for supporting the party's one-man rule.

The period between 2010 and 2013 (between the constitutional referendum and the Gezi protests) was politically very complex in a number of ways. According to Esen and Gumuscu, "by the end of 2010 the AKP had already pacified most of the veto-players in the system,"[67] and had already consolidated its power in structural and institutional terms. Yet I argue that the party's consolidation of power was not fully recognized in the public consciousness until after the AKP's third election victory, in 2011. In spite of its growing undemocratic practices, the AKP continued to reap the benefits of its long-time publicity strategy that presented the party as a champion of democratization inside and outside of Turkey. In other words, between 2010 and 2013, Turkey experienced a dissonance, a gap between perception and reality: while the AKP gradually removed the institutions that provided checks and balances, many citizens continued to perceive increasing democratization by looking at a number of democratization measures that in the end turned out to be only symbolic moves and distractions: the trial of Kenan Evren, the general responsible for the 1980 coup, was one such symbolic move.

Conservative women had diligently supported the party during the 2010 referendum. On the one hand, they believed that the AKP democratized the country to an unprecedented degree, particularly with its initiatives to respond to Kurdish demands. For example, TRT established the television channel TRT 6 in 2009 to broadcast in Kurdish, renamed as TRT Kurdi in 2015.[68] Indeed, a number of previously taboo issues (although only those issues selected to delegitimize the early republic) were openly discussed in the media in 2010. Yet, on the other hand, this openness did not translate into more rights for women because removing the headscarf ban was not a priority for the AKP. In 2010 the ban was de facto removed from the universities, but the door was still closed for women MPs wearing headscarves. It was frustrating for conservative women to see the government they had supported becoming more and more powerful and yet not responding to their demands.

As a result, 2011 witnessed the conservative women's most significant public clash with the AKP: the campaign of "No MP with Headscarf, No Vote." All three women columnists joined the campaign with high hopes[69] and were reprimanded by Erdoğan in return. Erdoğan blamed the women for creating "politics of tension" and using their wearing of the headscarf as a means of negotiation to be elected for the parliament.[70] Karaca wrote an open letter to Erdoğan and asked, "Since when has the struggle for rights been part of negotiation?" She argued that the women were aware that the party was about to be shut down because of the headscarf issue in 2007. Yet they were also aware of the amount of power concentrated in the hands of Erdoğan and the AKP. She argued that they were the ones who suffered most because of the polarization that he had created.[71] Hilâl Kaplan also responded to Erdoğan's criticisms and reminded him that in the past he had also been criticized on similar grounds.[72]

These years were also extraordinary because conservative women, like secular liberal democrats, clearly observed increasing authoritarianism and concentration of power in Erdoğan's hands. This observation applies to all conservative women in this study, but especially to Nihal Bengisu Karaca and Hilâl Kaplan.[73] In their pieces in 2011 and 2012, both columnists mentioned increasing authoritarianism and the AKP becoming part of the status quo as a problem.[74] Yet these criticisms never took the form of a "revolt" that could push the government to reconsider its controversial policies. First of all, women tried to strike a balance by criticizing Erdoğan and praising him at the same time; second, and more importantly, their insider criticisms aimed to protect the party from attacks and critiques coming from the opposition. Women used a protective critical voice to alert the party about potential criticism from its opponents. For example, Karaca grew furious when Erdoğan called an artist's statue "freakish."[75] She thought such attitudes would play into the hands of the secular opposition and contribute to the creation of secular shrines at such sites. Similarly, the conservative women were concerned that the AKP could lose votes for backing the wrong policies. Hilâl Kaplan criticized the AKP's nationalist language and argued that AKP's policies in the region pushed Kurds, who otherwise may vote for the AKP, to the Kurdish party.[76] She and other women journalists criticized the AKP regularly for not being able to solve the murder of the Armenian journalist Hrant Dink in 2007. Calls for justice accompanied concerns that the AKP's inability to solve the murder has been harmful for the party.[77]

In other words, criticisms coming from non-conservative circles drew the boundaries of women's criticisms of the AKP and Erdoğan, which has led to a series of contradictions in women's writings: women have criticized Erdoğan's increasing authoritarianism and his abandonment of democracy, and at the same time they persistently attacked the writers outside of the conservative circles who criticized Erdoğan for his departure from democratic practices. Karaca defended Erdoğan when Ahmet Altan called him a sultan,[78] and when Murat Belge called him dictatorial,[79] even though she had also complained about toughening politics and increasing authoritarianism.

I interpret women's insider criticisms in 2011 and 2012 also as an indication of internal unrest among the AKP's conservative constituents in those years. And I see that the feeling of democratic expansion in the general environment probably also gave them more confidence to express dissent. They expressed discontent on a number of issues: Turkey's policy in Syria and decrease in the quality of education,[80] the building of a controversial mosque at Istanbul's Çamlıca hill,[81] policies reshaping Istanbul,[82] detentions of elected Kurdish representatives,[83] police brutality,[84] Erdoğan's patronizing language,[85] the abandonment of democratic principles,[86] and increasing authoritarianism.[87] Karaca expressed concern about the exclusion of liberals,[88] and the creation of an environment of fear because of the Ergenekon trials.[89] Even though women were not satisfied by the party's democratic performance,[90] they continued to see the AKP as the only alternative for Turkey's democratization.[91] They called for caution and warned the party that the failure to pursue democratization reforms might lead to the AKP's own destruction.[92]

In 2011 Karaca wrote an article that might in retrospect impart an eerie feeling to any reader. In her article "Ya sonra" ("What about later"), Karaca criticized the AKP for becoming intolerant of criticism and listed a series of future issues that might confront the party if the AKP did not control its own power with checks and balances. She predicted the emergence of an "unorganized opposition," massive unrest and a government responding to that with more pepper gas and water cannons.[93] Karaca called the government to make sure that it did not suppress dissent. She said, "Turkey must turn into a huge İstiklal Street where five to six demonstrations and protests take place every day."[94]

Karaca's predictions did come true in 2013 with the eruption of the Gezi protests. Yet, instead of seeing the protests as a reaction to the AKP's intolerance, as she had predicted, Karaca interpreted the events through the AKP government's lens and saw the protestors as pawns of an imperialist conspiracy aimed to topple Erdoğan.[95] Her writing from that point onward has become propagandistic, aimed to defend the AKP and justify Erdoğan's growing authoritarian rule. After Gezi, Karaca's writing has entered a new phase, following a sharp turn. Her piercing insider criticisms came to an abrupt end following the Gezi protests.

The Gezi protests and Islamist female journalists

The Gezi protests started on May 31, 2013. The event that sparked the protests was the government's plan to build a mall in the middle of Taksim Gezi Park, one of the last green spaces in the center of Istanbul. Young protestors, university students who camped in the park with the hope of saving the park from demolition, were being gassed by the police between May 28 and 31. The heightened police aggression on the last day of May resulted in thousands pouring onto the streets in Istanbul in a matter of hours.[96]

People took to the streets not just because of the frustration caused by the ongoing police brutality at Gezi Park. During the months preceding Gezi, Istanbul's inhabitants experienced police violence, and they were gassed for the slightest opposition. Police gassed the protestors on May 1, Labor Day. On May 11, Beşiktaş football fans suffered under excessive police gas. At the same time, the AKP's urban transformation projects had ruthlessly restructured Istanbul and disregarded all the criticisms coming from the NGOs, universities, and residents. Istanbul's middle classes in particular lost the places they loved day by day and witnessed the replacement of these places with malls and other construction projects undertaken by large pro-AKP businesses.

Right before the Gezi protests took off, Erdoğan passed a new law that imposed severe restrictions on alcohol sales, and he handled this hot-button lifestyle issue, which indeed presents a test of tolerance for a conservative party, in a highly divisive way, insulting alcohol drinkers as drunkards. On top of this, he pushed the name Yavuz Sultan Selim, an Ottoman Sultan famous for his massacre of Anatolian Alevis in the sixteenth century, for Istanbul's proposed third bridge. Even though the decision greatly disturbed Turkey's Alevi community, the government did not step back. At the same time, in May 2013, families were leaving behind a very exhausting academic year. The new education system had overhauled the old one without proper preparation and had created great uncertainty about instructional quality. The resentments toward increasing restrictions on the media and the internet were also growing. The Gezi protests started against such a backdrop. The protests were a call for the government to stop imposing authoritarian policies, to respect difference, and to stop interfering with lifestyle issues.

The conservative women journalists did not see Gezi as a response to the AKP's growing authoritarianism. Instead, they saw the Gezi protests through the government's lens and framed it as an orchestrated "civil coup" organized by the Republican People's Party to overthrow Erdoğan and the AKP.[97] "Taksim rebellion" was another phrase they used to delegitimize the protests.[98] For the conservative women journalists, the government was the victim, not the protestors who suffered under heavy police violence. They saw the protestors through the government perspective as looters, as plunderers, and as part of a foreign and domestic coalition to bring down Erdoğan. The "coup attempt" analogy worked to misplace the power relations at work and actively promoted the AKP government's framing of the events.

To cast the protests as a "coup attempt," the conservative journalists appealed to the "sincerity" argument and tried to distinguish between those with sincere concerns about the park and those who wanted to create chaos.[99] Karaca argued that the young people who wanted to protect the park had a legitimate reason to do so and the few bad policemen who excessively gassed students at the park had to be held accountable.[100] But for her the unfolding of the events showed that the protests were not about protecting the park but about overthrowing Erdoğan by the forces of the old Turkey and their allies on the streets.[101] Karaca was right in pointing out that, once thousands poured to the streets, the Gezi protests were not about the park anymore. Yet she disregarded the AKP's authoritarian policies and Erdoğan's divisive language that led to the growing unrest in the first place (and about which she had previously expressed concern herself). Instead, she minimized Erdoğan's role in building up the tension and criticized the opposition for not recognizing his kind, funny, and compassionate side.[102] She framed the protestors as people who were troubled not with Erdoğan's style but his mere existence.[103] She argued that those who criticized Erdoğan for acting like a dictator had allied with domestic and foreign powers to overthrow him.[104] She showed the protestors' search for Gene Sharp's book *From Dictatorship to Democracy*[105] as an evidence of a dirty conspiracy, and argued that all the slogans used during the protests were designed not by the protestors themselves but by advertising agencies.[106]

Women wanted to distinguish Gezi from similar protest movements that had been taking place in the Middle East. Ayşe Böhürler had celebrated the protests in Egypt, Tunisia, and Yemen in 2011.[107] Gezi reminded her of those Arab Spring protests, but Böhürler wondered whether there might be more going on behind the scenes, despite her caution about conspiracy theories.[108] She concluded Gezi was an "accident" and argued that the protests made the conservatives like her feel that their "own neighborhood" was the safest.[109]

Gezi took place at an interesting juncture, at a critical point when Turkey's modern middle and professional classes, who had internalized secularism and were progressive in their lifestyle choices, were being increasingly pushed to the margins of the official discourse, were being frequently insulted by Erdoğan and his team, and were feeling deprived of voice and power day by day. In other words, the Gezi protests erupted at a certain tipping point when secular people started to wrestle with the impact of the AKP's authoritarian policies directed mainly at their lives; they felt their voices and demands would not be heard and lost completely what little trust they had had in the AKP.

Yet this was the same moment when conservative women felt the power balance in the country had finally turned in their favor.[110] On April 3, 2013, Karaca wrote about the court decision that overhauled the headscarf ban for lawyers. For her, this was a blissful and cheerful moment.[111] She and other conservative women writers interpreted Gezi as a secularist reaction directed against the "accomplishments" of the AKP that benefited and enriched the party's conservative constituents. Gezi, as the biggest protest movement in the history of Turkey, was something new, something hard to explain by reference to "old Turkey." Yet the women's writings clearly show that they saw Gezi as the return of the old Turkey, and felt truly scared that they would lose the rights and privileges they gained during the AKP government.

Meanwhile, the AKP's media propaganda pumped highly emotional stories about women wearing the headscarf who were harassed, verbally insulted, and attacked by protestors on the streets. Erdoğan himself accused the protestors of attacking women who wore the headscarf. Soon after Erdoğan's allegations about protestors attacking women wearing the headscarf, Elif Çakır, a conservative female writer at *Star* newspaper, published an interview with a woman who was allegedly attacked by the protestors in Istanbul, at Kabataş, one of the central and busiest nodes in the city, turning the alleged incident into an infamous point of contention. According to Çakır's story, protestors, topless and wearing leather gloves, attacked the woman who was walking with her baby, beat her, and urinated on her in one of Istanbul's busiest neighborhoods.[112]

Çakır faithfully defended her story in numerous television programs. Yet witnesses did not confirm her story and the details in the woman's narrative. The oppositional media suspected that the story had been forged by the pro-Erdoğan media to mobilize Erdoğan supporters around an emotionally charged topic. They turned out to be correct in their suspicions when the CCTV records were found. Conservative writers, on the other hand, continued to believe that this and similar stories were true. When the camera records were published, showing no attack, Karaca asserted that the CCTV records, which she found unclear and imperfect, were not enough for her to discredit the story.[113]

The story definitely worked in the government's favor and sealed the support of the women journalists wearing a headscarf. The incident pitted not just conservatives against the opposition but also men against women. Conservative women writers defended the story with feminist arguments. They argued that the woman's testimony should be enough to prove that the incident actually took place. Karaca asked whether it would be different if the woman in question had been wearing tight pants.[114] A number of secular liberal journalists sided with the conservative women and defended them until they figured out that the story was forged.[115]

Gezi as a turning point

Gezi, a turning point, made the contradictions in women's writing sharper. After Gezi, conservative women writers have gone to great lengths in creating and mobilizing arguments in defense of the AKP. Gezi created a clear shift in women's writing. For example, Karaca's topics were much more diverse before Gezi, and she used to write about the problems and anxieties of the secular population as well.[116] After Gezi she focused primarily on defending the AKP. Her insider criticisms about authoritarianism disappeared and her writing took the form of pro-AKP propaganda, regularly listing the accomplishments of the party.[117]

Probably aware of this shift herself, Karaca complained that AKP members and supporters were able to criticize Erdoğan before Gezi, but this changed afterward.[118] Instead of criticizing the AKP's growing undemocratic practices, she blamed the Gezi protestors for the disappearance of insider criticisms, for the heightened polarization in the country, and for the emergence of "Erdoğanism."[119] In spite of her admission that her own perspective suffered from polarized politics, she later argued that there was no polarization in Turkey and depicted polarized Turkey as a false accusation lobbed by the Gülenists toward the AKP.[120]

Before Gezi, Karaca had criticized police violence against the university students during Erdoğan's meeting with the university rectors.[121] Even though the police violence significantly escalated after Gezi, and the police were granted tremendous powers, she framed these developments in terms of the state legitimately protecting itself. Before Gezi, she had talked about democracy with reference to pluralism; after Gezi, she talked about democracy with reference to the majority coming out of the ballot box. How are we to explain this sharp turn in a conservative woman's position? Was she not sincere or authentic in her criticisms? What could be the reason for this immediate tightening of support behind Erdoğan? To understand the significant turn in women's position right after Gezi, we have to turn to another repeated pattern in women's writings.

Populist language in pro-AKP women columnists' writing

After Gezi, women started to emphasize the role of internal and external enemies that conspire against Erdoğan.[122] They framed the AKP as the defender of the nation against foreign interests. A populist, anti-colonialist discourse based on "foreign powers" was already present in women's writing in 2010.[123] Yet such populist and anti-colonialist language did not characterize their writing, and such references appeared only occasionally before the conflict in Syria. One particular article by Karaca was indicative of the coming shift in women's position and the dilemma that they created for themselves: she interpreted the conflict in Syria and speculated about a dirty plot (*kirli tezgah*) that involved the PKK (defined by her as a confederation of a number of countries), Kurdish leader Barzani, and the United States. She argued that Erdoğan was probably one of the targets of this plot. She asked whether the people of Turkey would be able to unite against this conspiracy and resist it, closing her article ominously: "No doubt there is another side to the issue: the danger of turning a blind eye to the government's mistakes in the name of resisting the conspiracy, and contribute to the loss of democracy. A very difficult period awaits us where [our] conscience will be under pressure from all fronts."[124]

Starting with the Syrian conflict in 2012, critical voices in Turkey were increasingly framed as the allies of foreign and Western powers who did not want a strong Turkey. The argument goes like this: Following Turkey's involvement in the conflict in Syria, Erdoğan has become an unpopular leader in the US, and there is now an international conspiracy against him to topple him. For conservative women, Gezi itself was the evidence of this conspiracy. In other words, conservative women seeing the AKP as part of their own neighborhood reverted back to conspiracy theories and a populist-nationalist discourse instead of pushing the government to change its repressive policies.

In the AKP's lingo, the term "higher intelligence" refers to a coalition of international and domestic powers who want Erdoğan to go. The term has become part of everyday language among AKP supporters and rank-and-file members as an explanatory framework. "Higher intelligence" refers to Israel one day, the US another; Germany or the UK on yet another day, or the West as a whole. "Global financial powers" are also seen as part of "higher intelligence." According to this conspiracy theory, these powers do not want Erdoğan because he strengthened the Turkish economy, criticized Israel for violating the rights of Palestinians in Gaza, and made Turkey a much stronger political player in the Middle East. In short, all the accomplishments of Erdoğan made him a target, and these accomplishments are now under threat.

The history of Western influence in the Middle East makes this conspiracy theory believable for many Turks, and conservative women journalists are no exception. They have no doubt that there is a conspiracy against Turkey.[125] They see it as a crystal-clear fact. This creates a logic where criticism is interpreted as an extension of the larger conspiracy. At best, critical voices are framed as naïve or idiotic people who cannot see the "obvious" plot against their own country. At worst, they are framed as part of the conspiracy, as traitors who ally with foreign powers against their own country and people.

As proponents of an Islamist right-wing discourse, it was already natural for women to see the world as divided into two camps: the people versus the status quo. The Westernized, Kemalist secular elite represented the status quo for them. The women extensively mobilized this division at critical junctures, for example, to garner support for the yes vote for the AKP's proposed constitutional amendments in 2010.[126] They have regularly situated themselves as part of "the people" and framed the AKP's opponents as having problems with "the people."

They frequently depicted the Kemalist and leftist intellectuals as alienated toward their own people and ignorant of the local culture.[127] After Gezi this way of seeing the world in two camps became much stronger and deeply entrenched in conservative women's writing. Before Gezi, the populist discourse was one among other discourses competing for their attention. After Gezi though, the language of populism became the most dominant and worked at the expense of all other ways of seeing and interpreting the world. Conservative women's discourse after Gezi shows all the characteristics of populism: "the people" have a common foreign enemy threatening the nation, and the "nation" is equal to Erdoğan's supporters. The nation not only faces an outside threat but is also threatened from the inside by an intellectual class that has a colonized mind and collaborates with foreign powers at the expense of the "nation." These changes in the discourse accompanied the propagation of the AKP's fascist slogan all over the country: "One Land, One Nation, One Flag, One State" (Tek Vatan, Tek Millet, Tek Bayrak, Tek Devlet).

The new enemies inside: Liberal intellectuals, academics, and the Kurds

Conservative women did not receive sympathy or support from the Kemalists.[128] This was not the case with the liberal democrats and intellectuals from the Left. Many liberal democrats critical of Kemalism had supported conservative women throughout the headscarf ban, helped them to gain legitimacy, and argued for their inclusion in the system. Therefore, the break with the liberals represented a fundamental shift not just in women's position but also in Turkish politics. In spite of collaboration on the headscarf issue, women and liberal democrats diverged on a number of other issues throughout the AKP's time in power, until 2011. In other words, collaboration went hand in hand with disagreements and conflicts.

While conservative women have collaborated with liberal intellectuals, they have also competed with them to set the terms of significant debates and define what counts as common sense. Throughout the AKP's time in power, conservative women have moved from being counter-elites[129] to new hegemonic elites, and established themselves as the voices of Turkey's conservative intellectuals. They have become the intellectual elite of the so-called new Turkey. To establish themselves as the new intellectual class in the media, these women had to discredit the secular, liberal intellectuals and the academics from the Left, and situate themselves as the voices of reason, objectivity, common sense, and "the people."

Women discredited the secular academic establishment and the intellectuals on the Left in two major ways: by creating a link between university professors and militancy[130] and by casting critical academics as foreign to the nation, as colonialists inside.[131] Women regularly worked on the binary between the local and the foreign. Binnaz Toprak, a professor of political science, became the target of criticism in 2008 because of her empirical study that presents a well thought-out criticism of conservatism and religion in Anatolian towns. Her study explored whether the entrenchment of religious conservatism has started a new process of othering for Turkey's vulnerable groups: youth, Alevites, gypsies, Christians, and nonpracticing, alcohol-drinking Muslims. Ayşe Böhürler was furious because the study did not include women wearing the headscarf among those vulnerable groups. She accused Toprak of treating the local element of the country as foreign and likened her to colonialists. She found Toprak unscientific and unobjective because Toprak's findings reinforced the stereotype that pious Muslims do not tolerate difference.[132]

Similarly, Böhürler compared two sociologists' comments about the Gezi protests: Nilüfer Göle, a Turkish sociologist who lives outside of Turkey, and Hüsamettin Arslan, who lived in Bursa, a city in West Anatolia.[133] The comparison appealed to the binary between the foreign and the local, marking Göle as an outsider. The "local" sociologist, Hüsamettin Arslan, in turn, interpreted the Gezi events in line with the AKP's perspective and endorsed the AKP government as the entity that has best understood the people since 1826.[134] In 2012, Hilâl Kaplan had implicated Göle as a local colonialist because of her comments on the relations between Islam and terrorism, and questioned her prestigious place among the conservative religious circles.[135] Göle remained dear to Islamist circles until she criticized the government during the Gezi protests in 2013. After Gezi, conservative women framed every attempt by the critical intellectuals to resist authoritarianism as collaboration with the colonialists and blamed the liberal intellectuals for having a colonized consciousness.[136] Turkey was never officially colonized, yet, women's frequent allusions to colonization works to reinforce the binary between the East and the West; and between foreign and local.

The fear of the West and the "foreign," with their corrupting influence, was extended even to young conservative women who got their education in the West because of the headscarf ban. Böhürler mentioned a meeting where she gathered with a group of conservative women who received their education in Western countries. She felt highly impressed by their qualifications, but she also became worried: Are they now intellectually alienated? Have their minds been occupied? She described, "remaining as ourselves" as the basic yardstick for contributing to society.[137] In this framework, a good education is useful only if the people who received that education fit into an essentialized definition of self. If even Western-educated conservative women are under suspicion, then the liberal intellectuals who lead a secular and "Westernized" lifestyle can be much more easily cast as the extensions of imperialist, colonial powers.

What, then, is local for conservative women? They construct an essentialist definition of the local with religion at its core,[138] making Islam a part of Turkish genetics.[139] Böhürler mentioned one's "cultural DNA"[140] as one of the factors behind religious belief and practice. Conservative women journalists react very strongly to the criticism of religion and personally attack liberal, secular, and left-wing intellectuals.[141] In that sense, conservative women's approach to religion and secularism presents one of the fundamental breaking points with the liberal democrats.

Conservative women columnists take Islam as the reference point in defining right and wrong, and challenge secularism as the norm.[142] They delegitimated Turkish secularism as "militant"[143] and argued for a secularism defined on the basis of the needs of religious conservatives. They blamed secularism for a variety of things that went wrong in Turkey. In an intricate argument, Kaplan even blamed secularism for the Armenian genocide during the First World War.[144] Whether conservative women challenge secularism as the norm or call for a different type of secularism, they fundamentally disagree with the liberal democrats in terms of what secularism should be about: In their view, secularism should protect believers and practicing Muslims. They are silent about the fact that secularism also protects nonbelievers, and nonpracticing Muslims, from religious oppression.[145] In their framework, secularism is developed out of the needs of Christian societies and is incompatible with Muslim societies.[146] Yet they offer no explanations of how nonbelievers' rights would be secured without secularism.

Conservative women attacked secular and liberal intellectuals especially when these intellectuals questioned the government's decision to incorporate a Qur'an course and a course on Mohammad's life as an elective into the middle school (fifth to eighth grades) curricula.[147] These courses were proposed in addition to the controversial mandatory course on religion that has been taught from a conservative perspective. The change in the curriculum followed Erdoğan's statement on February 1, 2012 that he wanted to educate "a pious youth,"[148] and for liberal democrats these courses, even when they were offered as electives, were a clear sign of Islamization and a breach of secular principles.

Their concerns were not unwarranted, considering that in large numbers of schools these courses could easily be offered as the only available "elective" courses, forcing the students to take them and negatively framing any students who refused.[149] Conservative women, on the other hand, approached this as a question of religious freedom and choice. Karaca called the liberal democrats and the Left "despots" and argued that they treat the Qur'an as "harmful content."[150] She was even more furious with the Kurds on the Left: they demanded education in their native language and received support from the Muslim democrats, yet they failed to support Muslim democrats in their demand for religious education.[151] These courses were also justified with reference to the "people," framing them as what the people want.[152]

The question of religious education is definitely part of the debates on lifestyle. In addition to the demands for changes in the curriculum, abstention from alcohol is one of the most important signifiers of a religious lifestyle, making the restrictions on alcohol consumption another hot-button issue.

Alcohol consumption, lifestyle issues, and Islamist female journalists

The debates around the AKP's efforts to restrict alcohol consumption have been central in polarizing AKP supporters and opponents. Restrictions on alcohol are no small matter. They directly influence the ways the young, secular middle classes socialize, the restaurants where they dine, and how much they spend. Alcohol is also widely consumed in the lower and lower-middle classes.

The AKP did not simply ban the consumption of alcohol. Instead, the party gradually instituted a number of measures that restricted access to alcohol. The imposition of very high taxes on alcohol sales skyrocketed prices and placed alcohol out of the poor's reach. It has become harder for businesses to keep or renew their alcohol licenses; alcohol became subject to time and zoning restrictions that made sales illegal in the vicinity of mosques and education institutions. The definition of "mosque" or "education institution" was kept broad and included prayer rooms or private institutions offering vocational training, eventually pushing businesses to move or close down. As property changed hands, the new owners of the market chains—wealthy conservatives—stopped selling alcohol, and drinkers were burdened with traveling the extra mile. Alcohol consumption became possible in small enclaves, mostly the neighborhoods run by the Republican People's Party, for very high prices. By 2017, alcohol prices rose so high that producing alcoholic beverages at home had become a widespread alternative.[153] Alcohol was removed from the opening reception of the parliament in April 2016.[154]

At the same time, in the AKP's popular discourse, Turkey's problems are blamed on an imaginary "whisky-drinking wealthy," linking alcohol consumption with Westernization and an alienated elite. In addition, AKP municipalities stopped serving alcohol in restaurants run by their municipal governments. These are popular places with affordable prices. Yet the absence of even light beer excludes secular people from these spaces, limiting the possibilities where people with different lifestyles could mingle and eat together sharing the same space.

The AKP's issues with alcohol go back a long time. When the AKP's predecessor, the Welfare Party, won Istanbul's municipal elections in 1994 with Erdoğan as mayor, one of the first things the new city government did was to enforce the removal of tables and chairs that belonged to businesses with alcohol licenses from the streets in the highly popular Beyoğlu district. Street life in Beyoğlu was the center of socialization for college students and young professionals, who interacted over glasses of beer or wine during the 1990s. This early attempt was resisted by the businesses and their clients, and the municipal government was not able to hit businesses with alcohol licenses at that time.

In 2011 Erdoğan reinstituted this measure forcefully and with success, leading to the closure of numerous businesses in the Beyoğlu district. This also involved the gradual transfer of these businesses into AKP-friendly hands. For the young, secular middle classes, one of the hardest blows came in the alcohol restrictions brought for concerts, festivals, and other public events in 2011. The most controversial measures with broad restrictions on the sale of alcohol materialized right before the Gezi protests in May 2013. Erdoğan's uncompromising attitude in defending the measures, casting people who consume alcohol as drunkards and alcoholics, was one of the triggers for the protests. Throughout the protests, Erdoğan referred to beer bottles allegedly left in a mosque as a way of discrediting the protestors.[155]

Throughout this process, conservative women writers responded to concerns over the restrictions as unwarranted and unreasonable. They instead argued that alcohol was available everywhere. In 2008, Ayşe Böhürler mentioned a meeting in Konya, a conservative Anatolian town, and complained that religious women could not find a hotel for their events that did not serve alcohol.[156] The following year, Nihal Bengisu Karaca responded to criticisms of the restrictions by referring to statistics that indicated a rise in the consumption of alcohol.[157] Hilâl Kaplan defended the restrictions by comparing alcohol with drugs and by casting secular people as hypocritical.[158] She framed the debate in terms of the state's legitimate role of drawing boundaries in favor of the "public good." Even though women used secular arguments to defend the restrictions, the debate cornered the secular parties, who lost the power and the courage to defend rights not condoned by religion for fear of alienating conservative voters.

When other lifestyle issues surfaced, women criticized the secular populace and liberals for unrealistic fears about Islamist politics. They frequently resorted to strawmen fallacies and exaggeration in defense of the AKP. Ayşe Böhürler responded to the concerns about the lifestyle issues by saying that she does not know anybody in her conservative circles who supports polygamy or defends cutting off hands—a reference to the Islamic law that punishes thievery by amputating the hand.[159] Karaca responded to criticisms of Erdoğan's "three children" comment by asking "Have we become subjects of chemical experiments to enable us [women] give birth to three children at once?"[160]

At the beginning of 2011, liberal democrats started losing their columns in conservative newspapers because of their opposition to the AKP.[161] Conservative women columnists openly discussed how to interpret their disagreements with the liberal democrats. Böhürler wrote that she followed the debates with sadness and criticized liberals for patronizing the conservatives. She argued that ideas like freedom and democracy do not belong just to liberals.[162] In another article, she criticized the liberal democrats for being unappreciative and not acknowledging the conservative newspapers' support when the Kemalists had closed the doors to the liberal democrats in the aftermath of February 28, 1997. According to Böhürler, these writers were leaving conservative newspapers not because they were fired but because of their own individual circumstances.[163] She also criticized them for hyping up polarization in the country.[164] The final, and the most critical, breaking point between the conservative women and the liberal democrats took place over the Kurdish issue in June 2011.

Kurdish question and conservative female journalists

In June 2011, Recep Tayyip Erdoğan targeted liberal democrat Nuray Mert and insulted her in a mass rally by twisting her last name to "Namert," meaning coward in Turkish. Nuray Mert was one of the most outspoken voices against the headscarf ban and the injustices of the February 28 period. She had received severe criticisms from Kemalist circles for legitimating Islamist conservativism in the name of democratic expansion in Turkey.[165] Nuray Mert had close friends among religious conservatives, including high-profile AKP representatives and conservative women journalists. She was writing at *Milliyet* at the time of Erdoğan's attacks. By then, she had been critical of the AKP government's policies for a while.

Mert became Erdoğan's target because of her comments on the Kurdish issue made at the Dersim Conference at the European Parliament.[166] Interestingly, the original comments did not even belong to her. With reference to sociologist Mesut Yeğen, she established parallels between the early republican policies toward Dersim and contemporary security policies in the Kurdish-majority regions. Dersim (renamed Tunceli in 1935) is an Anatolian town with considerable Alevi, Zaza, and Kurdish populations. The city is the location of a massacre committed by the early republican government. According to Mert's references, the Dersim massacre took place after the region was connected to the center with new roads, which facilitated the deployment of troops. Nuray Mert cautiously pointed at the parallels between Dersim and the AKP government's policy that focused on servicing the Kurdish cities with new roads. She argued that she did not expect a massacre similar to Dersim, yet both policies were based on a similar logic, and construction of roads could go hand in hand with policies based on violence and coercion.[167] Erdoğan's verbal attacks in June 2011 targeted these comments. Eight months later, in February 2012, Nuray Mert lost her job at *Milliyet*, which was bought by a pro-AKP businessman in April 2011.

Prime Minister Erdoğan's attacks on Mert and her eventual firing constituted a landmark in the relationship between conservatives and liberals. This was a divisive issue for conservative women within the context of pre-Gezi politics. Karaca strongly criticized both Erdoğan's attacks on Mert[168] and her firing next year.[169] She found Mert's comments extreme and made clear that she did not agree with her, yet she also argued that the prime minister's comments on the Kurdish issue called for such offensive language. Böhürler stayed silent about Erdoğan's attacks on Mert in June 2011, but she commented on her firing the next year in a defensive way by putting the blame on the media. Even though Mert was fired from a newspaper owned by a pro-AKP businessman, Böhürler pointed at the media of the "republican bourgeoisie" and their approach to the Kurdish issue.[170] She preferred to describe Mert's firing as "an interruption to her writing." Even though she did not agree with her, Böhürler was reluctant to give up on her friendship with Mert. She emphasized that she would always remain friends with those who did not give up on her in difficult times (recalling Mert's support after February 28, 1997).

Hilâl Kaplan's attitude toward Nuray Mert was different. In a series of articles between July 24 and August 21, 2011,[171] she attacked Mert and Ece Temelkuran (another leading female journalist) for their position on the Kurdish issue. According to her, both journalists at the time had an alliance with the Kurdish party BDP (Peace and Democracy Party) and Kurdish politicians closer to

"Kandil," the headquarters of PKK and the Kurdish guerrilla fighters. She argued that these writers did not want the Kurdish question to be solved by the AKP and were ready to accept any consequence,[172] a common argument among other conservative writers against the seculars and liberal democrats.[173] She called Temelkuran the "trumpeter of Kurdish nationalists."[174] Later she extended her attacks to Yıldırım Türker, a popular male writer on the Left who had defended Mert and Temelkuran. She mocked Ece Temelkuran as "Mrs. Conscience" and Yıldırım Türker as "Mr. Conscience."[175]

This series of articles aimed to question the intellectual legitimacy of these famous secular female journalists. Kaplan cast them as columnists whose influence on public opinion was greater than the "real intellectuals." She questioned their authority and moral responsibility by pointing at some of the shifts that, according to her, occurred in their position on the Kurdish issue.[176] For her, the only constant in the position of these journalists was their opposition to the AKP. Casting them as unreliable, she called on the Kurds to reconsider their alliance with them.[177]

Most interestingly, on the basis of her numerous columns on the Kurdish issue in 2011, Kaplan herself could easily be blamed for aligning with the terrorist organization and supporting Kurdish nationalism. Her attacks become meaningful when seen from the perspective of hegemonic struggle. The controversy emerged out of the Kurdish issue but was not only about the Kurds: it was about delegitimating the secular intellectual class and creating ambiguity around the terms of the debate. Kaplan's attacks were a prime example of the struggle over gaining intellectual hegemony. Liberal secular intellectuals tried to push back on these attacks and argued that Kaplan made Mert and Temelkuran targets for the Turkish ultranationalists and vulnerable to violence. Kaplan hit back by arguing that her critics were confused about the difference between showing someone as a target and the freedom of expression.[178] Kaplan did not comment when Nuray Mert lost her job five months after this debate. Even though Kaplan's attitude toward Mert was different from Böhürler's and Karaca's, all three conservative women attacked intellectuals on the Left and liberal democrats without giving specific names on many other occasions that involved the Kurdish issue.[179]

In numerous articles, conservative women have fervently supported the AKP's Kurdish–Turkish peace process (also called the "solution process") between 2009 and 2015.[180] All praised the AKP for its initiatives for peace. Ayşe Böhürler wrote in favor of developing a language of peace and asked for the violence to stop.[181] Kaplan and Karaca took part in the AKP government's public relations initiative in 2013 to convince the Turkish majority about the necessity of the peace process. They traveled from town to town and met with different constituents, trying to convince them about the government's peace process. The conservative women tried to do three things during these years: set the terms of the debate on the process by delegitimating criticism toward the AKP by the liberal democrats; legitimate the AKP's behavior in handling the process; and, finally, provide insider criticisms of the contradictions between the party's discourse and practice.

The women's insider criticisms toward the AKP were loud on the Kurdish issue, particularly in 2011 and 2012, the years in which their insider criticism was the strongest.[182] Kaplan criticized conservative Muslims for remaining insensitive toward the oppression of the Kurds and their pain.[183] They all criticized the AKP government following the Roboski/Uludere massacre where thirty-four Kurdish villagers smuggling cigarettes and other goods across the border were killed in a Turkish military airstrike in December 2011.[184] Kaplan criticized Erdoğan for "defending the rights of the state instead of the rights of his Kurdish brothers."[185] She even went further and apologized to the Kurds. The Roboski/Uludere massacre became another significant event, similar to the "No MP with Headscarf, No Vote" campaign that generated a lot of criticism among the conservative women toward the AKP government. Women also felt uneasy about the detention of around four thousand Kurds between 2009 and 2011 and criticized the government on these detentions for fear that this might alienate the moderate Kurds. Along with these insider criticisms, conservative women continued to see the AKP as the only party that could solve the Kurdish problem.

Tanıl Bora argued that the AKP's strategy during the peace process was based on creating a softening by granting rights to the Kurds, while removing the representatives of the Kurdish movement from the equation.[186] Conservative women's columns on the Kurdish issue confirm Bora's observation. Women supported the process within the AKP's framework, and their language consistently reproduced negative stereotypes about the Kurdish politicians. Similar to the ways the Kemalists questioned women on their sincerity in wearing the headscarf, conservative women questioned the Kurdish politicians on their sincerity about peace. They blamed them for blocking the peace process and abusing the good intentions of the government to solve the problem.[187] Böhürler and Karaca regularly distinguished between the good and the bad Kurds.[188] Böhürler designated Kurdish children as a vulnerable group abused by the PKK and bad Kurdish politicians, and in need of saving by conscientious Kurds.[189] In this framework, good Kurds were reasonable, wanted peace, supported the AKP's peace process[190] and did not insist on "unrealistic" demands such as asking for changes in the constitution for more inclusive language.[191] Good Kurds were also pious Muslims and mostly voted for the AKP or were willing to work with the party. Women emphasized religion as a common ground with the Kurds and advocated for solutions by framing them as Muslim brothers and sisters.[192]

Nihal Bengisu Karaca held up a leading Kurdish politician, Ahmet Türk, as the ideal Kurdish politician.[193] When Türk was attacked in 2010 and his nose broken, Karaca condemned the attack and praised him for his forgiving, hopeful, gentle, and local attitude. Earlier, in a feminist-sounding article, she had severely criticized an Islamist male author who diminished her struggle for the headscarf by characterizing her as a headscarved woman without gentleness and kindness.[194] Yet when it was the Kurds who struggled for rights, she praised "gentle" Kurds who would not create trouble for the establishment of which she was a part. The experience of oppression as a "woman" did not translate into empathy for the Kurdish politicians' struggle. She described Kurdish politicians who loudly criticized the AKP government as provocative and aggressive.[195] Selahattin Demirtaş, the leader of the Kurdish party HDP (People's Democratic Party) and a significant challenger to Erdoğan, has become a constant target of criticism over the years.[196]

Finally, following the breakdown of the peace process, women followed the government line, blamed the Kurds for the breakdown of the process, and attacked the signatories of Academics for Peace who asked the government to end its military operations in the region. On January 11, 2016, 1,128 academics published a statement asking the government to end the human right violations taking place during those operations. Erdoğan labeled the academics "the so-called academics," and called for government institutions to take action.[197] Soon after this call, a number of academics who signed the document were detained on charges of terrorist propaganda. Karaca and Kaplan were among the conservative female writers who attacked the academics. Kaplan called their statement "despicable" and described academics, who work mostly for state universities and earn middle- or lower-middle-class salaries, as "people who would get mad if they receive their valet service with five minutes' delay," associating the academics with wealth and luxurious consumption in a form of populist propaganda.[198] She called on the academics to resign from their positions in state universities and called them people without intellectual honor and dignity. Karaca, although unhappy about detentions, argued that the academics had to be disciplined by their institutions.[199]

To sum up this section, conservative women strongly disagreed with the secular, liberal, and leftist intellectuals on the government's policies about religious education, alcohol consumption, and the Kurdish question. The disagreement and break with Nuray Mert in 2011 was a critical turning point in conservative women's relationship with the liberal intellectuals. This break only deepened with time. The anti-intellectualism that was always present in these women's writing became stronger after the Gezi protests. A right-wing populist language became dominant in conservative women's writing following the protests. They equated the "nation" with the AKP supporters, and designated Kurdish politicians and critical intellectuals as threats to the nation. They regularly cast liberal and leftist intellectuals as "foreign," as representing the colonialist within. In other words, they used the critique of Western colonialism to nationalist ends. Conservative women's hostility toward the critical intellectuals and the Kurdish politicians drew the boundaries around their approach to democracy and the freedom of expression. When Selahattin Demirtaş, the leader of the pro-Kurdish HDP, was jailed on terrorism charges on November 4, 2016, none of the three leading conservative women journalists criticized the imprisonment of an elected representative.

Women and right-wing politics

Conservative women columnists regularly negotiated their position in relation to Islamism, conservatism, and right-wing politics in Turkey. In a reflective article in 2012, Ayşe Böhürler had difficulty in locating Turkish Islamism. According to her, Islamists are a very diverse group of religious people close to the Right. In her approach, political Islamism is an oppositional movement that emerged out of the Turkish Right. In spite of grudges against the state, in her view, the Right always prioritized protecting and defending the state as a religious and national duty. As a result, people on the Right were satisfied with being able to practice Islam inside the boundaries drawn by the state. Political Islamism (among other versions of Islamism) distinguished itself from the Right in its willingness to challenge the state in the aftermath of the 1980 military coup. Böhürler mentioned three influences on the oppositional stance of political Islamism: Turkish ultranationalists (*ülkücüler*), left-wing movements, and the Iranian Revolution.[200] What distinguished political Islamism, which Böhürler situates herself as part of, is its rejection of the Right's submissive attitude toward the authority of the state.[201]

Böhürler described the AKP in 2012 as a party that brought all the shades of the Right in Turkish politics together.[202] For her, the AKP pays attention to the equal representation of diverse groups on the Right.[203] The party's appeal and power comes from the fact that the AKP kept this spectrum on the Right as wide as possible, including even the versions of the Left that stood closer to the Right.[204] She described Ahmet Davutoğlu, the AKP's minister of foreign affairs at the time, and the party's long-time strategist, as representing that branch of Islamism that is closer to the center-right.[205] Böhürler's positioning of Islamism within the Turkish Right is in line with Tanıl Bora's approach to Islamism in Turkey: as a movement that emerged out of right-wing politics. In another instance, Böhürler unequivocally situated herself among the representatives of the Turkish Right.[206]

Women oscillated between situating themselves on the Right and criticizing the Right for its tendency to protect the status quo. In her article, "Right-Wing Muslim" in 2011, Hilâl Kaplan criticized the AKP for prioritizing right-wing politics over Muslim identity. She argued that the Right always protects the status quo and she found this in conflict with Islam.[207] Nihal Bengisu Karaca had also the same attitude toward right-wing politics and the AKP's position within it in Turkey. Yet women's distinguishing of Islamism from the right-wing attitude of protecting the state has to be put into the context of particular political events as well. In spite of their criticisms of the status quo, women fell into the right-wing discourse of protecting the state each time a scandal involving the AKP government came to the surface. For example, in 2012, Gülenists leaked conversations from a national security meeting, posting a number of audio files on YouTube. According to the tapes, high officials from the government discussed the possibility of forging a justification for a military operation in Syria.[208] The government was greatly disturbed by the leaks and blocked YouTube throughout Turkey.[209]

Conservative women journalists seemed more disturbed by the fact that this information became public than by the content of the tapes. Nihal Bengisu Karaca refused to discuss the content and referred to the "privacy of the state" while criticizing the circulation of the tape on YouTube.[210] Earlier in 2012, Böhürler discussed the conflict between the AKP and the Gülenists over Hakan Fidan, the head of the National Intelligence Agency, within the framework of "privacy" and saw the debates as exposing the family bedroom. She argued that discussing such private issues in public does not contribute to democracy. This was another moment that indicated women's return to the right-wing discourses. The Syrian conflict and the clash with the Gülenists were the two key issues that triggered the revival of right-wing arguments in women's discourse.[211]

In other words, even though the academic literature situated and named conservative women only in relation to religion and Islamism, women negotiated a position on the Turkish Right[212] and saw themselves as the successors of the previous generations of conservative women activists.[213] The dominant academic literature on the Islamist women failed to highlight the continuities between the current generation of conservative women and their forerunners in the 1960s. In her meta-analysis, Feyda Sayan-Cengiz pointed at the shortcomings of the narrative of "rupture" in the academic literature on the headscarf. Extending her analysis, I argue that the misleading emphasis on the "new" nature of Islamism overshadowed the movement's connection to the Turkish right-wing politics and women's position in it.[214]

With reference to Lila Abu-Lughod, Sayan-Cengiz also emphasized that romanticizing women's critical attitude within conservatism conceals the structural elements that shape their politics and subject positions.[215] Picking up this suggestion, I would like to emphasize that my argument calls for approaching these active women not as "Islamist women" or "Islamic feminists," but as actors who are part of the larger right-wing and conservative movements in Turkey. Situating Islamism as a form of right-wing politics helps to explain the women's regular recourse to right-wing discourses to justify the AKP's authoritarian policies.

Wounded conscience

In this chapter, I analyzed three prominent conservative women's columns to understand why they chose to support the AKP in spite of its growing authoritarianism. Before I started reading the women's columns closely, I had assumed that conservative women could not see the democratic failures of the AKP because of their closeness to and sympathy toward the party. I had assumed that when the women looked at the AKP, they saw something totally different than what I saw. Yet the results showed that the conservative women columnists have observed the same problems that the secular, liberal, and left-wing intellectuals have observed about the AKP government. They are keenly aware of the democratic deficiencies, rights violations, and polarization taking place under the AKP, and they support the party and Erdoğan nevertheless. Considering the role regularly attributed to women as "bridge-builders" or "transformative actors" in academic literature, this came as a big surprise. The evidence based on the women's columns over a period of eight years challenge the assumptions of the academic literature on Turkey's "Islamic feminists."

I looked for answers for two questions in this chapter. Let's go over these questions and the answers that I propose.

First, the liberal thesis on the transformative role of women within Islamist movements proved false. Liberals had attributed women a "bridging" role between the secular and Islamist circles. Yet conservative women failed to transform or democratize Islamism and the AKP. On the contrary, the AKP transformed women from actors who defended democracy into actors who defended authoritarian practices. Where did the liberal argument on the transformative role of conservative women go wrong?

To address this question, I argued that Turkey's liberals departed from modernist and orientalist assumptions to understand the role of conservative women in politics. They looked at women's relationship with religion to understand women's political position. With religion in mind, they encountered a number of "surprises" about conservative women: these women also engage with secularism, feminism, and Western philosophy, and they write about sex, too, although in subtle ways.[216] Liberal democrats looked at conservative women with an ideal "devout woman" in mind who lives strictly according to the book, and interpreted conservative women's departures from that ideal as "transformation." They disregarded the fact that Turkey's conservative women also grew up and received their education in secular Turkey and were willing to adopt more women-friendly interpretations of Islam. They mislocated conservative women in Turkish politics by attributing a revolutionary role in their criticisms toward the conservative male establishment.

My second question asked how the shift in women's language could be explained. Kemalists widely argued that the AKP's discourse of democratization was a form of deception: *takiyye*. *Takiyye* refers to Muslims living in un-Islamic societies having permission to hide their true intentions until they seize power. Liberals, for good reasons, had always countered the *takiyye* argument by emphasizing the futility of attempts to read intentions. How can a democracy ever function without a basic level of trust in the words of an opponent? Liberals underlined the conspiracy approach behind the *takiyye* argument, and they approached it with suspicion. I would also like to highlight the anti-Muslim sentiment behind the *takiyye* argument that makes it part of Islamophobic language. Yet women's shifting positions over time make one wonder if indeed Turkey's Kemalists had a point in insisting on a possible deception.

The evidence coming from the columns point in different directions. First, women's writing does provide evidence that they were strategic about challenging the system from within. Hilâl Kaplan openly argued that Muslims should use the language of liberal secularism to expose the failures of liberal secularism and open up room for a discourse that emphasizes Islam and justice. She referred to the Frankfurt School and suggested engaging in "immanent critique" to target liberalism " 'with its own weapons.' "[217] Pointing out such strategies that women openly discussed in the media does not prove outright deception or an Islamist conspiracy from the beginning.[218] It proves, though, that women had been part of a struggle to insert their point of view into the public debate and get control over it.[219] The struggle was taking place out in the open, with women even talking in their columns about which strategies to employ. I argue that the liberals' mistake was to underestimate this struggle, and the Kemalists' mistake was to frame it in Islamophobic language and use it to justify the deficiencies in Turkey's democracy.

Second, the columns show that women did not expect the AKP to have an authoritarian turn. They were initially (particularly between 2010 and 2013) disappointed by this turn for a number of reasons and expressed it openly. Karaca had supported constitutional changes in 2010, and she was very unhappy about it when the AKP used the amendments to gain control over the judiciary.[220] I argue that such expressions of disappointment and frustration have to be read together with women's strong commitment to Turkey's conservative neighborhood and their elite status inside the neighborhood. They are also among the beneficiaries of the new system. As a result, conservative women see the AKP leadership as part of their in-group, and they tolerate the party's misbehavior in ways that they would not tolerate were the same behavior exhibited by others. Women's writing beautifully exemplifies the "ultimate attribution error"[221] mentioned by social psychologists: When someone from the identified in-group misbehaves, the cause of that misbehavior is attributed to external factors. When someone from the out-group misbehaves, that is attributed to the character of the out-group. In other words, a very strong in-group identity shaped women's point of view and the way they framed the events. For example, when Erdoğan used tough language, Nihal Bengisu Karaca blamed the opposition for it. In contrast, when HDP representatives used tough language, she explained it with reference not to an external factor but to the representatives' aggressiveness (an internal characteristic).

Identity is not something fixed: it is something contextual and flexible. Yet when strong political or ideological commitment is at work, identities can become rigid and lead people to stick to their own neighborhoods. For millions of ordinary women in Turkey, Muslim identity is flexible and contextual: many women cover their hair, then uncover and recover depending on their life circumstances and needs. Yet for elite female ideologues active within conservatism, identity is mostly fixed and rigid. This rigidity leads them to withdraw to the confines of their discursive neighborhood and defend it when the neighborhood is under criticism.

In addition, these elite conservative women also play the role of identity police in moments of crisis and uncertainty. In 2007, Ayşe Böhürler strongly objected when some conservative women in the party considered taking off their headscarves in order to be elected to the parliament.[222] She encouraged women to "sacrifice" position and status in return for "honor" (or dignity). In 2011, she repeated the same argument when similar discussions took place. She found it acceptable to uncover for every other reason than becoming an elected representative and argued that the principle should come first.[223] She did not articulate which principle made it okay to abandon the headscarf to get a job but not okay to be elected for the parliament, which, in fact, is also a job. As one of the founders of the party, and an opinion leader, her stance on this was probably influential on women party members' decisions to keep or abandon the headscarf, particularly when this decision carried the risk of being framed as a woman without "dignity" or "principle."

Could things have been different? Can the results of my analysis be interpreted in a positive and promising way? I believe so. Women's writing between the 2010 Constitutional Referendum and the Gezi protests in 2013 showed that women freely expressed internal dissent when they did not feel under existential threat. This suggests that in a climate of perceived democratization, although accompanied by increasing authoritarianism at the structural level, conservative women felt more leverage to voice loudly their insider criticisms of the party. In that sense, with genuine democratization we could expect more insider criticisms and more diversity within the conservative neighborhood. The best sign of this was the establishment of a new conservative party, the Has Party (Halkın Sesi Partisi—People's Voice Party), in 2010. In 2012, Nihal Bengisu Karaca praised the Has Party and pointed to it as the new address of opposition outside the parliament.[224] She mentioned that conservatives vote for the AKP but love the Has Party. This also shows that before the Gezi protests, the AKP was facing challenges from its own conservative constituents, and democratization did not work in the party's favor. Gezi gave Erdoğan a new opportunity to unite Turkey's conservatives by constantly pointing at the new foreign and domestic threats. And this worked.

The columns of these three conservative women suggest that when they reached a fork in the road, they made a difficult decision: They decided to stay loyal to their in-group and retorted to the right-wing discourses to protect the new status quo that gave them new advantages. The Syrian crisis and the Gezi protests provided justification for the shift in their discourse. As mentioned earlier, in an article she wrote after the Syrian crisis, Karaca had articulated the choice that was waiting for them: supporting the government against foreign conspiracies and turning a blind eye to its mistakes at the cost of democracy. She mentioned this as a decision "where [our] conscience will be under pressure from all fronts."[225] In other words, Turkey's conservative women made a choice: they chose to defend a new conservative authoritarian regime and Erdoğan's one-man rule at the expense of a wounded conscience.

Conservative women are part of a struggle to redefine common sense and establish a new conservative hegemony. They challenged the established secular hegemony on a number of issues and actively worked to create a new normal, a new horizon in favor of conservative constituencies. The headscarf has become part of this struggle to define a new normal. For example, in 2013, Hilâl Kaplan turned the secular argument on the headscarf around and argued that "not wearing the headscarf is a political symbol."[226] Kaplan did not do this in a hostile manner. She did it in the context of defending the headscarf, and she discussed the power dynamics in defining "the political." Yet her point reveals the extent of the discursive struggle over the headscarf and all that is at stake. By 2018, many women not wearing the headscarf felt that the stakes are becoming higher each time the conservative men in power raise their voices with misogynist comments about women not wearing the headscarf.[227]

In new Turkey's polarized climate, the liberal intellectuals, leftist academics, and Kurds are not the only ones pushed outside of the nation. Feminists are another group not situated as part of "the people." The rise of the conservative female journalist went hand in hand with the rise of antifeminism and misogyny in the public discourse. Antiwomen comments from government officials and elected representatives have become common. More importantly, antifeminism has become institutionalized in Turkey. In the next chapter, I situate women's writing within the framework of feminist and antifeminist struggles. I focus on how conservative women allied with the AKP to marginalize feminism, and I explore ways to resist the new conservative gender hegemony in Turkey.

seminars, talks, and screenings.[25] Kaos GL established an LGBT library and also collaborated with academics to organize conferences and seminars in a number of Turkish universities.[26]

The AKP's initial years (2002–7) coincided with that period of expansion where the feminist movement in Turkey had started to reap the results of its two decades of struggle.[27] During these initial years, the AKP was still weak in relation to the secular establishment, and the party did not strain its relationships with the feminists, as it did not with the liberals. Since their success in civil code reform in 2001, feminists had been working on the amendments to the penal code "to establish a women-centred legal framework"[28] in matters of violence against women. During the debates on penal code reform in 2004, the AKP attempted to criminalize adultery, an early battle that the party could not win under pressure from the secular population, liberals, and feminists. In September 2004, the AKP-majority parliament accepted "more than thirty amendments"[29] to the penal code demanded by the feminists within the framework of the candidacy to the European Union. While the feminists celebrated their accomplishment, this gave the AKP the opportunity to frame some of these gains that did not conflict with the party's conservative gender ideology as its own. As for the other gains of feminism, the AKP was simply unwilling to implement them. Kandiyoti pointed at "the huge chasm between the laws that are intended to safeguard women's rights and their actual implementation."[30]

In 1994, the Welfare Party did not reward conservative women like Sibel Eraslan, who walked from door to door and carried the party to power. Yet Erdoğan's attitude was different when he established the AKP in 2002. The Welfare Party experience taught Erdoğan the importance of garnering and keeping support among women. He first opened up room, although not much, for successful conservative women like Ayşe Böhürler around the highest decision-making mechanisms of the party. This was a move that the conservative women saw as a significant expansion. Second, he did not shy away from giving his wife, Emine Erdoğan, and his daughter, Sümeyye Erdoğan, extensive power and visibility. Emine Erdoğan in particular, who has been very active among the party's female base, modeled a strong conservative woman who, in addition to her committed political activism, raised four children and has become her husband's biggest support. Emine Erdoğan is probably one of the most, if not *the* most, active First Lady that Turkey has ever seen. Third, the party continued to mobilize women on the ground through its hierarchical system that reaches out to women in the neighborhoods.[31] In addition, the municipalities run by the AKP provided training and short-term courses on a variety of subjects ranging from carpentry and gardening to courses on numerous foreign languages offered free of charge. These are services consciously modeled on the "People's Houses" (Halkevleri),[32] an early Kemalist project later picked up by the Left, that provided training and various other services in community centers. "People's Houses" were shut down by the 1980 military coup. The AKP's services modeled on this earlier experiment drew women in large numbers. The AKP's Istanbul municipality in particular became successful in reaching out women through its ISMEK Lifelong Learning Centers that helped women get out of the home and meet other women with similar interests.[33]

At the same time, the AKP gradually pushed the feminist organizations outside of the forums and decision-making processes on gender issues and strengthened conservative women's organizations.[34] KADEM was established, with Erdoğan's daughter Sümeyye Erdoğan as vice president, to promote the AKP's vision of gender conservatism over all of Turkey. Between 2004 and 2018, in addition to the services that aimed to garner lower-class women's support, the AKP implemented policies that defined women in relation to the family and motherhood. Erdoğan regularly advised young women against postponing marriage, advised families to have at least three children, and even called women who were not mothers "half women."[35] One of the most painful losses for the feminists came with the establishment of Ministry of Family and Social Policies in 2011, replacing the previous Ministry for Women and Family. The Directorate of Women's Status (Kadının Statüsü ve Sorunları Genel Müdürlüğü), which had been actively working on gender equality, was reorganized under this ministry. The feminists had long pushed for increasing the powers of this directorate by turning it into a ministry that focused on achieving gender equality in Turkey.[36] For feminists, the establishment of Ministry of Family and Social Policies represented a significant structural and institutional change that de-emphasized the equality between men and women, and categorized women's problems under the family. Indeed, from that point onward, questions of reproductive rights that directly involved women's bodies were regularly framed as "social policy issues" both by the government and by conservative women columnists. As feminists feared, the change in the naming of institutions also changed the terms of the debate. For conservative women, on the other hand, this was neither a political nor an ideological decision and they considered feminist concerns as unwarranted.[37]

Erdoğan has expressed numerous times that he does not support the idea of equality between men and women. According to Erdoğan's gender conservatism, men and women are created with different capabilities and they complement one another; they are equal in principle but not in practice. During its time in power, the AKP implemented concrete policies to actualize Erdoğan's perspective. The AKP discouraged cohabitation through tax fines and suppressed the burgeoning LGBT movement.[38] The party encouraged traditional marriage through institutional means, by distributing government benefits to newly married heterosexual university students. This was accompanied by the party's attack on co-ed student housing. The AKP government restricted women's access to abortions, making them de facto unavailable. Under the AKP, Turkey experienced a steady drop in international rankings on gender equality and women's employment outside of the home.[39] Quite symbolically, the AKP cracked down on the Beyoğlu neighborhood, which has long represented cosmopolitanism and liberal gender relations. The businesses, bars, clubs, and restaurants enjoyed by the university students and young professionals of the 1990s disappeared one by one, giving way to shopping malls or AKP-friendly businesses.

In Turkey, misogynist voices had never been successfully marginalized, yet feminist activism and Kemalist women's organizations had succeeded a great deal in pushing them back in the 1990s. During the AKP's time in power, misogynist voices moved into the mainstream and gained unprecedented access to public discourse and the media. It has become common to hear sexist comments from party members, AKP mayors and representatives, and the AKP's core supporters. The examples are too many to be recounted in detail here. One high-profile sexist comment came from Bülent Arınç, deputy prime minister at the time, when he described the ideal men and women. Arınç said that the ideal woman should be modest and not laugh out loud in public.[40] Another infamous comment came from Ömer Tuğrul İnançer, a famous religious leader who has been a regular guest in the state-run TRT's programs. İnançer shamed pregnant women who walked on the streets with their "not aesthetic" bellies.[41]

Among all these, the jump in the violence against women has been the most urgent issue calling for attention. Kandiyoti rightfully argues that "soaring levels of violence against women" are a symptom of "a crisis in the gender order" in Turkey.[42] Building on her argument, I suggest that this crisis in the gender order is the result of a conservative backlash against feminists' accomplishments in the 1990s. The expansion achieved in gender relations in the 1990s encountered a sudden conservative backlash led by the AKP in the subsequent decade and generated a crisis. The organization We Will Stop Femicide Platform[43] reported that in 2016 the majority of these murders took place when women wanted to walk away from their relationship or when they wanted to take an independent decision about their own life.[44] While women are empowered enough to walk away, the AKP's gender-conservative discourse encourages men to keep the women in their place, and some men who pick up that message even use violence to that end.

There is now contention among scholars writing about women wearing the headscarf regarding the degree to which the women writers wearing the headscarf are still vulnerable or not. Based on interviews with women columnists wearing the headscarf, Didem Unal argued that "pious women still feel vulnerable in the public sphere in contemporary Turkey," and she dismissed the opposite argument that emphasized the gains of "pious women" as "untrue."[45] I contend that taking women's claims at face value, without situating them within the broader political context, is problematic. Today, vulnerability is claimed both by women writers who support the AKP and by women who are marginalized by the AKP. This in itself is evidence that a hegemonic shift has been taking place and that claims of "vulnerability" have currency within the struggle for power and legitimacy. Conservative women's claims of vulnerability rhetorically work to conceal their gains made at the expense of secular, feminist, and Kurdish women's demands, as well as their alliance with a misogynist and authoritarian leader. In an environment where an authoritarian government has redefined the headscarf as part of ideal womanhood, it is harder to sustain the argument that women wearing the headscarf are still vulnerable in the current political climate in Turkey.[46] If conservative women writers have any vulnerability today, it does not come from their piety, identity, or headscarves. It comes from their sustained support for authoritarianism, as they probably will be among the first to lose their power when Erdoğan falls.

Conservative women's choice to wear the headscarf in Turkey today is protected and supported by an immensely powerful party and a man who has concentrated unprecedented power in his own hands. Yet women not wearing the headscarf find themselves more and more unprotected from assault and violence. In September 2016, a man attacked Ayşegül Terzi, a nurse in Istanbul, and kicked her in the face for wearing shorts. He was released three times by the courts following the incident. He was rearrested as a result of the reactions coming from the public, and was convicted of assault in September 2017.[47] Even more frustrating than the whole process was Prime Minister Binali Yıldırım's comments on the incident: he said the perpetrator could have just mumbled instead of attacking her.[48] Other women have also reported similar incidents where they were attacked either for their clothes or immodest behavior such as sitting with their legs crossed.[49] Women do not find a supportive and friendly police force when they suffer from such attacks where law enforcement is socialized to see some women as more virtuous than others. Alternative news organizations regularly report incidents where the police have protected the perpetrators instead of the women.[50] In her analysis of normalization of violence in Turkey, Kandiyoti mentioned that Erdoğan's comments following an incident where a woman demonstrator "was savagely beaten by the police" made it clear that "only the deserving (our sisters) are worthy of protection, the rest, and especially those with the audacity to break the norms of modesty and protest in public put themselves in jeopardy."[51]

Feminist activism in Turkey is fragmented and sporadic as I write. But, more importantly, it is marginalized and under heavy political pressure. Following the July 15 coup attempt in 2016, the government closed fifty-two Kurdish feminist organizations[52] in addition to other feminist organizations.[53] JINHA, by its own description the first news agency in the world run by women, was shut down.[54] Similar to the liberals and the Kurds, the AKP eventually designated the feminists a group alienated to the nation's values, and regularly attacked them when opportunities arose. Erdoğan's infamous statement in 2015 provided the best evidence of the culmination of hostility toward the feminists: "You know these feminists (. . .) [they] have nothing to do with our civilization, our faith, our religion. . . ."[55]

In short, the 1990s feminist dream of creating a shared ground on the basis of "sisterhood" has come to an end. Contrary to what the feminists hoped for, opening up more space for conservative women came at the price of marginalizing secular, leftist, and Kurdish feminisms. Sibel Eraslan, who called herself "a feminist with faith" in a 1995 *Pazartesi* interview, preferred to be a sister to conservative men like Erdoğan, not to the feminists.[56] The same is true for the other conservative female columnists who legitimate Erdoğan's authoritarianism and antifeminism. Scholars and feminists who called for caution about "Islamic feminism" have proved to be right in pointing at the limits of women's rights discourse as embraced by conservative women.[57] Sharing the same vision for the future, not sharing the same sex, makes women sisters. As of 2018, the feminist and conservative women's visions for the future are simply irreconcilable and make them not sisters but opponents.

Who represents "women's rights"?

Conservative women journalists have made a number of argumentative moves to discredit feminism and establish themselves as the representatives/carriers of women's rights in Turkey. In one of her articles, Böhürler declared, "The times of the old school feminists as women's rights defenders are over."[58] She framed the feminists as gaining a reputation for hating their country and complaining about it to the West at every opportunity.[59] She blamed them for looking down on their own people. This is an extension of the argument used to discredit the liberal intellectuals by likening them to "colonialists." According to Böhürler, "women who understand the society" have to be on the ground, not the ones looking down upon society.[60]

A common argument used among conservative women to discredit feminist women's groups is to call them subjective. Feminists who do not endorse or support the AKP's policies on gender are pushed into the realm of "subjectivity," making the definition of "objectivity" dependent upon supporting the AKP's policies. Feminists were praised when they supported the AKP, but when they did not, they were considered outside of "the people." Before the 2010 Constitutional Referendum, Ayşe Böhürler equated the Yes vote with "the people," making those who said no fall outside of "the people." She praised the leading feminist Şirin Tekeli (1944–2017) for supporting Yes but criticized the other feminists who supported the No campaign.[61] Three years later, Böhürler mentioned a gender equality symposium that took place in Paris in 2013. She praised the representatives of the government on their "extremely objective" approach and, by way of comparison, cast feminist women's right activists as partisan and unobjective.[62] Establishing a new hegemony is about defining a new common sense and pointing at the actors that represent the common sense. In their efforts to establish a new hegemony, conservative women pointed to themselves and the AKP government as the new representatives of "objectivity" and common sense.

Another strategy used to discredit feminism is to frame it as an aggressive, "women-centered" ideology.[63] In other instances, feminist demands are framed as too idealist and unrealistic. In a rather friendly article toward feminism, Nihal Bengisu Karaca argued that "feminists are fixated on an 'idealist' position that does not produce 'ideal' results for conservative women."[64] For her, conservative women activists represent the "realist" position by taking the assumed differences between men and women for granted.

Conflicting perspectives on the AKP's gender policies

The AKP clearly gained conservative women's hearts on a number of issues, receiving more of the women's vote than the men's in the 2014 elections that made Erdoğan president of Turkey. Around 55 percent of women voted for the AKP in that election.[65] In other words, the majority of women in Turkey seems to be persuaded to see the AKP from the conservative elite women's perspective. Let's look at the AKP's concrete policies from the conservative point of view and the controversies around them.

Among the conservative journalists I analyzed, Ayşe Böhürler stands out for her frequent emphasis on women's issues.[66] Her writing gives an insider's perspective on the AKP's policies on gender. From Böhürler's perspective, Erdoğan is a women's rights champion, and under the AKP women's rights have improved for all women to an extent that is unprecedented in the history of the modern Turkish republic.[67] Like other conservative women, she celebrated the removal of the headscarf ban in universities and in parliament and saw this as a huge improvement for women's rights.[68] In her writing, the AKP is the party that brought freedom to all women, whether they wore a headscarf or not.[69] Already in 2013, Böhürler was aware of the government's tendency to define the headscarf as part of ideal womanhood. In the article where she thanked Erdoğan for removing the ban, she also cautioned against turning the headscarf into a source of privilege.[70]

For Böhürler, the AKP championed increasing women's political participation at the local and national levels, particularly in Turkey's conservative towns.[71] She praised the AKP's Women's Branches and credited them for breaking "the elitist monopoly in women's movement" and mobilizing women even in villages to participate in politics.[72] To Böhürler's mind, the AKP did not discriminate on the headscarf and included women in equal proportions in the party's top decision-making mechanisms.[73] Böhürler argued that women are the AKP's biggest supporters both at the ballot box and in the field.[74] She praised the AKP for getting women beyond the boundaries of the family, giving them a voice, and engaging them in civil society and NGO work.[75]

For Böhürler, girls' education is another realm where the AKP had huge success. She complained that the party's efforts in this area has remained invisible and unacknowledged.[76] Böhürler argued, without evidence, that the AKP had its biggest success in the history of modern Turkey in terms of girls' enrollment in schools, and the party hugely invested in this area.[77] Her favorite example is from Harran, one of the most conservative towns in southern Turkey. She argued that the AKP had considerable success in this conservative town by opening girls' schools. She criticized the insistence by secular people on providing mixed-gender education that, according to her, kept the girls, whose families objected to sending their daughters to mixed-gender high schools, at home.[78]

The AKP indeed opened schools for girls in this region—vocational schools that educated girls in religion (e.g., an Imam Hatip high school for girls), information technologies, childrearing, and services for the sick and the elderly.[79] These are areas of study that clearly reflect the AKP's gender ideology. From the conservative perspective, the AKP respected people's values in Harran and responded to their demands within a democratic framework. It goes without saying that it is highly debatable whether this counts as "democratization" or "Islamization." These education policies have enabled the AKP to educate a new generation of women on conservative gender roles, and at the same time to argue that they are the champions of women's rights and democracy: they are the ones who increased girls' enrollment in schools and responded to the "people's" (i.e., conservative constituents') demands for segregated education.

Böhürler supported the AKP's trickle-down economics scheme for women.[80] She criticized the voices on opposition (mostly feminist groups) who decried the deregulation of the work place: Workplaces that employ more than 150 women are obliged to provide day-care services for their employees. In 2008, the AKP proposed to eliminate this obligation for employers. Böhürler supported the government's explanation that the elimination of the day-care obligation would relieve the employers of significant costs, which in turn might encourage the employers to employ more women. The Minister of Employment and Social Security, Böhürler's source, argued that the elimination of this obligation created opportunities for women to open day-care centers and provide these services themselves, which would be another way of increasing women's employment. Böhürler diligently supported this proposal and argued that all women should support it. For her, only "information based on prejudice and subjective judgements" would stand against supporting this proposal. From the perspective of feminists, who in Böhürler's terms were cast as prejudiced and subjective, this was a problematic proposal in a number of ways: it empowered the employer at the expense of the worker; there was no guarantee that the extra revenue going to the employer would be used to employ more women; and this was another instance proving the government's limited vision that aimed to provide opportunities for women mainly in caretaking jobs related to family and motherhood.

The AKP's "social policies" that include issues such as childcare, parental leave, and the care of the elderly have stirred up a lot of controversy. By creating panic over a "stagnating population," the AKP government instituted policies to encourage women to give birth to more children. Although some projections predict a stagnating population, according to feminist economist Gülay Toksöz, this is not as severe as the AKP government projects and does not warrant schemes encouraging women to bear children. The government pays for each child born in a family. In line with Erdoğan's "three children" comment, the amount of financial aid paid to a mother increases with the birth of each baby.[81] Depending on their social security premium payments, mothers can also be eligible for breastfeeding money.[82] The AKP also introduced flexible and part-time work hours for one of the parents, a controversial arrangement that according to feminists encourages temporary work and diminishes women's salary and benefits by half.[83]

Conservative women regularly emphasize the government's reports and Erdoğan's statements that show an increase in women's employment.[84] Yet the international reports to which feminists refer show a steady decrease in women's employment[85] and contradict the government's reports. Gülay Toksöz examined how the AKP government compiled data on women's employment and figured out the following: The Ministry of Family and Social Policies pays salaries to women who take care of sick and disabled family members at home. The AKP government counts this insecure, round-the-clock "job" as part of "women's employment."[86] The government also includes female domestic workers who work in the informal sector as cleaning professionals as "women's employment" as well. For feminists, this is outright trickery and deception.[87] A number of scholars (feminist or otherwise) have pointed out that the AKP's initiatives toward women's work take place within a larger neoliberal program that approaches women's work as a source of cheap labor complementary to men's position as the breadwinners.[88] These initiatives are designed to push women to unsafe jobs without benefits and to reinforce traditional gender roles, making homemaking a convenient and desirable option for women, while the feminist ideal of women's economic independence becomes less and less attainable.

Another disagreement over the facts is about the number of women's shelters: according to Böhürler, the AKP triumphed in this area as well.[89] Yet, secular women's groups and feminists emphasize the hostility and pressure from the government on women's shelters, the hardships women face during the application process, and the unwelcoming attitude of the personnel.[90] They draw attention to the shelters closed by the government,[91] and diminished funding or absence of initiatives to protect women suffering from violence.[92] Feminists' claims about women's shelters are supported by the wing of conservative women critical of the AKP government, as well. Berrin Sönmez pointed out that the government changed the name of the "shelters" to "guest houses," implying the abandonment of these places' basic function: protecting and empowering women.[93]

From a feminist perspective, the conservative women in this conversation do not propose a consistent and reliable project to improve women's rights. For example, Hilâl Kaplan asked for a civil code for believers that would legalize polygamy in a limited fashion.[94] She defended polygamy on the basis of Islamic law (*sharia*), yet she took the secular civil code as the norm for divorce. (Islamic law greatly advantages men during divorce.) In other words, conservative women are unwilling to give up the gains of the secular civil code, but they also want to be able to follow Islamic law, pushing for a dual system for marriage and family. For feminists, this type of arbitrary appropriation of secular and religious approaches to the civil code has great potential to put women at a severe disadvantage: What would happen if a woman wanted to divorce based on secular law and her husband wanted to divorce based on sharia law? The AKP allowed religious officials to conduct civil marriages in 2017.[95] This can be seen as a step toward Islamizing the civil code, fulfilling demands for a dual system that may lead to further Islamization of marriage and the family.

Finally, for Böhürler, the AKP has transformed conservative men for the better, making them more open to accepting women's participation in politics and economy.[96] Yet from the feminists' perspective, the AKP government has encouraged conservative men to keep women in their place more than any other government has. For feminists and Kemalist women's right activists, there is no doubt that sexist comments that regularly come from conservative men at the top levels of the government have the effect of both mainstreaming and normalizing misogyny. The disagreement between feminists and conservatives on this point is due to the fact that, in spite of their frequent criticisms,[97] conservative women are cautious about not alienating conservative men.

Perhaps the best example of conservative women tending to defend misbehaving conservative men from feminist criticism was Nihal Bengisu Karaca's attitude toward female protestors who took to the streets following Ömer Tuğrul İnançer's comments shaming them for freely walking on the streets while pregnant. İnançer made these comments on the state television channel TRT during a Ramazan talk show. Although Karaca herself was shocked by the comments, the reactions to İnançer's comments were so ruthless that she felt bad for criticizing him.[98] Karaca said she did not understand pregnant women who ran to the streets to protest against İnançer and went on to reprimand them with the following words:

Who stopped you and when? You want to give birth underwater and you do it. You want to get yourself filmed while giving birth and show it to your relatives and friends, and you do it. And since Demi Moore, you sexualize your pregnancy in every conceivable way. Who banned any of these? Who said anything? Who interfered with your lifestyle, your style of giving birth? Every day in this country someone imposes something either in the name of religion or in the name of modernity. Arguing that all these views reflect the government's position and are part of the government's "secret agenda" is not just unfair: this cannot be taken seriously at all.[99]

Pregnant women and feminist groups protested against İnançer with the feminist slogan "My body belongs to me." Conservative women find this slogan highly alienating because according to them, a woman's body belongs to God, not to the woman herself.[100] This position inevitably limits the reproductive choices available to a woman, underlining a very strong philosophical and ontological disagreement between feminists and conservative women.[101] As a result, particularly in such moments of ontological disagreement, conservative women find religiously conservative men closer to them than the feminists are. In her article, Karaca juxtaposed İnançer—"a valuable person"—with women who film their most private moments for sharing with friends and relatives, casting women protestors as morally questionable. Ayşe Böhürler also wrote an article about the incident and blamed the medium of television more than İnançer himself.[102] Both Karaca and Böhürler dismissed the fact that these comments were made on state-run television controlled by the AKP. To this day, İnançer, who also made his own programs for TRT, continues to be invited to speak on state-run television as a distinguished guest.

Feminists and conservative women agree on one significant issue, though. All the conservative women in this study were unequivocally against all forms of violence against women and did not try to justify it in any form.[103] They have even occasionally granted the feminists' role in problematizing violence against women.[104] Yet even though both feminists and conservative women agree on the urgency of violence against women as an issue,[105] they immediately disagree on the source of violence and the possible solutions. For feminists, it is clear that the AKP's leadership has normalized misogyny and the party's gender policies are responsible for growing violence against women. Conservative women cannot make sense of this claim and find it hostile. In their view, the AKP government did so much to prevent violence against women that it cannot be held responsible for the increase in women's murders.[106]

I have found one moment where Böhürler admitted that policies toward women under the AKP did not produce positive results. She accepted that rejection of the idea of equality between men and women is a problem that prevented results in favor of women.[107] She put the blame on the implementers who did not internalize the idea of equality between men and women. Yet, two years later, when Erdoğan spoke against the idea of equality between men and women at KADEM, she was one of the first who ran to his defense.[108] This is the exact dilemma that prompted me to write this book in the first place: Why do conservative women support "equality" and support misogynist men who denounce equality at the same time? This dilemma shows that the conservative understanding of equality between men and women is not the same as equality understood in feminist terms. Conservative women and feminists disagree on what constitutes misogyny and sexism. Policies on welfare, reproduction, family, and economics are all battlegrounds between them.

Conservative men in power see conservative women as their "deserving sisters"[109] and know that they have conservative women's support in major political and ontological battles. Therefore, while attacking feminists, conservative men respond to conservative women's criticisms and open up new spaces for them within the new power structure. For example, Karaca wrote an article complaining about the government excluding women journalists from foreign visits.[110] Following that complaint, she started to receive invitations from the Ministry of Foreign Affairs to join these travels. In time, women journalists wearing the headscarf became regular guests, accompanying Erdoğan and AKP ministers on foreign travels and reporting the events from their perspective. This gave them access to power, as they could offer exclusive interviews with Erdoğan and the other ministers. Although the government did not necessarily plan for conservative women's inclusion in the circles of power, they responded to their criticism, and accommodated them. This, in turn, made the conservative women the beneficiaries of a new system, which worked in the AKP government's favor because highly educated conservative women supported and defended the government on multiple platforms.

As a result, conservative women, even those critical of the AKP, do not feel the adverse effects of conservative men's misogynist discourse as much as women who do not fit into the new "ideal womanhood." They tend to see men's sexist talk as empty rhetoric not having a real influence on women's lives.[111] The AKP's actual policies on gender disprove that claim.

The institutionalization of antifeminism in Turkey

The AKP's time in power did not just produce a series of attacks on feminism. This period also witnessed "the institutionalization of antifeminism"[112] in

Turkey through the establishment of KADEM, the Association of Women and Democracy.[113] KADEM is a government-organized nongovernmental organization with Erdoğan's daughter Sümeyye Erdoğan as a board member and vice president. I would like to draw attention to the fact that KADEM picked a name that sounds similar to the successful feminist organization KA.DER, established in 1997, one of the organizations that represented the institutionalization of feminism in Turkey.[114] On November 24, 2014, Recep Tayyip Erdoğan delivered a very controversial speech at KADEM's first International Congress on Women and Justice and made it clear that he does not espouse the idea of equality between men and women. With Erdoğan's direct support behind the organization, KADEM quickly opened branches in twenty-one cities throughout Turkey and keeps expanding. All of the three leading conservative women whose columns I analyzed in this study congratulated KADEM and celebrated its establishment.[115]

KADEM was established on March 8, 2013. The exclusion of feminist and LGBT organizations from the debates on gender-based violence quickly followed, in December 2014, with the Ministry of Family and Social Policies' decision to select NGO representatives to monitor Turkey's progress exclusively from KADEM and other pro-government conservative women's organizations.[116] Feminist and LGBT organizations reported that the government regularly created barriers to block their participation. KADEM itself adopted an exclusionary language toward feminist organizations in Turkey in spite of feminist organizations' long-time support for the headscarf. KADEM's then-director Sare Aydın Yılmaz accused feminists of leaving them alone during their struggles for the headscarf,[117] a false claim[118] that not only caught feminists by surprise but also puzzled some Kemalist women's rights organizations.[119] The most symbolic indicator of KADEM's hostility to feminism was the lawsuit opened by Sümeyye Erdoğan against the leading feminist Pınar İlkkaracan because of her criticisms. In other words, KADEM's establishment sealed the end of "sisterhood" between conservative women and Turkey's feminist organizations. KADEM emphasizes difference feminism and promotes the concepts of "gender justice" and "gender complementarity" as opposed to gender equality in national and international platforms.[120] Family is prioritized in the organization's discourse and activities. In all this, KADEM represents a new chapter in patriarchy.

KADEM's philosophy derives from postcolonial feminism with an added emphasis on Muslim women's difference, and women from KADEM utilize the arguments of postcolonial feminism to support a conservative, right-wing political agenda. KADEM's philosophy rests on the opposition to the West. The organization's discourse casts Turkey's feminists as Westernized women alienated from their religion. Even though it claims to be "independent" from the government, KADEM openly supported the Yes campaign to increase Erdoğan's powers in the April 2017 referendum and defined the abolition of the headscarf ban as a major advancement in women's rights. KADEM's propaganda videos equated the Yes vote to saying yes to women's advancement and democracy.[121] The image of a woman wearing a headscarf who confidently enters in a classroom was juxtaposed with the images of women who succeed in stereotypically male professions like auto racing and construction.

I find Ronnee Schreiber's work on conservative women's organizations in the United States highly relevant for situating KADEM within a field of women's rights organizations. Schreiber argued that—not being able to defy feminism in a climate where feminism's gains have become normal for the wide majority of women—conservative women's movements have appropriated the language of feminism to use it for conservative ends.[122] Schreiber calls it "righting feminism." KADEM's propaganda videos in favor of increasing Erdoğan's powers do exactly the same thing: repurposing the language of feminism to gain support for a conservative, right-wing government and its reinterpretation of "women's rights." During this process, KADEM frames feminism as Western and therefore foreign, yet at the same time depicts the gains of secular and feminist women's struggles as their own.

KADEM actively promotes its vision of gender justice in international forums, signaling the emergence of a conservative alliance among women from different religions. A number of studies point to the struggles taking place between the progressive and conservative NGOs in the transnational arena. Kristin Blakely focused on the conservative women's organizations from Canada and their efforts to redefine gender issues in conservative terms.[123] Within this contested sphere, Turkey's religiously conservative women are discovering their commonalities with the other religiously conservative women around the world,[124] and also strive to take a leadership role in defining "women's rights" in Muslim countries. Zehra Yılmaz, who studied conservative NGOs, argued that a new global gender regime is in the making and this new regime is defined on the basis of the needs of the neoliberal economy.[125] According to her, women's caretaking services in the NGO sector compensate for the elimination of social security networks while reinforcing the traditional patriarchal structure, and therefore constitute one of the desirable features of this new regime based on an alliance between Islam and neoliberalism.[126] Conservative women's right organizations like KADEM are candidates to be the influential actors of this new gender regime that Yılmaz depicts. Looking at the columns of conservative journalists who cherished the establishment of KADEM, the contours of a new conservative gender order can be depicted thus: this new order rejects extreme religious practices like stoning and female genital mutilation[127] and develops a language with which to criticize violence against women, yet it sees "women's rights" as identical to "conservative women's rights," redefining the meaning of the concept. As I argued earlier, categories like East and West have lost their analytical power for understanding and explaining the complex alliances that can emerge in this new transnational sphere.

Turkey's mainstream conservative women, exemplified by the leading columnists of focus here and by KADEM, may look progressive and "feminist" if their selective appropriation of the feminist language is taken at face value without considering their support for a repressive regime. Arat, for example, traced the "feminist" and "secular" arguments in conservative women's writings. She saw the existence of these tropes, tropes that were predetermined in her theoretical approach, as a promising potential in women's columns. My analysis enters into a productive conversation with Arat's most recent work.[128] I fundamentally disagree with her about the "feminist" or "secular" potential of conservative women's activism, particularly with respect to conservative women in the mainstream supporting the AKP government. I find Arat's concern about polarization and her willingness to search for dialogue understandable, yet her theoretical framework based on "Islamist women versus secular women" fails to explain the co-optation of feminist arguments by the "Islamist women" who support an authoritarian government.[129]

Women's rights in Turkey are increasingly being discussed with reference to religion in Turkey today.[130] And conservative women's "secular" arguments are part of a political regime that has narrowed down the secular realm.[131] Secular references are not valuable in themselves and do not indicate that women embrace secularism. These references should, rather, be seen as rhetorical devices for carving new spaces for conservative women within their own conservative circles. By looking at conservative women's "feminist" arguments, Arat suggested that "[d]espite differences, there are grounds for solidarity between Islamist and secular women concerning women's rights, particularly in a context of increasing encroachment on democratic rights."[132] My reading and analysis suggests the opposite. Solidarity is undermined in an environment where conservative women and feminists have not only different visions about what constitutes "women's rights" but also where feminists and secular women's rights activists (including Arat and her colleagues, like Binnaz Toprak) are delegitimized and marginalized by a repressive regime supported by conservative women. As long as mainstream conservative women defend an increasingly authoritarian government that encroaches on democratic rights, it is futile to search for grounds of "solidarity" with them.

Solidarity can be possible only with those women who, independent of what they wear, distance themselves from an authoritarian, repressive regime and its leader. My reading suggests that there are other ways of building solidarities both to resist authoritarianism and to defend "women's rights" from the perspective of a liberal democratic and secular standpoint in Turkey.

Possibilities for the future of feminism in Turkey

In this book, I have identified the images and narratives that are used to delegitimate Turkey's secular system and cherish Erdoğan's authoritarianism as "democracy," as representing "the people." The current repressive regime can be pushed back with the creation of counter-narratives in the popular discourse, a challenging task considering the government's repressive mechanism and heavy hand that so far has suppressed any form of dissent.

The Gezi protests were an attempt to push back this repressive regime at a moment when the regime had not yet fully entrenched itself. This attempt to stop authoritarianism, which in my reading corresponds to Gramsci's "war of manoeuvre" has failed.[133] I believe (in the aftermath of the June 24, 2018 elections where the AKP sealed the system change that would work in its favor, and entrenched its hegemony probably for decades to come) we are at a moment that calls for Gramsci's "war of position," a long-term struggle to undermine the authoritarian conservative hegemony. I suggest four proposals to resist this repressive mechanism, and focus particularly on how to reach out to women.

First of all, as many scholars of hegemony have pointed out, hegemonies rise and fall and any hegemony can be defeated. Conservative women know this best, and we have to learn from their success. Today's conservative women in right-wing politics are reaping the benefits of long decades of hard work and struggle to defeat Kemalist hegemony and mobilize women around conservatism. They have walked from door to door to "win hearts and minds," listened to women, and created connections between women's everyday concerns and conservative politics. Turkey's feminists have to accept the fact that with the help of conservative women, the AKP has become successful in mobilizing half of Turkey's women and expanded its base tremendously, particularly among poor women.

A large number of academics, journalists, and intellectuals are in prison at the moment. Others face the risk of jail time for opposing the government. Antonio Gramsci's ideas written from prison have never been so relevant. To use Gramsci's terminology, conservative women ideologues claimed "moral and intellectual leadership," first through writing novels and then by acquiring media power to discredit liberal and leftist intellectuals in the media. They presented their headscarf, which is a strong component of the ideology of the religious right, as part of the age-old traditions of "the people," and they used the symbolic meanings of the headscarf to communicate the message "We are like you." They have succeeded a great deal in garnering support, yet they have not fully established their intellectual and moral leadership because their support for authoritarianism situates them on a shaky ground. Millions of women have voted for the AKP, but it is not necessarily the case that the women who have voted for the AKP are conservative or will remain so. Turkey's secular feminists can win them back. While acknowledging conservative women's success in helping the party reach out to around 55 percent of women, we should be careful about not designating them as the natural representatives of these constituents.

Arat assumed that conservative columnists wearing the headscarf are "the opinion leaders" of 70 percent of women in Turkey who also cover their hair.[134] This rather straightforward-looking assumption fails the test of evidence, though. According to Çarkoğlu and Toprak's studies in 1999 and 2006,[135] the number of women wearing a form of headscarf in Turkey fluctuates. In 2006, 63.5 percent of women covered their hair with a form of headscarf when they walked onto the streets, a drop from 72.7 percent in 1999.[136] Only 3.9 percent of women in their study mentioned the headscarf as an inseparable part of their identity.[137] Even when we accept 70 percent as a rough estimate of women who cover their hair in some way, only 55 percent of women, many of whom do not wear a headscarf, voted for the AKP in 2014. This shows that a considerable segment of women who do wear the headscarf in Turkey do not see the AKP as representing their interests and do not identify with the pro-AKP conservative women columnists just because they wear the headscarf. Arat assumes that conservative women are the carriers of "feminist" arguments and women's rights discourses to this extremely large group of headscarf-wearing women. This assumption also defeats, from the start, the attempts to build feminist and secular counter-narratives by willingly offering "intellectual and moral leadership" to conservative women, enabling them to define women's rights on their own terms and communicate their version of equality to younger generations of women. Wearing the same headgear does not necessarily indicate similarity in beliefs and political positions. Conservative ideological struggles succeeded in making the connection between the headscarf and religious conservatism seem natural, normal, and inevitable. But there is nothing "natural" about this connection, and counter-narratives could unsettle the assumption that the AKP and conservative women stand for "the people's" values and traditions, one of which is symbolized by wearing a headscarf.

In other words, and this is my second proposal, secular women and feminists have to reclaim representing women's rights instead of accepting defeat from the start and leaving the whole ground for the conservative agenda. Accepting the "natural" leadership of conservative women also strengthens and justifies their claim that secular feminists are foreign to the "nation" and the nation's values. It goes without saying that secular feminists are as local as the conservative women. We need narratives and discourses to resist the conservative narratives that regularly push feminists outside of the nation and the nation's values. To put it differently, we need counter-narratives that localize secularism and feminism, emphasizing their inseparable place in local culture and history.[138]

In pro-AKP conservative women's discourse, feminists are framed as the allies of the West, alienated from their own culture and religion. Secularism is also cast as a foreign imposition. Yet, in 1999, almost 90 percent of the respondents in the representative sample in Çarkoğlu and Toprak's study were in favor of the Turkish civil code that has defined women's rights from a secular framework.[139] Secularism in Turkey has been part of the lived experience, and it is as local as Islam can be. For that reason, postcolonial critiques that characterize secularism as an imposition of the West, as something foreign to Muslim societies, fall short of explaining the contemporary presence of secularism as a lived experience in Turkey. My third proposal is therefore that it is necessary to cease framing secularism as a "foreign" imposition. The theoretical frameworks based on a binary between the West and the East reinforce exclusionary conservative discourses and provide them with the scholarly justification to project Turkey's secular intellectuals as allies of the "colonial powers." Secularism might have traveled to Turkey from the West during the eighteenth and nineteenth centuries, but by the end of the twentieth it had become an inseparable part of the local culture.

Secular feminists have reached out to young women before. Duygu Asena's little book *The Woman Has No Name*, published in 1986, went through forty editions within a year[140] and reached millions of young women. Asena's book has faced censorship and a conservative backlash over the last thirty years. Her story, and those of other leading feminists, have been great sources of inspiration for women and men wanting to resist a conservative gender regime and authoritarian policies. As did they, we have to reach out to young women and popularize feminism. Secular feminism on the Left today faces the challenge of reaching out to young women and winning hearts and minds by articulating connections between feminism and women's concerns in even the most conservative towns. I find Ayşe Böhürler's emphasis on Harran as an example of conservatives' accomplishment to reach out to young women significant. The feminist struggle will not be complete without gaining the support of women who grew up in conservative families and in conservative towns.

Young women will not be reached by purely academic literature. My fourth proposal is that novels, short stories, blogs, cartoons, and popular genres might indeed have more power in unsettling conservative narratives and exposing the cracks in conservative arguments. Literary and artistic concerns should be set aside in producing narratives countering conservatism from an anti-essentialist and antiracist feminist perspective. At the moment, a number of attempts to push back the AKP's religious conservatism in Turkey fall into other varieties of nationalist narratives and frame the AKP as carriers of "Arabization." This is another way to push an opponent outside of the "nation" and the "local"—by reproducing anti-Arab racism. While countering religious conservatism, feminism should be wary of the danger of falling into exclusionary nationalist discourses, and careful not to reproduce racism and anti-Muslim discourses.

More and more women and men in the opposition have developed a fear of Islam in Turkey today. This is Islamophobia in a Muslim-majority society, not in a society where Muslims constitute a small minority. Yet we need to acknowledge that Islamophobia in Turkey is caused not by "ordinary" practicing Muslims but by the religious right who politicized Muslim identity and gained power. To win women (and men) back, feminism should stay away from Islamophobic arguments. The fear of Islam can be countered by depoliticizing Islam and by explaining the AKP's authoritarianism not with reference to "Islamism" but with reference to the politics of the religious right. If it is really necessary to use the term, "Islamism" should not be treated as a unique category on its own but as a subcategory of the religious right, with affinities to right-wing politics based on Christian, Jewish, Hindu, and Buddhist identities.

There are a number of challenges for feminism in Turkey at the moment, and I'd like to emphasize three here: The first is an existential struggle. Like all other silenced groups in Turkey, feminists try to continue to exist under the AKP's suffocating mechanisms of repression. Producing counter-narratives within this environment is a big challenge, with risks of censorship and imprisonment. I don't have an easy answer to the difficult question of how to produce counter-narratives while at the same time staying under the radar of government censorship and repression. Second, feminists might benefit from re-evaluating their own narratives with a critical eye to see what has worked and what has not in terms of reaching out to women and men. Feminism needs strategies to garner men's support as well. Defining men in essentialist terms as an antagonistic group is counterproductive to the feminist goals.[141] Finally, the meanings of feminism are multiple and contested, not just by conservatives but also by feminist men and women. Are we talking about feminism for a businesswoman or feminism for a poor woman? A debate inside feminism about the future direction of feminism and its potential against authoritarianism might prove useful. At the radical end of the spectrum, even temporarily abandoning feminism (and other identity claims) to create a front against authoritarianism might be an option.

The good news is that, in spite of heavy repression, feminists are not alone in fighting against authoritarianism. First of all, feminism has extended its base among Kemalist women who were not sympathetic to feminism before. Nil Mutluer[142] notes that Kemalist women who had not seen themselves as "feminists" have come to embrace feminism during the AKP's time in power. Second, based on the findings of her fieldwork, Berna Turam suggested that in Turkey, "the new axis of conflict was shifting from Islamism versus secularism toward the defense of a deeper democracy versus authoritarianism."[143] This shows that a number of allies are there to push authoritarianism back and reclaim democracy and rights, not just for pro-AKP conservatives, but for all citizens of Turkey.

Who are the new allies against authoritarianism?

Nil Mutluer distinguished between "conservative" and "reformist" wings of Kemalist feminism. In her work, "conservative"[144] refers to those Kemalist women who "embrace the Kemalist understanding of laicism and the image of modern women attached to it without questioning. The reformists, by contrast, seek to rethink Kemalism under the guidance of Western democratic values."[145] The reformist branch differs from Kemalist hardliners in their approach to the headscarf. Mutluer mentions a surprising "general trend" among the Kemalist women, both conservative and reformist "to recognize headscarved women's right to public existence."[146] This shows the degree to which the headscarf has become normalized and accepted even by its fiercest opponents in Turkey. The Kemalist women on the reformist wing are natural allies of a left-wing feminism in terms of resisting nationalist and anti-Kurdish discourses of various kinds, sexism, and authoritarianism.

Even though the headscarf has become the signifier of ideal womanhood under the AKP, it seems that the garment has lost its actual political power on two fronts: it has lost its power to divide Kemalist women, and it has lost its power to unite conservatives. The elimination of the ban also eliminated the strong cause that brought conservative women together. The AKP's authoritarian policies have divided conservative women further and turned existing differences into clear divisions. As opposed to the pro-AKP conservative-wing represented by the women columnists I analyzed in the previous chapter, conservative women who are bothered by the AKP's authoritarianism have become vocal following the AKP's institution of a nationwide state of emergency[147] after the failed coup attempt in July 2016. In other words, dissenters are not just the seculars, liberal democrats, feminists, and Kurds but also the critical conservative Muslims who speak out against injustice. A number of conservative Muslim NGOs, initiatives, and platforms oppose the AKP government and suffer from censorship and repression in return.[148] For example, Ömer Faruk Gergerlioğlu, the former chair of the Islamist human rights organization Mazlumder, received a sentence of two and half years in jail for his pro-peace comments on the Kurdish issue made on social media. Gergerlioğlu was charged for propagating for the terrorist organization.[149] He was elected to the parliament for the HDP in the June 24, 2018 national elections, and his jail sentence was postponed.

I see *the critical wing of conservative women* among the potential allies for resisting authoritarianism, although with a note of caution, as I will explain in the following sections in this chapter. The critical wing has been more sympathetic toward feminism and more comfortable with calling themselves "feminists." They wear the headscarf and are clearly part of the conservative circles in their own self-positioning, yet they have been increasingly critical of the AKP's authoritarianism. Hidayet Şefkatli Tuksal and Berrin Sönmez are two leading female columnists who represent the critical wing. Both of them had leading roles in the influential conservative women's organization Başkent Kadın Platformu (Capital City Women's Platform) in Ankara, an organization that occasionally allied both with the Kemalist and leftist women's organizations in national and international platforms on women's issues.

Hidayet Şefkatli Tuksal became well known with her book on misogyny in Islamic traditions.[150] It was indeed her dissertation thesis, published later as a book, that gave the term "Islamic feminism" widespread currency among liberals in Turkey. For a while, Tuksal was the only well-known conservative female author who was not bothered by the term "feminist," and she has made a name for her critical stance within her own camp. Tuksal wrote in the *Star*, a pro-AKP newspaper, and left the publication in a controversial way in 2011. Critics of the AKP believe that she was fired following her piece that was harshly critical of Erdoğan's attitude toward the liberal democrats. Tuksal has repeatedly denied that, saying she resigned from the newspaper by her own choice.[151] Similar to Hilâl Kaplan, she wrote in *Taraf* for a while—the anti-Kemalist liberal newspaper.[152] She has been writing in the online newspaper *Serbestiyet*, with occasional long breaks, since 2013. She has been critical of the violations of rights and the rule of law under the AKP without trying to justify these violations, while retaining her insider's voice.

Berrin Sönmez started writing in the oppositional online newspaper *Gazete Duvar* soon after the failed military coup. As opposed to the conservative columnists in the pro-AKP wing, she actively campaigned against increasing Erdoğan's powers in the April 2017 referendum and supported the No vote. She came together with other critical conservatives to establish The Platform for Rights and Justice (Hak ve Adalet Platformu). For her, this platform represented those who stand against oppression even when the oppressor is "one of their own."[153] The platform aimed to reach out to the AKP constituents who were undecided about their votes for the referendum. This platform included two leading female politicians who wear the headscarf: Fatma Bostan Ünsal, one of the founding members of the AKP, and Hüda Kaya, a member of the pro-Kurdish HDP. Both women come from conservative circles, and they are loud critics of the AKP. Tanıl Bora called Fatma Bostan Ünsal "a consistent human rights advocate."[154] She is one of the Academics for Peace who criticized the government for its policies of violence against the Kurds and was fired from her university by executive order soon after the failed coup attempt in 2016.

Hüda Kaya's anti-authoritarian activism, on the other hand, deserves a whole book in itself. Kaya is a leading member of the pro-Kurdish left-wing HDP, a member of the parliament, and a long-time critic of the AKP's oppressive policies. Kaya's left-wing activism and her rather exceptional story underlines the point that women wearing the headscarf do not necessarily keep to Islamist or conservative politics. Kaya suffered severely under the headscarf ban and the oppression that took place following the February 28 directives in 1997. She was imprisoned a number of times for her activism around the headscarf. She was even charged with terrorism and, together with her three daughters, faced the death penalty in 1999. It would be safe to say that Kaya suffered because of the headscarf ban more than any other conservative woman, yet this did not make her an AKP supporter. On the contrary, she has translated her experience of oppression into a defense of the rights of Kurdish citizens who have suffered from state violence both under the Kemalists and the AKP. Kaya supported the Academics for Peace in front of the courts during trials and actively protested against the AKP government.

Hüda Kaya's party, HDP, and the Kurdish movement in general have been very successful in reaching out to Kurdish women and encouraging their participation in politics during the last two decades. Their experience also calls for careful analysis in order to learn from their success in mobilizing women. As Mona Tajali has noted, "HDP's feminist gender ideology sets it apart from all the other major political parties in Turkey, including the secular Kemalist party, the Republican People's Party (CHP)."[155] HDP follows a co-leadership system that requires a man and a woman co-chair the party. The party adopted "50% gender quota and a 10% quota for LGBT candidates for the June 7th, 2015 elections,"[156] and carried a number of leading feminists to the parliament. In that sense, HDP has become a strong ally for feminism in Turkey, yet the party suffers from heavy repression as both (now former) co-chairs have been jailed on terrorism charges since November 4, 2016.

A feminist alliance with the reformist wing of Kemalist women, who are more open to dialogue with the Kurds, looks less complicated and more straightforward still than an alliance with the conservative women critics. The headscarf issue might constitute a fragile point, the Achilles' heel, of a potential alliance between feminists and the critical wing of conservative women. Feyza Akınerdem's work voices the concerns of a younger generation of conservative women who feel closer to Hidayet Şefkatli Tuksal's version of conservatism, distanced from the AKP and sympathetic to feminism. Akınerdem is one of the writers of *Reçel* blog (Jam-blog, established in 2014), which represents a younger generation of conservative women's search to combine piety with a "feminist sensibility."[157] Akınerdem embraces feminism and does not see a conflict between feminism and her practice of wearing the headscarf. She is critical of the views that underline the contradictions between piety and feminism.

Yet Akınerdem's conversations with a group of feminists coming from various branches of feminism have reflected some unresolvable tensions between religion and feminism. These conversations were published in the now-defunct feminist magazine *Amargi* in 2012, as part of a series of feminist debates. During these debates, following Akınerdem's talk on "pious" and "Islamic" feminism, women discussed the breakdown of the online feminist initiative We Are Taking Care of Each Other (Birbirimize Sahip Çıkıyoruz), which aimed to bring women with different identities together on the basis of "womanhood" in 2008.[158] A number of issues that led to the breakdown of the group were based on religion and caused some feminists to distrust women who wore headscarves. Apparently, around that time, Hilâl Kaplan caused a crisis of confidence in women wearing the headscarf among the feminists when an Islamist male columnist published Kaplan's letter written to him saying that she spent time with feminists, gays, and lesbians in order to proselytize for Islam among them.[159] In the initiative, a participant suggested that they not talk about the headscarf issue at all for a while. Another participant mentioned that to avoid conflict with the religious women the initiative focused only on "public" issues at the expense of problematizing the family. Alcohol consumption arose as an issue, and a Ramazan dinner stirred controversy, alienating an Alevi feminist who did not follow Ramazan and who had suffered from the regular exclusion of her own religious practices by the Sunni majority. The power asymmetry between the religious and atheist women was another issue. The feminists who viewed the headscarf as a reflection of patriarchy preferred not to participate in this initiative at all. Women wearing the headscarf, on the other hand, were bothered by the questions that frequently tested them on whether they would lend support to those rights that conflicted with their religious belief.

These debates have indicated that solidarity with conservative women, even with the critical wing that is against authoritarianism, is rife with complications and might invite the suspension of criticisms toward the family, religion, and the headscarf. The question is, should differences on potentially offensive or explosive topics be suspended until the reinstitution of a democratic regime? Would the suspension of differences be necessary to build a coalition against authoritarianism, or would that narrow the space even further for feminism in a climate where it already suffers from the encroachment of religious conservatism?

I do not have a straightforward answer to these questions. Yet I would like to clarify my own position on the relationship between religion, the headscarf, and feminism while I still have the chance. I take courage from pro-AKP conservative columnist Ayşe Böhürler's assertion that once the ban is eliminated we will be able to discuss more freely whether the headscarf is indeed a religious requirement for Muslim women.[160]

Feminism and religion: an uneasy relationship

Wearing a headscarf on religious grounds and claiming feminism at the same time indeed presents a contradiction—in theory. Most feminisms assume that men and women do not have fixed natures and they can change through socialization and education. At the very basic level, I see feminism as a political attempt to denaturalize men's bad behavior that has been normalized and has come to be accepted as part of men's nature for centuries. Yet the religious injunction regarding the headscarf is based on the opposite position, which assumes a fixed nature for men and women, created by God. Claiming feminism and the headscarf at the same time places women at the juncture of these two opposite assumptions that call for opposing political projects on gender. It is an effort to ride two horses going in different directions at once. The religious injunction on the headscarf is full of contradictions that conservative Turkish women, either in the mainstream or in the critical wing, do not seem willing to discuss. Yet we need to discuss the contradictions that involve a practice that is made desirable for millions of young women.

The basic promise of the headscarf is to protect women from men's bad behavior by not calling for it, or "provoking" it. Yet, as numerous scholars have already pointed out, the practice has burdened the woman to protect herself instead of instituting strong sanctions against bad behavior by men. In addition, as thousands of women wearing the headscarf in and outside Turkey can testify, the headscarf fails to fulfill its promise of protection. Even women who wear the burqa and other forms of head-to-toe covering suffer from rape and sexual assault. In other words, an injunction by God does not deliver its promise as long as men continue to stick to their bad behavior. When men do change their behavior, the need for women to cover their bodies in more extensive terms immediately disappears. In this bright scenario, women would feel safe no matter what they wear. The religious rationale behind the headscarf is strongly bound up with men's behavior. The practice does not protect women in settings where men do not see women as their equals and widely misbehave, and it loses its rationale in settings where men do see women as their equals and behave well. The question then is, why would an omniscient God come up with a command that miserably fails to deliver on its promise? Would not that be attributing weakness to an almighty God?

Claiming the headscarf and feminism at the same time underlines the contradictions in "God's command" in bold. Such contradictions can be resolved only if we regard the headscarf as a contingent historical and cultural—not sacred or divine—practice. Addressing these contradictions might not be desirable for conservative women, as it makes the practice less immune to criticism by taking away its sanctity, making it a form of clothing equal to all others, a choice among other equal choices. Many conservative women will not be happy about seeing the headscarf on an equal footing with other forms of dress. Claims for the sanctity of the headscarf might accompany the claims for privilege that deny equal status to another woman's choice to wear a spaghetti-strap top and a miniskirt.

I understand that young critical conservative women who claim both the headscarf and feminism desire to rework the meanings of religion at this specific point in history by taking their own needs and contexts into account. This only proves the point that what is considered sacred or divine is mutable, and derives from the historical, political, and cultural considerations of a given period.

Following Foucault's contributions to feminism, I see the headscarf, as conceptualized in religion, as part of a regime of surveillance and self-discipline that aims to police women's behavior and sexuality. I see it closely linked to the institutionalization of patriarchy through religious texts. Sandra Lee Bartky's quote can be rewritten with the headscarf practices in mind:

> The woman who checks her makeup half a dozen times a day to see if her foundation has caked or her mascara run, who worries that the wind or rain may spoil her hairdo, who looks frequently to see if her stockings have bagged at the ankle, or who, feeling fat, monitors everything she eats, has become, just as surely as the inmate of the panopticon, a self policing subject, as self committed to relentless self surveillance. This self surveillance is a form of obedience to patriarchy. It is also the reflection in woman's consciousness of the fact that she is under surveillance in ways that he is not, that whatever else she may become, she is importantly a body designed to please or excite. There has been induced in many women, then, in Foucault's words "a state of conscious and permanent visibility that assures the automatic functioning of power."[161]

Replace Bartky's makeup-wearing woman with a woman wearing the headscarf, monitoring herself and trying to make sure that she does not show any piece of hair, any part of skin, calculating what portion of a wrist, ankle, or neck could be exposed to the men on the street. It does not matter whether the regime of control mentioned in this quotation has been internalized on the basis of beauty, capitalism, or religious belief. In the end, these regimes of self-discipline control women in ways that they do not control men. In the case of religion, such regimes of self-discipline ask women to internalize God's eye, making the police into part of her very being. Indeed, the expression "placing the police inside you," popular among religious circles in Turkey, summarizes Foucault's and Bartky's point better than any other example. Used positively, the expression refers to refraining from bad behavior for fear of God, reducing the role of "God" to simple policing.

I am not saying that as a woman who does not wear a headscarf, I consider myself free from submission to multiple regimes of self-discipline and patriarchal control. What I am saying is that, contrary to what many religious Muslim women would have me believe, the headscarf is not outside of the realm of male domination and patriarchy. It does not constitute a sacred exception. On the contrary, as I have tried to show in this book, it lends itself very usefully to authoritarian men, like Erdoğan, who aim to establish a gender hegemony based on religious conservatism, disadvantaging women who will not follow the rules of "modesty." In addition, conservative women, whether critical or mainstream, in defense of their own choice to wear the headscarf, tend to de-emphasize the instances where the headscarf is imposed on women. Studies indicate that once women cover their hair, they feel pressure to stay covered. According to the findings of Çarkoğlu and Toprak's study, 45.5 percent of women who wear a headscarf in Turkey say that if they decide to uncover their hair, they will be forced to re-cover because of social pressure, or pressure coming from their families.[162] The headscarf may be a free choice for religiously conservative women. Yet as long as stepping away from the headscarf remains a tough choice for around half of women wearing it, feminists have every right to question the conservative narratives that situate the headscarf mainly within the realm of "choice."

Feyza Akınerdem complained about the AKP's hijacking of the concepts such as piety and conservatism.[163] The AKP hijacked the headscarf as well. Will the critical conservative women be able to take the headscarf back from the hands of the AKP and the other conservative women who support the party's authoritarianism? This is another question whose outcome might influence any potential alliance with the critical wing of conservative women. Young critical conservatives' writing on the Reçel blog tells me that they have been working on reclaiming the headscarf from the AKP.[164] Yet, their commitment to their Muslim identity and the headscarf limit critical conservative women's power to question the new regime. When they criticize the AKP, they face harsh criticisms from their own circles for not appreciating the AKP's efforts in removing the ban.[165] In addition, as headscarf-wearing women, they ask for further legal protection against discrimination in the workplace,[166] a proposal that might place women not wearing a headscarf under severe disadvantage in a climate of religious conservativism. The Reçel blog has generated a new excitement among Turkey's secular liberal democrats, celebrating young conservative women's embracing of feminism. I want to share their excitement and believe they are not mistaken this time. Yet, my reading of women in conservatism and the new political structure in Turkey makes me cautious. It remains to be seen whether a new platform like the

Reçel blog might develop into a broader criticism of power and authoritarianism or stay as a younger venue for "insider criticism" within conservative circles, limited to helping young conservative women to vent their frustrations.[167]

Finally, I must add that I have always been a critic of the headscarf ban in universities. Yet this does not mean that I support and accept the premises behind the headscarf as a religious practice. Coming back to my question about suspending differences, I believe feminists should not shy away from pointing out the failures of religious discourses in delivering the promises they have made to women. A critical approach to religion is crucial in a period where religious discourses have increasingly been mobilized to oppress and exclude others all over the world, not just in Turkey and not just on the basis of Islam. There is a thin line to walk between establishing a meaningful alliance against authoritarianism and protecting the remaining secular space.

Conclusion

In this chapter I have argued that pro-AKP conservative women have not been sisters to the feminists and that solidarity is not possible with them as long as they continue to support an authoritarian government. Mainstream conservative women have caused a crisis of confidence in their relationships with feminists which will probably last for decades. Yet this does not fully apply to the critical wing of conservative women. Although an alliance with them also poses risks and hardships for feminists, they are potential partners against authoritarianism and racism in Turkey—anti-Kurdish racism being the most urgent at the moment. The reformist wing of Kemalist feminists and Kurdish feminists are among those who could be allies in resisting authoritarianism.

I have argued that to fight the AKP's new gender hegemony, feminists need to reclaim the representation of "women's rights" instead of willingly conceding that ground to conservative women. They have to reclaim the positions of intellectual and moral leadership. They need to insert their own vision of rights with the goal of reaching out to young women even in the most conservative towns to "win hearts and minds." We need narratives to localize feminism and secularism and popularize them, making them into natural elements of Turkey's culture. Producing novels, blogs, poems, graphic novels, short stories, and popular literature will be crucial to regaining the intellectual upper hand for feminism. Any feminist woman or man who has a story to tell should tell their story by any means available. We should not shy away from exposing the failures of religious discourses to deliver on their promise to protect women, and while doing that we have to avoid falling into Islamophobia. Secularism, feminism, and Islam are all equally part of Turkey's culture, and we have to watch out for the creeping influences of nationalism, racism, and anti-Muslim sentiments during this struggle.

Under the climate of repression, quiet solidarities emerge between unlikely groups. Little developments, silent alliances between women wearing and not wearing the headscarf, have been taking place as positive signs of resistance against authoritarianism. In a series of interviews published by *Bianet*, Hadiye Yolcu, a young religious woman wearing the headscarf, predicted a potential process of discrimination against women not wearing the headscarf and asserted that when the day comes, she will do everything in her power to defend them against oppression.[168] Emine Uçak, a female journalist wearing the headscarf from the online news site *Sivil Sayfalar* [*Civil Pages*] made an interview with Nil Mutluer of Academics for Peace who lost her job after signing the petition and now leaves in exile in Berlin.[169] Uçak and Mutluer talked about building solidarities against different forms of oppression. Muslim groups on the Left have been working to create new alliances to question and resist the AKP's version of conservatism. The Platform for Labor and Justice (Emek ve Adalet Platformu),[170] established in 2010, organizes seminars and talks that establish links among people from different social and cultural groups who have suffered from the AKP's oppression. A sister platform, Muslims Against Violence Against Women (Kadına Şiddete Karşı Müslümanlar)[171] run by the Reçel blog's co-editor Rümeysa Çamdereli, actively questions gender policies in the "new Turkey" and brings together feminist scholars and critical conservative women.[172] The We Are Equal Women's Group (Eşitiz Kadın Grubu),[173] and other secular feminist groups try to resist the government's gender policies and authoritarianism by following the court cases and disseminating news about gender oppression. These platforms are active on Twitter and, like any other online activism in Turkey as I write, they are vulnerable to suppression. Yet, in spite of their limited influence, they constitute spaces to develop counter-hegemonic discourses and potential new alliances to resist the AKP's conservative authoritarianism.

Although there is reason for growing pessimism under growing violence and repression by the AKP government, there is also hope. In this chapter, I referred to the ideas offered by Gramsci to fight against a fascist regime. I would like to close the chapter with his famous motto on the "pessimism of the intellect and optimism of the will." The source of my pessimism in this book stems from the pro-AKP conservative women's alliance with an authoritarian government. I do not see any reason to sugarcoat this detrimental alliance just because conservative women use "feminist" arguments in defense of an anti-democratic regime. Yet I know that, even though severely suppressed, the energy, wisdom, intellectual resources, and willingness are there to push back the depressing encroachment of authoritarian politics on millions of lives in Turkey.

Conclusion—Toward a New Gender Equilibrium

Shifting hegemonies

By following newspaper images, this book aimed to show that a new gender hegemony has been in the making in Turkey since the AKP's acquisition of power in 2002 and that conservative women who support the AKP are the carriers of this new hegemony. The analysis of news photographs shows that as a symbol of this new gender-conservative era, the headscarf has moved from the margins to the mainstream, and has become part of the image of desirable womanhood. Accompanying that shift, leading conservative women columnists have moved from religious to center-right newspapers and utilized leftist, feminist, and postcolonialist arguments in favor of the AKP governments. Their unending support for an authoritarian government and a misogynist leader came as a big surprise to the liberal democrats in Turkey who saw conservative women as agents of democratization. I have argued that these women's positioning in the academic literature as "Islamic feminists" caused liberal democrats to mislocate conservative women's right-wing politics as progressive.

I therefore suggested that we read the images of headscarves within the context of conservative, right-wing politics in Turkey. I questioned the analytical possibilities of the term "Islamist women" and proposed that the struggles over the headscarf distracted attention from the women's political position as significant actors within right-wing politics. I argued that conservative women's relatively progressive stance on women's issues led scholars and liberal journalists to see them as feminists even though conservative women have supported a misogynist authoritarian leader and his policies. I believe focusing on the term "conservative women" instead of "Islamist women" will open new analytical possibilities, the most important of which would involve shifting the focus away from religion, and the headscarf itself, and toward right-wing politics. The term "conservative women" includes women who do not cover their hair yet stay active in right-wing politics either as politicians or columnists. I hope other researchers will be willing to follow up on this theme to explore further the relationship between women and right-wing politics.

As I tried to understand why Turkey's mainstream conservative women support Erdoğan, I started to pay more attention to conservative women in the United States. It was striking that conservative women in the Unites States and in Turkey have supported similar policies and used similar arguments in defense of these policies.[1] In times of controversy, conservative women supported conservative men diligently in spite of men's sexism. Trump received 42 percent of women's votes in the United States in spite of allegations of sexual misconduct against him.[2] The mobilization of women around right-wing politics is not a phenomenon unique to Turkey or the United States. A growing number of studies on conservative women worldwide—including Latin American, African, and Asian countries[3]—indicate that one of the defining problems for feminism and other progressive movements in the twenty-first century will be how to get back the constituents lost to right-wing, xenophobic, and racist policies for various reasons.

The shifts in existing hegemonies in the world underline the shortcomings of some of our well-established categories and the struggles taking place around them. "Muslim" is such a contested and ambiguous category. That is why it makes more sense to look at how the term is mobilized and toward what kind of a political project it is mobilized. During the run-up to the presidential elections in 2016 in the United States, two leading Muslim women, both covering their head, stood at opposite ends of the political spectrum. Saba Ahmed, the president of the Republican Muslim Coalition,[4] devotedly supported Donald Trump, while Linda Sarsour devotedly campaigned for Bernie Sanders, and she was the co-chair of the Women's March organized in protest against Donald Trump's inauguration in 2017. Neither "Muslim" identity nor the practice of headscarf united these two women. They pursued opposing visions for the future, and supported competing political projects. Yet, because of the overwhelming signifying power of the headscarf, when we see the pictures of these two women, we automatically place them in the same category, "Muslim," overlooking their political stance that matters much more in shaping the future than their religious practice. In that sense, the headscarf, as a powerful signifier of Muslim women, has been a red herring that has distracted attention from similarities in right-wing, as well as progressive, women's movements across borders independent of religion.

Toward a new gender equilibrium: a new gender hegemony

The image of ideal womanhood has dramatically changed in Turkey since 2002. Old Turkey's ideal woman did not wear a headscarf and did not define herself primarily in relation to her Muslim identity. She valued secular education and women's rights within a secular framework. She performed piety in the privacy of her home if she wanted. Although the system constrained her with marriage and family, she had some room to explore her sexuality outside of these institutions. The rise of the conservative women's voices implies a significant shift in the image of ideal womanhood in Turkey. New Turkey's ideal woman wears a headscarf and emphasizes her Muslim identity. Although she challenges conservative men from time to time, she finds feminist women's demands for equality unrealistic. She encourages women to participate in the economy, politics, and social life—but within a framework favored by conservative politics that identifies family and motherhood as a woman's primary responsibility.

Until the late 2000s, it was customary to look at the books and columns of the Islamist men to understand what I prefer to call the religious right in Turkey. The term "Islamic intellectual" referred to Islamist men.[5] By 2018, women columnists from the religious right had moved to the mainstream and become significant intellectual actors of Turkish conservatism by actively legitimating the AKP's hegemony in Turkey. They carried their own definition of women's rights to the center of politics. This conservative backlash came right after a period of expansion during the 1990s and caused, in Kandiyoti's terms, a crisis in the gender order of Turkey. In the aftermath of the June 24, 2018 elections that solidified the AKP's power in Turkish politics, we may expect the stabilization of a new gender order in favor of conservative women. In other words, we might expect a new gender equilibrium to be established in Turkey in the long run at the expense of the feminists and women who do not believe in or practice religion.

In this new state of affairs, the mainstream pro-AKP conservative women's voices and preferences might be pivotal in defining what constitutes women's rights. Yet, even though they are among the winners of a new gender regime, there is a caveat for pro-AKP conservative women. There is no guarantee that they will be able to control the direction of this new equilibrium. The campaign "No MP with Headscarf, No Vote" showed that even when they are sympathetic to conservative women's demands, conservative men are the people who have the final say on when and how these demands will be realized. In realms where conservative women clash with men, we can expect the men's preferences to dominate. These women's commitment to conservative politics weakens their hand. Conservative men take their support for granted and take their concerns into consideration only when they see fit.

There is also no guarantee that mainstream conservative women will remain among the winners in the long run. There are other groups on the religious right who would not be pleased at all with conservative women's demands for social, economic, and political participation. If the AKP's conservatism tolerates and protects their religious fanaticism in return for votes, this will have negative repercussions for pro-AKP mainstream conservative women as well. They already encounter hostility from the more radical branches of the religious right.[6] The wave of criticisms and gender-based insults directed against Hilâl Kaplan when she had her photograph taken in a church shows that there is a base that would be willing to support a far more restrictive gender regime. It is simply a matter of how much power those radical voices might acquire over time under the AKP regime. In fact, before the elections on June 24, 2018, Ayşe Çavdar depicted these groups as the conservative women's nightmare and argued that conservative women find protection in Erdoğan against these radical groups.[7]

The question that is in the minds of many in Turkey as of this writing is, can we expect the headscarf to be compulsory for all women in Turkey at some point in the future, as it is in Iran? During the 1990s, Turkey's liberal democrats would laugh at that question and argue that Turkey would never be like Iran. With most prominent liberal democrats either in jail or in exile as I write, it has become harder to laugh at that question.

The AKP's policies on alcohol provide a good case with which to think about this question. The party did not ban alcohol but marginalized its consumers in the discourse by associating them with alienated elites, and they made alcoholic beverages difficult to find and very expensive to buy. The party so far has used the same strategy for the headscarf. That is why I do not expect the headscarf to be legally mandatory for all women in Turkey. Yet, within the AKP's new gender order, wearing the headscarf will probably be the key for social and cultural approval for women. Even though it might not be compulsory, young women will find themselves in an environment that makes them feel they fit better and will be more loved and respected if they wear the headscarf, making the headscarf the natural, normal, and desirable option. The pro-AKP conservative columnists wearing the headscarf legitimate this new order and also provide role models about how women should conduct themselves under a conservative gender regime.

Even though I do not expect the headscarf to be compulsory, I expect that women, even though they do not adopt the headscarf, will find themselves under pressure to wear more conservative clothes: longer skirts, longer sleeves, higher necks, more loose-fitting cuts, and so forth. I expect this both as a result of regular conservative propaganda and the threat of violence. The nurse Ayşegül Terzi's story of being kicked in the head for wearing shorts[8] shows that in "new" Turkey's misogynist climate male perpetrators feel encouraged to target women for not wearing "modest" clothes on the street. Such incidents might create a chilling effect, making it an act of courage for women to dress as they wish. As a result, more modest and conservative clothes might feel safer for women, both physically and politically.

By conservative women's own observations, the headscarf has become a safe choice for women. In 2014, Ayşe Böhürler complained that in the past wearing a headscarf meant taking a risk for one's belief, but it does not anymore. She blamed the women picking up the headscarf in increasing numbers in the aftermath of elections won by the AKP, arguing that they did so to get things done more readily for themselves.[9] Not surprisingly, she did not blame the AKP for creating an environment where women would feel that things would be more convenient for them when they adopted the headscarf. This complaint by a leading conservative woman indicates that the headscarf facilitates interactions with the government for women and their families. Clearly, even the conservative women in power will not be able to have control over its function and meanings in the long run. The headscarf acquires new meanings along the way that challenge conservative women's ongoing struggle to define it in religiously conservative terms.

Images of contradiction: changing connotations of the headscarf

The meaning work in relation to the headscarf is never complete. In an environment where the headscarf becomes the new normal, we can expect the weakening of its religious meaning, actually producing circumstances that are not desired by the conservative ideologues of the headscarf at all. The mainstreaming of the headscarf strips it of its religious meanings and turns it into a garment that women use functionally or instrumentally, to make their lives easier at home or at work.

When women wear the headscarf in a way detached from religion, a number of images that look contradictory receive more and more attention: the image that I mentioned at the very beginning of this book, the photograph of a young woman belly dancing while wearing a headscarf, was an early example of such images of contradiction. The number of controversies over such "contradictions" has been growing: women who wear the headscarf and become intimate (kiss or flirt) with their boyfriends at parks; women who combine the headscarf with tight jeans or see-through clothes; women who wear the headscarf and heavy makeup at the same time; women who wear the headscarf while smoking in public. The list goes on. These images show that these women do not necessarily associate the headscarf with piety, at least not in the sense defined by religious conservatives—as adherence to the particular interpretation of the book. As Feyda Sayan-Cengiz has suggested, this may indicate to a chasm between the religious practices of lower- and middle-class women.[10] It may be a sign of a "new religiosity," as suggested by Zehra Yılmaz.[11] Women may be using the headscarf as a new area of negotiation and resistance in their lives. For example, a woman might accept that she must wear a headscarf to find a job but put on makeup to compensate for the concession she has made.

Smoking, drinking, intimacy in public, intimacy outside of marriage, or wearing tight clothes are (arguably) all deemed religiously inappropriate behavior. The ways such "contradictory" images are interpreted by different constituents shape the connotations of the headscarf and indicate emerging conflicts over its meaning not just between the secular population and conservatives but also within conservative circles.

Secular constituents who feel their lifestyle is under threat seize such moments and tie the meaning of headscarf to "religious hypocrisy." Such pictures of contradiction regularly circulate on social media to emphasize the inconsistencies of a religious world view. In an age where cell phones are ubiquitous, secular people do not miss opportunities to document such moments and circulate them on social media. These images are also used to emphasize the point that only secularism can guarantee and protect the freedoms of women to wear headscarves and passionately kiss their boyfriends in public at the same time. This point was best reflected in Şafak Pavey's speech delivered in the parliament on October 31, 2013. Pavey, a female parliamentarian from the Republican People's Party (CHP), is a poster child for Turkish secularism, with her successful international career as a diplomat. In her speech, which went viral for days, she emphasized that it was the secular Atatürk reforms that made it possible for headscarf-wearing young women to enjoy moments of intimacy in public spaces.[12] Pavey delivered her powerful speech on the day when four female AKP parliamentarians walked into the parliament wearing headscarves, putting an end to the exclusion of the headscarf from the parliament. This was made possible with the consent of the other parties in the parliament, including Pavey's CHP. The four parliamentarians were not wearing the headscarf when they were elected, and they decided to put it on after having gone on pilgrimage that year.

The images of contradiction divide the conservatives at multiple levels. The controversy that arose in the summer of 2017 is a typical example revealing the tensions within them. On August 3, 2017, Hayrettin Karaman, a prominent religious scholar, wrote an article criticizing women wearing the headscarf for smoking in public.[13] Karaman implied that smoking was a sign of availability, an invitation to men, which conflicted with how women wearing the headscarf should conduct themselves in public. Conservative women have been bothered by conservative men dictating how headscarf-wearing women should conduct themselves in public. They have long complained that conservative men have different standards of piety for men and women, and place the bar very high for women. While severely critical of men like Karaman, conservative women's columns indicate that they themselves are confused by women who cover their hair without religious reasons, and they try to make sense of such images of contradiction.[14]

Another image of contradiction seized upon by the seculars is that of the young woman wearing a headscarf who drives an SUV on Bağdat Avenue. The seculars see that image as contradictory because SUVs are considered an exhibition of wealth and a symbol of conspicuous consumption. Bağdat Avenue, home to high-end global brands and boutique shops, has been a symbol of an upper-middle-class luxurious lifestyle. While conservative women try to push back and defend the young women with headscarves driving SUVs, they are divided on how conservative women should respond to the increasing wealth in Turkey's conservative neighborhood. As the AKP's time in power has tremendously enriched conservative circles, the relation between faith, religious practice, and conspicuous consumption brings new questions to the table. In conservative circles, women's bodies and the headscarf have become a new realm of displaying wealth and upward social mobility. The debates on Muslim women's relationship to wealth, brand names, and fashion are therefore rife with tension; these debates make women wearing the headscarf into targets of criticism and reveal divisions among conservative women.

A number of articles by Ayşe Böhürler also indicate disagreements between her and a younger generation of conservative women on the meanings of headscarf in relation to politics and consumption. Böhürler has complained about the lack of political consciousness among younger women who adopt the headscarf, and she has accused them of conformism. For her, the young women seem to have confused rising standards of living with gains in women's rights. She rated them high on consumption consciousness and low on political and social consciousness.[15] In another article, she expressed her discomfort caused by the appearance of a young woman wearing a headscarf in a commercial for sports cars. According to Böhürler, that was not what they struggled for.[16] Böhürler and other conservative writers rigorously resist "reducing the headscarf to consumption"[17] and emphasize the religious significance of the headscarf as symbolizing "good morals," not a "good lifestyle."[18] The appearance of the fashion magazines on the print market targeting women wearing the headscarf—and produced by women wearing the headscarf—was a common point of criticism expressed by all three conservative women journalists covered in this study.[19]

The images of contradiction occupy the younger generation of conservative women as well. An article published on the Reçel blog, run by young conservative women wearing the headscarf, mentioned a case where a young woman in a headscarf was photographed at a bar, allegedly drinking vodka.[20] The author harshly criticized the secular individuals who circulated the image as proof of religious hypocrisy for their hatred and bigotry, and she used a feminist language while doing that. This was a typical moment where young conservatives have reproduced the old antagonisms without acknowledging the shift in power, missing the chance to create space for the criticism of power and authoritarianism. In an interesting twist, the adoption of feminist language went hand in hand with undermining the actual consequences of increasing religious conservatism. The real problem here is that during the AKP's time in power, the spaces where both alcohol drinkers and nondrinkers could mingle together without being stigmatized were eliminated. Bars are one of the few remaining spaces that can host a group of friends composed of drinkers and nondrinkers, making women wearing the headscarf immediately noticeable. We can expect that the presence of women wearing the headscarf in such places will continue to stir controversy, especially as these spaces have been pushed more and more into enclaves within the cities.

Finally, at times of major hegemonic shifts, the matter of who is marginalized and who is not is deeply contested, and different groups struggle with each other to claim the position of the marginalized. Erdoğan has driven his power from his ability to claim marginalization, to speak to the marginalized, to represent them, and to promise to heal their wounds. Yet, by 2019, he has been at the very center of power for the last seventeen years and he has concentrated tremendous power in his hands. The challenge for him and his party is to claim marginality in discourse despite the real power they have acquired. Even though wearing the headscarf has become a source of safety and power, the AKP government will try to keep its meaning linked to marginalization and victimization, which they did during the Gezi protests. Conservative women who struggled against the headscarf ban to support women's education are now in the weird position of claiming marginalization on the basis of attacks against the proverbial girl who wears a headscarf and drives an expensive SUV in Istanbul's posh neighborhoods. This is a difficult position to sustain in the long run, especially when thousands of dissidents are silenced and put in jail by the new regime and half of the population is pushed outside of "the nation" in the AKP's polarizing and exclusionary discourse.

Yet the fear of the ban returning keeps mobilizing women wearing the headscarf around Erdoğan in spite of disagreements and discontent. During the run-up to the elections on June 24, 2018, Ayşe Böhürler tweeted that the opposition aims to revert the gains accomplished in favor of women wearing the headscarf. This was a regular theme that popped up in pro-AKP propaganda. Having lost their former supporters outside of the AKP, the party is now the only choice left for a big majority of these conservative women. They are afraid of headscarves being banned again. And the fear of the ban prevents them from seeing the adverse effects of the AKP on other women's lives. Because of this fear, they read the current political landscape of Turkey as if it were the same as it was two decades ago. Indeed, in a climate where the Kemalist position seems justified in pointing to the dangers of a gender ideology based on religion, what happens if the AKP loses power? Would the ban come back? Has this debate moved beyond a certain threshold that would make it pointless for conservative women to fear for the return of the ban? How would democrats and feminists take a position on this after having the experience of living under the AKP?

It is true that for Turkey's secular constituents on the Left and on the Right, the headscarf has become one of the signifiers of AKP's authoritarianism and repression, triggering existential anxiety and everyday conflicts. I notice more and more that my friends on the Left, who formerly supported the inclusion of the headscarf and saw it as a harmless choice, often express feelings of irritation and disillusionment toward the garment. People who formerly supported women's decision to cover their hair mention quarrels with women wearing headscarves on the streets and in everyday encounters. While the headscarf is becoming the "normal" and desirable option for women, it also encounters resistance. Moreover, the "new" Turkey has placed women wearing headscarves under a new political burden to "show" that they distance themselves from the AKP and do not support authoritarianism.

Along with such tension, there is evidence that the debate has moved at least beyond a certain threshold.[21] Headscarved women's right of access to university education or representation in the parliament has been widely accepted without further controversy. Yet the ban has not been removed by creating consensus within democratic mechanisms. Even if the issue might have been resolved for university students and women parliamentarians, the debate will most likely continue for schoolchildren and within certain professions, not just between neighborhoods but also within conservative circles. For example, conservative women are divided about letting school-age girls to cover their hair.[22] Should wearing a headscarf be about acquiring the habit from a young age or making a conscious decision about piety after age eighteen or twenty-one? Should it be the family's decision for a young girl, or an adult woman's decision? These are all points of contention even within conservative circles, making them open to further debate. At the same time, the images of headscarves on Istanbul's billboards have increasingly come to stand for "diversity." Advertisements for universities in particular, try to emphasize their "diverse" student body by simply juxtaposing the image of a girl wearing headscarf with a girl not wearing it. Although, it remains to be seen which image will come to signify "diversity" in the future in Turkey: an image of a woman wearing headscarf, or an image of a woman without headscarf.

The disconnect

I am still in touch with a small group of conservative women for whom my grandmother had prayed and cried during the height of the headscarf ban in the 1980s. They were young university students at the time, and today their daughters are attending university. In spite of our differences today, they have never abandoned me and my family. We are divided by politics more than ever and try to leave the divisive issues at the door in order to protect years-long friendships.

When I talked to one of the age-old friends from this small group in the summer of 2016, I realized the disconnect between her world and my world. Although she was critical of the AKP on numerous points, she just could not make sense of the resentment toward the AKP. She could empathize with the Kurds, yet the suffering of the secular population was totally invisible to her. She never frequented the spaces that secular people loved and cherished, so she was not aware of the crackdown on such spaces. She never bought alcohol, and the skyrocketing alcohol prices were not on her radar. On the contrary, she was able to find more and more places for her taste and lifestyle. The government's conservative gender policies that encouraged young people to marry early did not bother her, as her son and daughter married soon after they graduated from university. As a lawyer, she was never able to perform her profession because of the ban, but her daughter found a reasonably good job where she could wear the headscarf soon after her graduation. The brutal repression that depressed half of the population in Turkey has not touched her life in any form. Her biggest complaint was about the secular individuals who verbally assaulted a friend of hers who was driving an SUV on Bağdat Avenue.

The next year, I learned that she was undecided about supporting Erdoğan in the 2017 presidential referendum. I do not know if she voted yes or no. But I know that it is mostly in the hands of women like her to shift the balance of power in Turkey by withdrawing their support from a repressive regime. Turkey's way out depends on our ability to create a space to identify and resist authoritarianism together.

Notes

Preface and Acknowledgments

1 I covered my hair with a headscarf between the ages of twelve and twenty-seven, some fifteen years.

2 Berk Esen and Sebnem Gumuscu mentioned Hungary and Thailand as "other cases of democratic backsliding." Berk Esen and Sebnem Gumuscu, "Rising Competitive Authoritarianism in Turkey," *Third World Quarterly* 37, no. 9 (2016): 2. Britta Ohm compared the media management and manipulation strategies of India's Narendra Modi and Turkey's Recep Tayyip Erdoğan: Britta Ohm, "Organizing Popular Discourse With and Against the Media: Notes on the Making of Narendra Modi and Recep Tayyip Erdoğan as Leaders-Without-Alternative," *Television & New Media* 16, no. 4 (2015): 370–7.

3 Ayşe Esra Özcan, "Visualization of Gender in the Turkish Press: A Comparative Analysis of Six Turkish Newspapers," IRC-Library (Bremen: Information Resource Center der Jacobs University Bremen, 2010). Available online: https://opus.jacobs-university.de/frontdoor/index/index/docId/279 (accessed December 8, 2018).

4 Esra Özcan, "Women's Headscarves in News Photographs: A Comparison Between the Secular and Islamic Press During the AKP Government in Turkey," *European Journal of Communication* 30, no. 6 (2015): 698–713.

Introduction

1 Ertuğrul Özkök, "Modern Mahrem mi Demiştiniz?" *Hürriyet*, August 6, 2005. Available online: http://www.hurriyet.com.tr/modern-mahrem-mi-demistiniz-340283 (accessed December 8, 2018). Özkök's title refers to the book by Nilüfer Göle, *The Forbidden Modern* (Ann Arbor, MI: University of Michigan Press, 1996). For the news story that Özkök refers to, see: *Hürriyet*, "Göbeği Açık Türbanlı Kızlardan Oryantal," July 27, 2005. Available online: http://www.hurriyet.com.tr/gundem/gobegi-acik-turbanli-kizlardan-oryantal-38752064 (accessed December 8, 2018). The story does not include the image anymore. In 2005, I had saved the hardcopy image published on the same day in another newspaper, *Posta*, owned by the same media group as *Hürriyet*.

2 Ayşe Çavdar, "Erdoğan Neyi Güncelliyor?" *Artı Gerçek*, March 14, 2018. Available online: https://www.artigercek.com/erdogan-neyi-guncelliyor?t=1521020412 (accessed December 8, 2018).
3 In her analysis of the dominant features of the literature on Islamist women, Feyda Sayan-Cengiz beautifully criticized the "rupture" approach. Feyda Sayan-Cengiz, *Beyond Headscarf Culture in Turkey's Retail Sector* (Basingstoke: Palgrave Macmillan, 2016).
4 Zehra Yılmaz retains the term "Islamist" yet, she also emphasizes the "Islamist" women's activism during the 1970s. Zehra Yılmaz, *Dişil Dindarlık: İslâmcı Kadın Hareketinin Dönüşümü* (Istanbul: İletişim Yayınları, 2015). For the early phases of "Islamist"/conservative women's movement see also Tanıl Bora, *Cereyanlar, Türkiye'de Siyasi İdeolojiler* (Istanbul: İletişim Yayınları, 2017), 800–1.
5 Deniz Kandiyoti, "The Travails of the Secular: Puzzle and Paradox in Turkey," *Economy and Society* 41, no. 4 (2012): 513–31.
6 Nilüfer Göle, Yeşim Arat, Aynur İlyasoğlu, and Ayşe Saktanber are among the scholars who use the term "Islamist women." Nilüfer Göle, *The Forbidden Modern: Civilization and Veiling* (Ann Arbor, MI: University of Michigan Press, 1996); Yeşim Arat, *Rethinking Islam and Liberal Democracy: Islamist Women in Turkish Politics* (Albany, NY: State University of New York Press, 2005); Aynur İlyasoğlu, *Örtülü Kimlik, İslamcı Kadın Kimliğinin Oluşum Öğeleri* (Istanbul: Metis Yayınları, 1994); Ayşe Saktanber, *Living Islam: Women, Religion and the Politicization of Culture in Turkey* (London: I.B. Tauris, 2002).
7 Didem Unal, Canan Aslan Akman, and Margot Badran are among the scholars who use the variations of the term "Islamic feminist." Didem Unal, "Vulnerable Identities: Pious Women Columnists' Narratives on Islamic Feminism and Feminist Self-Identification in Contemporary Turkey," *Women's Studies International Forum* 53 (2015): 12–21; Canan Aslan Akman, "Islamic Women's Ordeal with the New Face(s) of Patriarchy in Power: Divergence or Convergence over Expanding Women's Citizenship," in *Gendered Identities: Criticizing Patriarchy in Turkey*, ed. Rasim Özgür Dönmez and Fazilet Ahu Özmen (Lanham, MD: Lexington Books, 2013), 113–45; Margot Badran, "Understanding Islam, Islamism, and Islamic Feminism," *Journal of Women's History* 13, no. 1 (2001): 47–52.
8 Berna Turam prefers the term "pious women," sometimes "pious feminists." Elifhan Köse, Didem Unal, and Feyza Akınerdem are also among the scholars who use the term. Berna Turam, *Gaining Freedoms: Claiming Space in Istanbul and Berlin* (Stanford, CA: Stanford University Press, 2015); Berna Turam, "Turkish Women Divided by Politics: Secularist Versus Pious Non-resistance," *International Feminist Journal of Politics* 10, no. 4 (2008): 475–94; Elifhan Köse, *Sessizliği Söylemek* (Istanbul: İletişim Yayınları, 2012); Feyza Akınerdem, "Dindar Kadınlar ve Feminizm—Yakınlıklar ve Uzaklıklar," in *Amargi, Feminizm Tartışmaları* (Istanbul: Kumbara Sanat Atölyesi Araştırma Dizisi—2, 2012).

9 The term "conservative women" is more popular in Turkish media than in academia.

10 Even though Handan Koç uses the term "Islamist women," she aligns Islamism as part of right-wing politics; Handan Koç, *Muhafazakarlığa Karşı Feminizm* (Istanbul: Güldünya Yayınları, 2015). Ayşe Saktanber also wrote about the "Islamist women" within the context of Turkish right-wing politics: Ayşe Saktanber, "Whose Virtue Is This? The Virtue Party and Women in Islamist Politics in Turkey," in *Right-Wing Women: From Conservatives to Extremists Around the World*, ed. by Paola Bacchetta and Margaret Power (New York: Routledge, 2002), 71–83.

11 Yeşim Arat, "Islamist Women and Feminist Concerns in Contemporary Turkey," *Frontiers* 37, no. 3 (2016): 125–50.

12 Nilüfer Göle saw a significant potential in women's activism not just to transform Islamism but also the public sphere in Turkey, Nilüfer Göle, "Islam in Public: New Visibilities and New Imaginaries," *Public Culture* 14, no. 1 (2002): 173–90.

13 Arat, "Islamist Women and Feminist Concerns."

14 Ibid., 135.

15 Ronnee Schreiber, *Righting Feminism: Conservative Women and American Politics* (New York: Oxford University Press, 2008).

16 Kristin Blakely, "Transnational Anti-Feminist Networks: Canadian Right-Wing Women and the Global Stage," in *New Perspectives on the Transnational Right*, ed. Martin Durham and Margaret Power (New York: Palgrave Macmillan, 2010), 171–86.

17 Bora, *Cerayanlar*, 437. Bora, acknowledged the left-wing varieties of Islamism and indeed, Anti-Capitalist Muslims of İhsan Eliaçık falls into this category. Kandiyoti, with reference to Feroz Ahmad's *The Making of Modern Turkey* (London: Routledge, 1993), mentioned how in the 1960s the conservative Right mobilized religion as an ideological counterforce against the socialist and democratic forces: Kandiyoti, "The Travails of the Secular," 518. It may be useful here to talk about the similarities and differences between the Islamist-right, center-right and nationalist-right. Islamist-right has annihilated the center-right in Turkey. The nationalist-right is represented in Turkish politics by MHP (Nationalist Movement Party) which regularly allies with the AKP particularly against the Kurds. A group of politicians from MHP who were unhappy about their party's alliance with the AKP left the party to establish *İyi Parti* (Good Party) on October 25, 2017, under Meral Akşener's leadership, the first female head of an ultranationalist party.

18 Köse, *Sessizliği Söylemek*, 9–10. Köse argues that pious women writers' antifeminism reveals itself in this selective appropriation of feminism.

19 Esra Özcan, "Conservative Women in Power: A New Predicament for Transnational Feminist Media Research," in *Feminist Approaches to Media Theory and Research*, ed. Dustin Harp, Jaime Loke, and Ingrid Bachmann (Cham: Palgrave Macmillan, 2018), 167–81.

20 Schreiber, *Righting Feminism*.

21 There is a vast literature on Islamic feminism. For a brief introduction to the latest debates see *Samyukta*'s special issue on Islamic feminism, edited by Margot Badran: *Samyukta: A Journal of Gender and Culture* 17, no. 1 (2017). See also, Margot Badran, *Feminism in Islam, Secular and Religious Convergences* (Oxford: Oneworld, 2009).

22 Sibel Özbudun, *Kadınlar: İslam, AKP ve Ötesi* (Ankara: Ütopya, 2016). İpek Merçil, "İslam ve Feminizm," in *Cinsiyetli Olmak: Sosyal Bilimlere Feminist Bakışlar*, ed. Zeynep Direk (Istanbul: Yapı Kredi Yayınları, 2007), 106–17.

23 Berna Turam often uses the term: Turam, "Turkish Women Divided by Politics."

24 Conservative women columnists frequently criticize other "pious" Muslims and criticize them for using religious practices for showmanship and PR, something that they can easily be criticized for. For example, see: Ayşe Böhürler, "Dini mesajlar," *Yeni Şafak*, December 27, 2014. Hilâl Kaplan, "Ramazan'ı uğurlarken . . . ," *Yeni Şafak*, August 29, 2011.

25 For more information on Anti-Capitalist Muslims see: Güldem Baykal Büyüksaraç, "'All Dominion Belongs to Allah . . . Capital Get Out': The Issue of Social Justice and Muslim Anti-Capitalists in Turkey," *Crosscurrents* 66, no. 2 (2016): 239–52.

26 Nihal Bengisu Karaca named İhsan Eliaçık as an "anomaly": Nihal Bengisu Karaca, "İslam Konferansına sabotaj mı?" *Habertürk*, May 10, 2014. Karaca had quoted him as a theologian and thinker in 2010: Nihal Bengisu Karaca, "Seyahat Özgürlüğü ve Suudi Arabistan Meselesi," *Habertürk*, January 6, 2010.

27 Nagehan Alçı is a well-known militant pro-AKP journalist writing in Habertürk. She does not wear a headscarf.

28 Clarisse Berthezène and Julie V. Gottlieb (eds.), *Rethinking Right-Wing Women: Gender and Conservative Party, 1880s to the Present* (Manchester: Manchester University Press, 2018), 2.

29 Margaret Power, *Right-Wing Women in Chile: Feminine Power and the Struggle Against Allende, 1964–1973* (University Park, PA: Penn State University Press, 2002).

30 Berthezène and Gottlieb, *Rethinking Right-Wing Women*.

31 Raffael Scheck, *Mothers of the Nation: Right-Wing Women in Weimar Germany* (Oxford: Berg, 2004).

32 Tanika Sarkar and Urvashi Butalia, *Women and Right-Wing Movements: Indian Experiences* (London: Zed Books, 1995). Kalyani Devaki Menon, *Everyday Nationalism: Women of the Hindu Right in India* (Philadelphia, PA: University of Pennsylvania Press, 2010).

33 Blakely, "Transnational Anti-Feminist Networks."

34 Schreiber, *Righting Feminism*.

35 Kathleen M. Fallon and Julie Moreau, "Righting Africa? Contextualizing Notions of Women's Right-Wing Activism in Sub-Saharan Africa," in *Women of the Right: Comparisons and Interplay Across Borders*, ed. Kathleen M. Blee and Sandra McGee Deutsch (University Park, PA: The Pennsylvania State University, 2012), 68–80.

36 Karla J. Cunningham, "Gender, Islam, and Conservative Politics," in *Women of the Right: Comparisons and Interplay Across Borders*, ed. Kathleen M. Blee and Sandra McGee Deutsch (University Park, PA: The Pennsylvania State University, 2012), 81–97. Saktanber, "Whose Virtue Is This?"

37 Ferruh Yılmaz, "From Immigrant Worker to Muslim Immigrant: Challenges for Feminism," *European Journal of Women's Studies* 22, no. 1 (2015): 37–52. Sara R. Farris, *In the Name of Women's Rights: The Rise of Femonationalism* (Durham, NC: Duke University Press, 2017).

38 Sema Maraşlı is a writer from the radical wing who believes women are naturally submissive. Conservative columnist Nihal Bengisu Karaca, a mainstream conservative columnist, criticized her views on gender in "İnsan memeli bir hayvan mıdır?" *Habertürk*, January 13, 2012. Karaca criticized another conservative writer who defended polygamy, in: "Statüko bekçisi dindar kadınlar," *Habertürk*, May 25, 2011.

Chapter 1: Old Versus New Turkey

1 Deniz Kandiyoti, "The Travails of the Secular: Puzzle and Paradox in Turkey," *Economy and Society* 41, no. 4 (2012): 514.

2 Ibid., 527.

3 Ibid., 514.

4 For Qasim Amin's ideas see, Leila Ahmed, *A Quiet Revolution: The Veil's Resurgence, from the Middle East to America* (New Haven, CT: Yale University Press, 2011), 19, 24.

5 Ümit Cizre (ed.), "Introduction," *Secular and Islamic Politics in Turkey: The Making of the Justice and Development Party* (New York: Routledge, 2008). The term "secular establishment" is used throughout the book. Hilal Elver also uses the term "secular establishment." See: Hilal Elver, *The Headscarf Controversy: Secularism and Freedom of Religion* (Oxford: Oxford University Press, 2012), 26.

6 For more information see: İştar Gözaydın, *Diyanet: Türkiye Cumhuriyeti'nde Dinin Tanzimi* (Istanbul: İletişim Yayınları, 2009).

7 Neşet Çağatay, a well-known professor of history of Islam asked the student either to take her headscarf off or to leave the classroom. Hatice Babacan, the rejected student, was also taking a class from the father of Reha Muhtar, a famous journalist. Reha Muhtar recounted the story in his column: Reha Muhtar, "Hey sen başörtülü kız. . ." *Vatan*, September 17, 2007. Available online: http://www.gazetevatan.com/reha-muhtar-137315-yazar-yazisi--hey-sen-basortulu-kiz----/ (accessed December 8, 2018). Hatice Babacan's nephew, Ali Babacan, served as the Deputy Prime Minister for Economic and Financial Affairs under the AKP.

8   Scholars have expressed their views on headscarf in the following videos:
    Prof. Beyza Bilgin-Örtünme. Available online: https://www.youtube.com/
    watch?v=z3JUdpyhD0o, at 0:55–2:15. Odadaydım Belgeseli-Ölümcül Kitap.
    Available online: https://www.youtube.com/watch?v=gtNM6wVlV2k, at 1:13–3:55
    (both accessed December 8, 2018).

9   The program's first episode, broadcast in 1980, was made public for a while in TRT's
    online archive: http://www.trtarsiv.com/izle/131428/inanc-dunyasi-1-bolum (now
    defunct). For an episode from 1986, see: https://www.youtube.com/
    watch?v=OxgWbgGL110 (accessed April 25, 2019).

10 Hayrettin Karaman, who writes in pro-AKP *Yeni Şafak* at the moment, has been
    such a leading figure.

11 Bahattin Akşit, "Imam-Hatip and Other Secondary Schools in the Context of
    Political and Cultural Modernization of Turkey," *Journal of Human Sciences* 5, no. 1
    (1986): 25–41.

12 For the "Anatolian Islam" thesis, see, Ali Çarkoğlu and Binnaz Toprak, *Türkiye'de Din,
    Toplum ve Siyaset* (Istanbul: Tesev Yayınları, 2000), 17. Available online: http://tesev.
    org.tr/wp-content/uploads/2015/11/Turkiyede_Din_Toplum_Ve_Siyaset.pdf
    (accessed December 8, 2018).

13 Elif Batuman, "The Head Scarf, Modern Turkey, and Me," *New Yorker*, February 8–15,
    2016. Available online: https://www.newyorker.com/magazine/2016/02/08/cover-
    story-personal-history-elif-batuman (accessed June 11, 2019).

14 Ayşe Böhürler, "Elalem Korkusu!" *Yeni Şafak*, December 27, 2008.

15 I heard this myself from a distant relative who covered her hair in traditional style.
    I was thirteen and was covering my hair with a headscarf.

16 Nesrin Tuna (Interview with Sibel Eraslan), "Ben İmanlı Feministim," *Pazartesi:
    Special Issue on Religion*, July–September 2007, a compilation of previously published
    articles on religion. This interview originally appears in September 1995, issue 6.
    According to the conservative writer Sibel Eraslan's account, many families
    threatened to reject their daughters if they continued to cover their hair and risk
    their university education.

17 Hilâl Kaplan, "Neden İslamcı değilim?" *Yeni Şafak*, August 13, 2012; Hilâl Kaplan,
    "Hz. Muhammed (s.a.v.) İslamcı mıydı?" *Yeni Şafak*, August 24, 2012. In these
    articles, Kaplan defines "Muslim" as an inherently political subject, as someone who
    organizes all their social and political activities on the basis of Islam.

18 Kandiyoti, "The Travails of the Secular," 523, original emphasis.

19 For a selection of Cemalnur Sargut's videos see: https://www.youtube.com/user/
    cemalnursargut (accessed December 8, 2018).

20 Ayşe Esra Özcan, "The New Configurations of Islam in Contemporary Turkey: The
    Case of Yaşar Nuri Öztürk," unpublished MA thesis, Boğaziçi University, Istanbul,
    2000.

21 Fulya Atacan, *Cerrahiler* (Istanbul: Hil Yayınları, 1990). Fulya Atacan, the student of legendary Turkish female sociologist Mübeccel Kıray, is one of the scholars who lost her job under an executive order as part of the government's attempt to crack down on academia after the failed coup attempt of July 15, 2016.

22 Çarkoğlu and Toprak, *Türkiye'de Din, Toplum ve Siyaset*, 16.

23 Ibid.

24 Ibid., 19.

25 Ayşe Öncü, "Turkish Women in the Professions: Why So Many?" in *Women in Turkish Society*, ed. Nermin Abadan-Unat, Deniz Kandiyoti, and Mübeccel Kıray (Leiden: E.J. Brill, 1981), 181–93.

26 For more information on the tutelary role of the Turkish military see: Yaprak Gürsoy, "From Tutelary Powers and Interventions to Civilian Control: An Overview of Turkish Civil–Military Relations Since the 1920s," in *Turkey's Democratization Process*, ed. Carmen Rodríguez, Antonio Ávalos, Hakan Yılmaz, and Ana I. Planet (Abingdon: Routledge, 2014), 253–73. Ergun Özbudun, "Democracy, Tutelarism, and the Search for a New Constitution," in *Turkey's Democratization Process*, ed. Carmen Rodríguez, Antonio Ávalos, Hakan Yılmaz, and Ana I. Planet (Abingdon: Routledge, 2014), 293–311.

27 Kandiyoti, "The Travails of the Secular," 518.

28 For more information on Gülenism, see Berna Turam, *Between Islam and the State: The Politics of Engagement* (Stanford, CA: Stanford University Press, 2007).

29 For more information on the Second Republic movement see: Tanıl Bora, *Cereyanlar: Türkiye'de Siyasi İdeolojiler* (Istanbul: İletişim Yayınları, 2017), 55; Metin Sever and Cem Dizdar, *2. Cumhuriyet Tartışmaları: Yeni Arayışlar, Yeni Yönelimler* (Istanbul: Başak Yayınları, 1993).

30 The accusation against Erdoğan was "incitement to hatred on the basis of religious and racial differences."

31 Kenan Çayır, "The Emergence of Turkey's Contemporary 'Muslim Democrats,'" in *Secular and Islamic Politics in Turkey: The Making of the Justice and Development Party*, ed. Ümit Cizre (New York: Routledge, 2008), 62–79.

32 Metin Heper, "A 'Democratic Conservative' Government by Pious People: The Justice and Development Party in Turkey," in *The Blackwell Companion to Contemporary Islamic Thought*, ed. Ibrahim M. Abu-Rabi' (Malden, MA: Blackwell, 2006), 345–61.

33 Nora Onar, "Kemalists, Islamists, and Liberals: Shifting Patterns of Confrontation and Consensus 2002–06," *Turkish Studies* 8, no. 2 (2007): 273–88.

34 Berk Esen and Sebnem Gumuscu, "Rising Competitive Authoritarianism in Turkey," *Third World Quarterly* 37, no. 9 (2016): 1582. Others pointed out the manipulative strategies that AKP employed before the elections: Cenk Aygül,

"Electoral Manipulation in March 30, 2014 Turkish Local Elections," *Turkish Studies* 17, no. 1 (2016): 181–201.

35 For debates over the AKP representatives' wives and first ladies wearing the headscarf see: Dilek Cindoğlu and Gizem Zencirci, "The Headscarf in Turkey in the Public and State Spheres," *Middle Eastern Studies* 44, no. 5 (2008): 791–806.

36 In the Turkish parliamentary system, the president had a symbolic role and was expected to be impartial, above party politics. It was clear that Abdullah Gül, one of the founders of the AKP, would not uphold such impartiality.

37 Ümit Cizre (ed.), *Secular and Islamic Politics in Turkey: The Making of the Justice and Development Party* (New York: Routledge, 2008). The edited volume questions the AKP's potential to democratize Turkey.

38 Selim Temo, "Bir 'bölüm'ün serencamı," *Radikal 2*, September 19, 2010. Available online: http://www.radikal.com.tr/radikal2/bir-bolumun-serencami-1019912/ (accessed December 8, 2018).

39 For more information on the topic see: Berk Esen and Sebnem Gumuscu. "Building a Competitive Authoritarian Regime: State–Business Relations in the AKP's Turkey," *Journal of Balkan and Near Eastern Studies* 20, no. 4 (2018): 349–72.

40 *BİA News Desk*, "TRT'nin Cumhurbaşkanı Adayı 'Adaleti,' " July 10, 2014. Available online: https://m.bianet.org/bianet/siyaset/157100-trt-nin-cumhurbaskani-adayi-adaleti (accessed December 8, 2018).

41 Around a hundred media organizations (newspapers, television stations, and radio stations) were shut down because of their alleged links to Fethullah Gülen. Rengin Arslan, "15 Temmuz darbe girişimi: 100'den fazla gazete, televizyon kapatıldı," *BBC Türkçe*, July 28, 2016. Available online: http://www.bbc.com/turkce/haberler-turkiye-36913856 (accessed December 8, 2018).

42 *Reporters without Borders*, "Verdict Imminent in Trial of 29 Turkish Journalists and Media Workers," February 22, 2018. Available online: https://rsf.org/en/news/verdict-imminent-trial-29-turkish-journalists-and-media-workers (accessed December 8, 2018). For the crack down on academia after the July 15, 2016 coup attempt see, Umut Özkırımlı, "How to Liquidate a People? Academic Freedom in Turkey and Beyond," *Globalizations* 14, no. 6 (2017): 851–6.

43 Humeyra Pamuk and Ece Toksabay, "Purge of Academics Leaves Future of Turkish Universities in Doubt," *Reuters*, March 1, 2017. Available online: https://www.reuters.com/article/us-turkey-security-academics/purge-of-academics-leaves-future-of-turkish-universities-in-doubt-idUSKBN1684DE (accessed December 8, 2018).

44 Celal Başlangıç, " 'Kendinden olmayanı yok etme rejimi' geliyor," *Gazete Duvar*, January 17, 2017. Available online: https://www.gazeteduvar.com.tr/yazarlar/

2017/01/17/kendinden-olmayani-yok-etme-rejimi-geliyor/ (accessed December 8, 2018). Başlangıç reported the deportation of an Italian journalist. On the same day, the *New York Times* reported the deportation of another foreign correspondent, Rod Nordland: Rick Gladstone, "Veteran Times Reporter Denied Entry to Turkey," January 17, 2017. Available online: https://www.nytimes. com/2017/01/17/world/europe/rod-nordland-turkey.html (accessed December 8, 2018).

45 *Reuters*, "Turkey's Powerful New Executive Presidency," June 22, 2018. Available online: https://www.reuters.com/article/us-turkey-election-factbox/turkeys-powerful-new-executive-presidency-idUSKBN1JI1O1 (accessed December 8, 2018).

46 Peter Kenyon, "Turkey's State of Emergency Ends, While Erdogan's Power Grows and 'Purge' Continues," *NPR*, July 26, 2018. Available online: https://www. npr.org/2018/07/26/632307755/turkeys-state-of-emergency-ends-while-erdogans-power-grows-and-purge-continues (accessed December 8, 2018).

47 *Hürriyet Daily News*, "Separation of Powers an Obstacle, Says Erdoğan," December 18, 2012. Available online: http://www.hurriyetdailynews.com/separation-of-powers-an-obstacle-says-erdogan-37052 (accessed December 8, 2018).

48 *Diken*, "Erdoğan'ın hayali: Anonim şirket nasıl yönetiliyorsa, Türkiye de öyle yönetilmeli," March 15, 2015. Available online: http://www.diken.com.tr/erdoganin-hayali-anonim-sirket-nasil-yonetiliyorsa-turkiye-de-oyle-yonetilmeli/ (accessed December 8, 2018).

49 Aygül, "Electoral Manipulation in March 30, 2014 Turkish Local Elections," 182.

50 Ferruh Yılmaz, *How the Workers Became Muslims: Immigration, Culture, and Hegemonic Transformation in Europe* (Ann Arbor, MI: University of Michigan Press, 2016), 194.

51 Cihan Tugal, "In Turkey, the Regime Slides from Soft to Hard Totalitarianism," *openDemocracy*, February 17, 2016. Available online: https://www.opendemocracy. net/cihan-tugal/turkey-hard-totalitarianism-erdogan-authoritarian (accessed December 8, 2018). Ayşe Kadıoğlu, "Coup d'État Attempt: Turkey's Reichstag Fire?" *openDemocracy*, July 16, 2016. Available online: https://www.opendemocracy.net/ ay-e-kad-o-lu/coup-d-tat-attempt-turkey-s-reichstag-fire (accessed December 8, 2018).

52 Diyanet TV; see: https://www.diyanet.tv.

53 *BBC Türkçe*, "Erdoğan: Boğaziçi Üniversitesi Bu Ülke ve Bu Milletin Değerlerine Yaslanamadığı İçin Hedeflerine Ulaşamadı," January 7, 2018. Available online: http://www.bbc.com/turkce/haberler-turkiye-42597325 (accessed December 8, 2018). David Matthews, "Erdoğan Attack Sparks Fears over Future of Turkish Universities," *The Times Higher Education*, January 18, 2018. Available online:

https://www.timeshighereducation.com/news/erdogan-attack-sparks-fears-over-future-turkish-universities (accessed December 8, 2018).

54 *Hürriyet*, " 'İmam hatip lisesi sayısını 440'tan 1017'ye çıkardık,' " January 28, 2015. Available online: http://www.hurriyet.com.tr/imam-hatip-lisesi-sayisini-440-tan-1017-ye-cikardik-28069992 (accessed December 8, 2018).

55 *T24*, "İmam hatipli sayısı 11 yılda 10 kat arttı," December 19, 2014. Available online: http://t24.com.tr/haber/imam-hatipli-sayisi-11-yilda-10-kat-artti,280937 (accessed December 8, 2018).

56 *BIA News Desk*, "Erdoğan: İmam Hatiplerde Hamdolsun 1 Milyon 300 Bin Öğrenci Var," September 29, 2017. Available online: https://m.bianet.org/bianet/siyaset/190233-erdogan-imam-hatiplerde-hamdolsun-1-milyon-300-bin-ogrenci-var (accessed December 8, 2018).

57 For more information on the Islamization of the education system see, Deniz Kandiyoti and Zühre Emanet, "Education as Battleground: The Capture of Minds in Turkey," *Globalizations* 14, no. 6 (2017): 869–76.

58 Freedom House, "Turkey, Freedom of the Press 2014." Available online: https://freedomhouse.org/report/freedom-press/2014/turkey (accessed April 25, 2019).

59 For media concentration and ownership before the AKP changed the media structure in Turkey see: Doğan L. Tılıç, *Media Ownership Structure in Turkey* (Ankara: Çağdaş Gazeteciler Derneği, 2000). Christian Christensen, "Concentration of Ownership, the Fall of the Unions and Government Legislation in Turkey," *Global Media and Communication* 3, no. 2 (2007): 179–99. Andrew Finkel, "Who Guards the Turkish Press," *Journal of International Affairs* 54, no. 1 (2000): 147–66. Dilruba Çatalbaş, "Freedom of Press and Broadcasting," in *Human Rights in Turkey*, ed. Zehra F. Kabasakal Arat (Philadelphia, PA: University of Pennsylvania Press, 2007), 19–34. Ceren Sözeri and Zeynep Güney, *The Political Economy of the Media in Turkey: A Sectoral Analysis* (Istanbul: Tesev, 2011).

60 As of 2004 Doğan Media Group (DMG) had control over 60 percent of the top five newspapers, 38 percent of all newspapers, and they had 62 percent of the newspaper advertisement market share in Turkey; see Christensen "Concentration of Ownership," 188.

61 In its initial years, while the Kemalist establishment was still in power and the AKP was on friendly terms with the European Union, the AKP passed laws that seemed to be expanding media freedom. But, at the same time, they passed other laws to limit that freedom. For example, as part of EU regulations, the AKP passed a new Press Law that looked promising in 2004; yet, restrictive measures in the Turkish Penal Code (particularly Article 301) which came into effect in 2005 led to the prosecution of journalists, writers, and publishers on the charge of insulting Turkishness.

62 Tasarruf Mevduatı ve Sigorta Fonu (TMSF—The Government Agency for Public Funds / Savings Deposit Insurance Fund) is a crucial government institution that has transferred media power to pro-AKP owners.

63 For more information on the shift in Turkish media see, Murat Akser and Banu Baybars-Hawks, "Media and Democracy in Turkey: Toward a Model of Neoliberal Media Autocracy," *Middle East Journal of Culture and Communication* 5, no. 3 (2012): 302–21. Esra Arsan, "Killing Me Softly with His Words: Censorship and Self-Censorship from the Perspective of Turkish Journalists," *Turkish Studies* 14, no. 3 (2013): 447–62. Bilge Yesil, *Media in New Turkey: The Origins of an Authoritarian Neoliberal State* (Urbana, IL: University of Illinois Press, 2016).

64 *Bia Haber Merkezi*, "Demirören Yazılı Basında Birinci Sıraya Yükseliyor," March 23, 2018. Available online: http://bianet.org/bianet/siyaset/195466-demiroren-yazili-basinda-birinci-siraya-yukseliyor (accessed December 8, 2018).

65 Salih Bayram, "Reporting Hijab in Turkey: Shifts in the Pro- and Anti-Ban Discourses," *Turkish Studies* 10, no. 4 (2009): 511–38. Çiler Dursun, "The Struggle Goes On: The Discursive Strategies of the Islamist Press in Turkey," *Journal of Contemporary European Studies* 14, no. 2 (2006): 161–82. Songül S. Gül and Hüseyin Gül, "The Question of Women in Islamic Revivalism in Turkey: A Review of the Islamic Press," *Current Sociology* 48, no. 2 (2000): 1–26.

66 Constanze Letsch, "Turkish Journalists Face Secret Trial for Revealing Arms Deliveries to Syria," *The Guardian*, March 25, 2016. Available online: https://www.theguardian.com/world/2016/mar/25/turkish-journalists-can-dundar-erdem-gul-secret-trial-revealing-arms-deliveries-syria (accessed December 8, 2018).

67 Some of the other small oppositional online news sites are: Sendika.org, *Gazete Karınca*, Medyascope, Demokrathaber.org, Siyasihaber4.org, Ötekilerin Postası (available online: https://www.facebook.com/10.posta/), and IleriHaber.org. *BirGun Gazetesi* is another oppositional newspaper survivor in the print press.

68 *Committee to Protect Journalists*, "Second Worst Year on Record for Jailed Journalists," December 18, 2013. Available online: https://cpj.org/reports/2013/12/second-worst-year-on-record-for-jailed-journalists.php (accessed December 8, 2018).

69 In addition to all these restrictions, AKP immediately bans news reporting following violent events or attacks. The news organizations are not allowed to report on the event. According to Reporters Without Border's World Press Freedom Index, Turkey ranked at 157 out of 180 countries in 2018. See *Reporters Without Borders*, available online: https://rsf.org/en/ranking (accessed December 9, 2018).

70 *Reporters Without Borders*, "Enemies of the Internet 2014," Available online: https://rsf.org/sites/default/files/2014-rsf-rapport-enemies-of-the-internet.pdf (accessed December 9, 2018).

71 *The Guardian*, "Turkey Blocks Wikipedia Under Law Designed to Protect National Security," April 29, 2017. Available online: https://www.theguardian.com/world/2017/apr/29/turkey-blocks-wikipedia-under-law-designed-to-protect-national-security (accessed December 9, 2018).

72 *Hürriyet Daily News*, "Turkish Parliament Approves Law Giving TV Watchdog Authority over Internet Broadcasts," March 22, 2018. Available online: http://www.hurriyetdailynews.com/internet-broadcast-law-passed-in-turkish-parliament-amid-censorship-outcry-129139 (accessed December 9, 2018).

73 Carlotta Gall, "Erdogan's Next Target as He Restricts Turkey's Democracy: The Internet," *New York Times*, March 4, 2018. Available online: https://www.nytimes.com/2018/03/04/world/europe/turkey-erdogan-internet-law-restrictions.html (accessed December 9, 2018).

74 *Committee to Protect Journalists*, "In Turkey, Draft Bill Would Give New Censorship Powers to State Regulator," February 22, 2018. Available online: https://cpj.org/2018/02/in-turkey-draft-bill-would-give-new-censorship-pow.php (accessed December 9, 2018).

75 *Freedom House*, "The Future of Turkish Democracy," July 15, 2014. Available online: https://freedomhouse.org/article/future-turkish-democracy (accessed December 9, 2018).

76 Murat Yetkin, "The New Media (Dis)order in Turkey," *Hürriyet Daily News*, May 20, 2015. Available online: http://www.hurriyetdailynews.com/the-new-media-disorder-in-turkey.aspx?pageID=238&nid=82654 (accessed December 9, 2018).

77 Gülseren Adaklı, "Türkiye'de Medya Sahipliği Kamuya Açık Bir Bilgi Alanı Mı?" *Bia News Desk*, March 31, 2017. Available online: https://bianet.org/bianet/bianet/185011-turkiye-de-medya-sahipligi-kamuya-acik-bir-bilgi-alani-mi (accessed December 9, 2018).

78 Dağhan Irak, "A Close-Knit Bunch: Political Concentration in Turkey's Anadolu Agency Through Twitter Interactions," *Turkish Studies* 17, no. 2 (2016): 336–60. See also Esra Arsan, "AA! Muhbir," *Evrensel*, March 31, 2017. Available online: https://www.evrensel.net/yazi/78780/aa-muhbir (accessed December 9, 2018).

79 TRT announced the CHP's "Justice Walk" in 2017 as "the so-called Justice Walk."

80 *Yunus Emre, Diriliş,* and *Payitaht Abdülhamid* are some of the programs that glorify the Ottoman past. *Payitaht Albulhamid* (2017), glorifies Sultan Abdülhamid, who was notorious for his repressive rule. The series justify repression and the elimination of freedom of press under his regime.

81 On TRT's website, the religious programs are listed in a separate section, giving the impression that only a limited number of programs focus on religion. Yet, religion has become the main topic of a large variety of other programs. For example, Pelin Çift's popular talk show titled "Beyond the Agenda," gives the impression of a political talk show, yet, it is mainly about religious issues debated with theologians.

82 *Gazete Karınca*, "Memuriyet Şartını Taşımıyor: Bilal Erdoğan'ın Arkadaşı İbrahim Eren TRT Genel Müdürü Oldu," July 10, 2017. Available online: http://gazetekarinca. com/2017/07/memuriyet-sartini-tasimiyor-bilal-erdoganin-arkadasi-ibrahim-eren-trt-genel-muduru-oldu/ (accessed December 9, 2018).

83 Sinan Tartanoğlu, "Basın Artık Resmen Saray'ın Emrinde," *Cumhuriyet*, July 24, 2018. Available online: http://www.cumhuriyet.com.tr/haber/siyaset/1036301/Basin_artik_resmen_Saray_in_emrinde.html (accessed December 9, 2018).

Chapter 2: The Headscarf as a Contested Terrain in Turkish Media and Politics

1 Ahmet Davutoğlu became prime minister on August 28, 2014 after Erdoğan became the new president. He stayed in office until May 24, 2016. Davutoğlu resigned from his position claiming that his resignation was not his choice.

2 For Binali Yıldırım's speech see: "Binali Yıldırım'ın Boğaziçi Üniversitesi Anısı." Available online: https://www.youtube.com/watch?v=Bh1ZwKYWQjk (accessed December 15, 2018).

3 *Reuters*, "Mixed-Sex Student Housing Becomes Turkish PM's Latest Bugbear," November 5, 2013. Available online: https://www.reuters.com/article/us-turkey-erdogan-students/mixed-sex-student-housing-becomes-turkish-pms-latest-bugbear-idUSBRE9A410N20131105 (accessed December 15, 2018). Jamie Dettmer, "Turkey's Leader Condemns Coed Dormitories," *Daily Beast*, November 12, 2013. Available online: https://www.thedailybeast.com/turkeys-erdogan-condemns-coed-dormitories (accessed December 15, 2018). Nihal Bengisu Karaca, "Bülent Arınç'ın sitemi," *Habertürk*, November 10, 2013: In this article conservative female columnist Karaca talked about the problems of university students and added that they are also a "source of complaint" in all Anatolian cities.

4 Leila Ahmed's account on the emergence of the Islamic headscarf in Egypt is similar to the emergence of Islamic headscarf in Turkey. The style is very similar too. Leila Ahmed, *A Quiet Revolution: The Veil's Resurgence, from the Middle East to America* (New Haven, CT: Yale University Press 2011).

5 "İrtica/irticaci" (reaction/reactionaries) were pejorative terms commonly used to refer to the religious groups critical of Turkish secularism. Dinci (religionist) was another such term. The term "Islamist" was not part of the vocabulary of the secular establishment during the 1960s and 1970s.

6 The conservative women whom I know of from my childhood and who suffered during the headscarf ban in the 1980s told me their stories in these terms. They started covering their head at their father's request and only after that they started looking for its rationale, finding it in the Qur'an.

7 Istanbul University is located in Istanbul's historic district which is full of mosques.

8 Hatice Babacan, the student in that case, completed her education while wearing headscarf, although in another faculty, not in the Faculty of Theology; see Reha Muhtar, "Hey sen başörtülü kız . . . ," *Vatan*, September 17, 2007. Available online: http://www.gazetevatan.com/reha-muhtar-137315-yazar-yazisi--hey-sen-basortulu-kiz----/ (accessed December 8, 2018).

9 Ayşe Böhürler, "Kimlik kriterleri," *Yeni Şafak*, August 31, 2013. In this article, conservative columnist Ayşe Böhürler talks about how the Iranian Revolution excited them during the 1980s. The revolution showed that America was not invincible. Böhürler lamented that the Iranian Revolution that was meant to expand freedoms came to restrict freedoms later. She complained about the term "Iranist" (*İrancı*) in another article: Ayşe Böhürler, "İrancı olmak," *Yeni Şafak*, January 12, 2013.

10 Ayşe Böhürler, "Fikri Sabitler," *Yeni Şafak*, October 16, 2010. In this article, Böhürler talks about how a secularist journalist criticized women wearing the headscarf for imitating Iranian women's black head-to-toe covering. The women interviewed by Feyda Sayan-Cengiz mentioned how they were insulted by secular people telling them to go to Iran; see Feyda Sayan-Cengiz, *Beyond Headscarf Culture in Turkey's Retail Sector* (Basingstoke: Palgrave Macmillan, 2016), 107–8. Naming "Iran" among other Muslim nations that impose the headscarf is not coincidental; it reflects a deep-seated fear of losing secular freedoms and rights, and becoming subject to an imposed headscarf. The fear of "becoming like Iran" is still widespread among secular circles in Turkey, and seems to have a more legitimate ground under the authoritarian AKP rule.

11 For a history of the ban see, Anna C. Korteweg and Gökçe Yurdakul, *The Headscarf Debates: Conflicts of National Belonging* (Stanford, CA: Stanford University Press 2015); Alev Çınar, *Modernity, Islam, and Secularism in Turkey: Bodies, Places, and Time* (Minneapolis, MN: University of Minnesota Press, 2005).

12 Sayan-Cengiz, *Beyond Headscarf Culture*, 40.

13 Tanıl Bora looked at conservative women's movements, rather, in a continuum: Tanıl Bora, *Cerayanlar: Türkiye'de Siyasi İdeolojiler* (Istanbul: İletişim Yayınları, 2017). Although with an emphasis on her fashion, Rustem Ertug Altınay's work is a rare example focusing on Şule Yüksel Şenler, a leading conservative female icon from the 1960s: Rustem Ertug Altınay, "Şule Yüksel Şenler: An Early Style Icon of Urban Islamic Fashion in Turkey," in *Islamic Fashion and Anti-Fashion: New Perspectives from Europe and North America*, ed. Emma Tarlo and Annelies Moors (London: Bloomsbury Academic, 2013). Zehra Yılmaz also paid attention to different generations of "Islamist" women in her work: Zehra Yılmaz, *Dişil Dindarlık: İslâmcı Kadın Hareketinin Dönüşümü* (Istanbul: İletişim Yayınları, 2015). The women were rarely seen as activists of right-wing politics, though.

14 "Türban," before being picked up by Turkish secularists as a derogatory term for the Islamist headscarf, referred to headgear similar to that worn by Hindu men. For more information on "turban vs. headscarf" debates, see: Çınar, *Modernity, Islam, and Secularism in Turkey*, 78–81; Korteweg and Yurdakul, *The Headscarf Debates*; Salih Bayram, "Reporting Hijab in Turkey: Shifts in the Pro- and Anti-Ban Discourses," *Turkish Studies* 10, no. 4 (2009): 511–38.

15 For information on Saylan in English, see: Daniella Kuzmanovic, "Imbued with Agency: Contesting Notions of the Extraordinariness of Türkan Saylan," in *Politics of Worship in the Contemporary Middle East*, ed. Andreas Bandak and Mikkel Bille (Leiden: Brill 2013), 171–90.

16 Nermin Abadan-Unat (1921–) is another legendary figure from this generation. For one of her publications, see: Nermin Abadan-Unat, *Women in the Developing World: Evidence from Turkey*, Monograph Series in World Affairs, 22/1 (Denver, CO: University of Denver Press, 1986). Necla Arat (1940–) is another icon for secularist women in Turkey, see: Tansu Bele, *Necla Arat, Cumhuriyet Kadının Aydınlık Yüzü* (Istanbul: Kaynak Yayınları, 2013).

17 Bayram, "Reporting Hijab in Turkey."

18 For contradictions over the images of "the village woman" in Turkey see: Emine Onaran İncirlioğlu, "Images of Village Women in Turkey: Models and Anomalies," in *Deconstructing the Images of "the Turkish Woman"* ed. Zehra F. Arat (New York: St. Martin's Press, 1998), 199–223.

19 Conservative women's efforts to distinguish themselves from "traditional" or village women generated a whole area of study on Muslim women's fashion. They are in fact too many to list here. For examples, see Barış Kılıçbay and Mutlu Binark "Consumer Culture, Islam and the Politics of Lifestyle," *European Journal of Communication* 17, no. 4 (2002): 495–511; Banu Gökarıksel and Anna Secor, " 'Even I was Tempted': The Moral Ambivalence and Ethical Practice of Veiling-Fashion in Turkey," *Annals of the Association of American Geographers* 102, no. 4 (2012): 847–62; Özlem Sandıkçı and Güliz Ger, "Veiling in Style: How Does a Stigmatized Practice Become Fashionable?" *Journal of Consumer Research* 37, no. 1 (2010): 15–36.

20 For an example see, Ayşe Böhürler, "Tu-kaka," *Yeni Şafak*, February 23, 2008. In this article, Böhürler connects the headscarf to almost anything, including one's "cultural DNA," but politics.

21 In *The Headscarf Debates*, Korteweg and Yurdakul mentioned that there is also a class dimension in the pro-secular rejection of headscarf. The authors quoted Merve Kavakçı, the first Islamist representative with a headscarf, who argued that the pro-seculars accept the headscarf when it is worn by the women who clean their houses, but not when it is worn by women who study with them at the university (Korteweg and Yurdakul, *The Headscarf Debates*, 59). Merve Kavakçı's argument seems to make sense at first glance, yet, her own classist attitude and the ways she

distinguishes herself from the poor women wearing headscarf should not go unnoticed. Kavakçı, as an upper-middle-class educated conservative woman is also in a position to employ lower-class women wearing traditional styles of headscarf to clean her house, and does not cover her hair in their style.

22 Another landmark media event during this period involved a young girl with a headscarf, Fadime Şahin. In a highly mediatized police operation to a radical group known as Aczimendis, Şahin was found together with the Aczimendi leader, making her an important actor of a sex scandal within an Islamist sect. In the following weeks, Şahin told the story of how she was deceived in numerous television interviews. As these media events heightened the fear of Islamization, the military started to send warning messages to the government. First, in a seemingly routine military tank transfer, they re-routed the tanks through Sincan, a town famous for radical Islamist activity. The Islamist groups argued that the media coverage was forged to generate reactions against them.

23 February 28 was not a "coup" in the traditional sense. The following article published in a pro-AKP newspaper talks about February 28 from the perspective of the Islamist right-wing. Yusuf Selman İnanç, "Feb. 28: A Military Coup Never to be Forgotten," *Daily Sabah*, February 27, 2014. Available online: https://www.dailysabah.com/ politics/2014/02/28/feb-28-a-military-coup-never-to-be-forgotten (accessed December 15, 2018).

24 In July 2017, Merve Kavakçı was appointed as the Turkish Ambassador to Malaysia.

25 Ruşen Çakır and Fehmi Çalmuk documented these contradictions in *Recep Tayyip Erdoğan: Bir Dönüşüm Öyküsü* (Istanbul: Metis, 2001).

26 *Cumhuriyet*, "Türkan Saylan'a İftira Belgelendi," September 12, 2015. Available online: http://www.cumhuriyet.com.tr/haber/turkiye/366745/Turkan_Saylan_a_ iftira_belgelendi.html (accessed December 15, 2018). Nil Mutluer mentioned how the Kemalist hardliners excluded Saylan because of her slogan "neither sharia nor coup" during the Republican People's Party's rallies against the AKP in 2007. Nil Mutluer, "Kemalist Feminists in the Era of the AK Party," *The Turkish AK Party and Its Leader: Criticism, Opposition and Dissent*, ed. Ümit Cizre (New York: Routledge, 2016), 40–74.

27 Mehmet Altan, Ali Bayramoğlu, Murat Aksoy, and Nazlı Ilıcak were among these journalists. Tanıl Bora in *Cereyanlar* mentions Ali Bayramoğlu as the first liberal writer who moved to the conservative newspaper *Yeni Şafak*. Ali Bayramoğlu was also the last liberal to leave the newspaper in 2016.

28 During the height of the February 28 measures that became a symbolic landmark for AKP, 42 percent of the Turkish population said there was pressure on religious Muslims and 65 percent of those who said so mentioned the headscarf. See Ali Çarkoğlu and Binnaz Toprak, *Türkiye'de Din, Toplum ve Siyaset* (Istanbul: Tesev Yayınları, 2000), 69.

29 In the 1990s, many Turkish liberals were enchanted by Bill Clinton's and Tony Blair's departure from the Left, pursuing business friendly politics. For more information on Turkey's liberal democrats see Bora, *Cereyanlar*.

30 Nilüfer Göle, *The Forbidden Modern: Civilization and Veiling* (Ann Arbor, MI: University of Michigan Press, 1996).

31 I talk about these years in more detail in: Esra Özcan, "Turkish Women in Islamism: Gender and the Mirage of 'Islamic Feminism,'" *Samyukta: A Journal of Gender and Culture* 17, no. 1 (2017): 182–92.

32 Nilüfer Göle was inspired by Shmuel Noah Eisenstadt's "multiple modernities" approach: Shmuel Noah Eisenstadt, "Multiple Modernities," *Daedalus* 129, no. 1 (2000): 1–29.

33 To be fair to Göle, with her argument, she was criticizing the Kemalists and asking them to be more inclusive and tolerant of difference. The Kemalist position saw "takiyye" behind every move by the "Islamists." Takiyye (*taqiyya* in Arabic), in this context, refers to concealing one's true intentions until the time is ready for political take-over.

34 In the media, Nuray Mert and Gülay Göktürk were among the leading female liberal democrats questioning the headscarf ban. In academia, Nilüfer Göle, Fatma Müge Göçek, Binnaz Toprak, and Yeşim Arat were influential in the debates, among other scholars.

35 Nilüfer Göle, *The Forbidden Modern*, 17.

36 I discuss this point further in Chapter 6. The use of a headscarf for fashion is a divisive issue between the current generation of pro-AKP conservative women and a younger generation of conservatives who are more at ease with seeing the headscarf just as a form of dress.

37 Metis Publishing in Istanbul produced a number of books critical of the ban and gave voices to women impacted by the ban. The socialist publication *Birikim* also provided a significant forum for women.

38 *Mahrem Exhibition* and the conference *Modern Mahrem: Islamic Veiling and Secularism* at Bilgi University in Istanbul (October 18–19, 2007) was a very good example of an intellectual, Göle in this case, helping women to gain access to public debate in prestigious forums. Three leading conservative women, Sibel Eraslan, Nihal Bengisu Karaca, and Hidayet Şefkatli Tuksal, gave talks at the conference.

39 For examples on these debates see, *Birikim*, special issue on İslam, Kadın ve Özgürleşme [Islam, Woman and Emancipation] (September 2000).

40 Conservative columnist Ayşe Böhürler situated conservative women as fighting on two fronts in numerous articles in *Yeni Şafak*: "Çevre Baskısı," June 2, 2007; "Araf," August 25, 2007; "Olduğum Gibi Görünme Hakkı İstiyorum," January 20, 2008; "Önce İlke . . . ," April 9, 2011.

41 Feyda Sayan-Cengiz criticized the ways in which "transformation" has been defined mainly in relation to consumption and fashion in the dominant literature on headscarf in Turkey: Sayan-Cengiz, *Beyond Headscarf Culture*, 43–4.

42 For some examples, see: Banu Gökarıksel and Anna Secor, " 'Even I was Tempted' "; Özlem Sandıkçı and Güliz Ger, "Veiling in Style"; Yael Navaro-Yashin, "The Market for Identities: Secularism, Islamism, Commodities," in *Fragments of Culture: The Everyday of Modern Turkey*, ed. Deniz Kandiyoti and Ayşe Saktanber (New Brunswick, NJ: Rutgers University Press, 2002), 221–53.

43 Nilüfer Göle and Ludwig Ammann (eds.), *Islam in Public: Turkey, Iran and Europe* (Istanbul: Bilgi Publishing, 2006).

44 I focus on one major example, the case of Nuray Mert, in Chapter 4 of this book.

45 Sayan-Cengiz, *Beyond Headscarf Culture*, 25–54.

46 For the relations between Alevism, Sunni Islam, and the state in Turkey see: Kabir Tambar, *The Reckoning of Pluralism: Political Belonging and the Demands of History in Turkey* (Stanford, CA: Stanford University Press, 2014).

47 Carla Kaplan, "Identity," in *Keywords for American Cultural Studies*, ed. Bruce Burgett and Glenn Hendler (New York: New York University Press, 2007), 123–7. Available online: https://keywords.nyupress.org/american-cultural-studies/essay/identity/ (accessed December 15, 2018).

48 For a discussion on the rise of authoritarian capitalism in the world, see: Peter Bloom, "Authoritarian Capitalism in Modern Times: When Economic Discipline Really Means Political Disciplining," *openDemocracy*, July 22, 2015. Available online: https://www.opendemocracy.net/can-europe-make-it/peter-bloom/authoritarian-capitalism-in-modern-times-when-economic-discipline-rea (accessed December 15, 2018).

49 According to Feyda Sayan-Cengiz, the dominant literature on headscarf in Turkey, with its emphasis on politics of difference, neglected the structural influences on women's choices to wear the headscarf: Sayan-Cengiz, *Beyond Headscarf Culture*, 50–2.

50 The feminist magazine *Pazartesi* is a good example for that. Aynur İlyasoğlu's *Örtülü Kimlik: İslamci Kadın Kimliğinin Oluşum Öğeleri* (Istanbul: Metis Yayınları, 1994), is another attempt to establish dialogue with the Islamist women on the basis of "womanhood."

51 Handan Koç, *Muhafazakarlığa Karşı Feminizm* (Istanbul: Güldünya Yayınları, 2015). Sibel Özbudun, *Kadınlar: İslam, AKP ve Ötesi* (Ankara: Ütopya, 2016). İpek Merçil, "İslam ve Feminizm," in *Cinsiyetli Olmak: Sosyal Bilimlere Feminist Bakışlar*, ed. Zeynep Direk (Istanbul: Yapı Kredi Yayınları, 2007), 106–17.

52 I will talk about the case of a violent attack toward a woman wearing shorts in more detail in Chapter 5 of this book.

53 For more information about these debates see, Dilek Cindoğlu and Gizem Zencirci, "The Headscarf in Turkey in the Public and State Spheres," *Middle Eastern Studies* 44, no. 5 (2008): 791–806.

54 For more information on this case, see: Hilal Elver, *The Headscarf Controversy: Secularism and Freedom of Religion* (Oxford: Oxford University Press, 2012), 76–81.

55 Yeşim Arat mentions how the AKP propagates conservative interpretations of Islam that advise headscarves for girls through mandatory religious courses at the expense of alternative interpretations of Islam and alternative gender roles: Yeşim Arat, "Religion, Politics and Gender Equality in Turkey: Implications of a Democratic Paradox?" *Third World Quarterly* 31, no. 6 (2010): 874.

56 *Radikal*, "Gürsel Tekin'den Kılık Kıyafet Yönetmeliğine Tepki," September 23, 2014. Available online: http://www.radikal.com.tr/politika/gursel-tekinden-kilik-kiyafet-yonetmeligine-tepki-1214403/ (accessed December 15, 2018). Gürsel Tekin, the CHP's Secretary General at the time, argued that "our religion" requires religious practice to be a conscious decision.

57 The case of Sevan Nişanyan, a famous atheist, exemplifies this point. Nişanyan faced hostility in a television program hosted on a secular media channel by the secular journalist Enver Aysever: "Ateizm ve Dinler Sevan Nişanyan Aykırı Sorular." Available online: https://www.youtube.com/watch?v=qqxKzbPpnA0&t=800s (accessed December 15, 2018).

Chapter 3: Transformation of the Representations of the Headscarf in Religious and Secular Newspapers

1 *Cumhuriyet*, "Şüküfe H. Türkiyede ilk kadın hukuk Dr.u," December 11, 1928 (11 Kanunuevvel 1928), front page. This is one of the first issues of *Cumhuriyet* that appeared in Latin alphabet.

2 *Cumhuriyet*, "Manken kizlar," December 26, 1928, 3.

3 Ali Gevgilili, "Türkiye Basını," *Cumhuriyet Dönemi Türkiye Ansiklopedisi*, Vol. 1 (Istanbul: İletişim Yayınları, 1983), 222.

4 Ayşe Esra Özcan, "Visualization of Gender in the Turkish Press: A Comparative Analysis of Six Turkish Newspapers," IRC-Library (Bremen: Information Resource Center der Jacobs University Bremen, 2010). Available online: https://opus.jacobs-university.de/frontdoor/index/index/docId/279 (accessed December 8, 2018).

5 Ibid., 119.

6 Ibid.

7 Ibid., 150.

8 For women's representation in the news worldwide, see: Margaret Gallagher, *Who Makes the News? Global Media Monitoring Project 2005* (London: WACC, 2005). Available online: http://cdn.agilitycms.com/who-makes-the-news/Imported/reports_2005/gmmp-report-en-2005.pdf (accessed December 18, 2018). Margaret Gallagher, Amie Joof, Nidya Pesántez, and Mindy Ran, *Who Makes the News? Global*

Media Monitoring Project 2010 (London: WACC, 2010) Available online: http://cdn.
agilitycms.com/who-makes-the-news/Imported/reports_2010/global/gmmp_
global_report_en.pdf (accessed December 18, 2018). Sarah Macharia, *Who Makes
the News? Global Media Monitoring Project 2015* (London: WACC, 2015). Available
online: http://cdn.agilitycms.com/who-makes-the-news/Imported/reports_2015/
global/gmmp_global_report_en.pdf (accessed December 18, 2018).

9 Women were not represented as news subjects as often as men, they were depicted
either as sex objects or as wives and mothers. See Olcay E. İmamoğlu, Yeşim (Yasak)
Gültekin, Bahar Köseoğlu, and Afife Çebi, "Representation of Women and Men in
Turkish Newspapers," *Journal of Human Sciences* 9, no. 2 (1990): 57–67; Ayşe
Saktanber, "Women in the Media in Turkey: The Free, Available Woman or the Good
Wife and Selfless Mother," in *Women in Turkish Society: A Reader*, ed. Şirin Tekeli
(Atlantic Heights, NJ: Zed Books, 1991), 154; MEDIZ—Women's Media Watch
Group, *End to Sexism in the Media* (Istanbul: Çağın Matbaacılık, 2008). Available
online: http://www.bianet.org/bianet/medya/107742-mediz-raporu-medyada-
yonetimde-olmayan-kadin-haberlerde-nesne (accessed December 18, 2018); Hülya
Uğur Tanrıöver, "Medyada Kadınların Temsil Biçimleri ve Kadın Hakları İhlalleri," in
Kadın Odaklı Habercilik, ed. Sevda Alankuş (İstanbul: IPS İletişim Vakfı Yayınları,
2007), 151–68. Available online: http://bianet.org/files/static/bia_kitaplar/
kadinodaklihabercilik.pdf (accessed December 18, 2018).

10 News about the headscarf was presented in a male-dominated framework in both
Islamist and secular newspapers: Seda Mengü, Murat Mengü, and Necla Odyakmaz,
"Ideological Formation in Turkish Newspapers: An Analysis of the News About the
Headscarf Issue," *Journal of Arab & Muslim Media Research* 2, no. 3 (2009): 223–39; Iclal
Cetin, "Veiled Representations: Political Battles Around Female Sexuality in Turkish
Print Media," *Feminist Media Studies* 10, no. 4 (2010): 409–19. Women with headscarves
were not on the front pages of Islamist newspapers even when the headscarf ban had
become a national debate, see MEDIZ, *End to Sexism in the Media*, 86.

11 Yeşim Arat, "Feminism and Islam: Considerations on the Journal Kadın ve Aile," in
Women in Modern Turkish Society, ed. Şirin Tekeli (London: Zed Books, 1991),
66–78. Feride Acar, "Women in the Ideology of Islamic Revivalism in Turkey: Three
Islamic Women's Journals," in *Islam in Modern Turkey: Religion, Politics and
Literature in a Secular State*, ed. Richard Tapper (London: I.B. Tauris, 1991), 280–303;
Songül Sallan Gül and Hüseyin Gül, "The Question of Women in Islamic Revivalism
in Turkey: A Review of the Islamic Press," *Current Sociology* 48, no. 2 (2000): 1–26.

12 Acar, "Women in the Ideology of Islamic Revivalism," 286–7; Gül and Gül, "The
Question of Women," 20.

13 Nuran Hortaçsu and Elvan Melek Ertürk, "Women and Ideology: Representations of
Women in Religious and Secular Turkish Media," *Journal of Applied Social
Psychology* 33, no. 10 (2003): 2034.

14 Ibid.

15 Gallagher, *Who Makes the News?* 52; İmamoğlu et al., "Representation of Women and Men," 61.

16 Salih Bayram used a keyword search in his study of discourses on headscarf. Salih Bayram, "Reporting Hijab in Turkey: Shifts in the Pro- and Anti-Ban Discourses," *Turkish Studies* 10, no. 4 (2009): 511–38.

17 Paul Messaris and Abraham Linus, "The Role of Images in Framing News Stories," in *Framing Public Life: Perspectives on Media and Our Understanding of the Social World*, ed. Stephen D. Reese, Oscar H. Gandy, and August E. Grant (Mahwah, NJ: Lawrence Erlbaum Associates, 2001), 220.

18 Stuart Hall, "The Determinations of News Photographs" in *The Manufacture of News: Social Problems, Deviance and the Mass Media*, ed. Stanley Cohen and Jock Young (London: Constable, 1982), 234, original emphasis.

19 Trischa Goodnow, "Using Narrative Theory to Understand the Power of News Photographs," in *Handbook of Visual Communication: Theory, Methods and Media*, ed. Ken Smith, Sandra Moriarty, Gretchen Barbatsis, and Keith Kenney (Mahwah, NJ: Lawrence Erlbaum Associates, 2005), 360–1.

20 Özcan, "Visualization of Gender in the Turkish Press."

21 Ibid., 149.

22 Ibid., 153.

23 Ali Çarkoğlu and Binnaz Toprak, *Değişen Türkiye'de Din, Toplum ve Siyaset* (Istanbul: Tesev Yayınları, 2006), 24. The authors reported the percentage of women who did not wear headscarf on the street.

24 Özcan, "Visualization of Gender in the Turkish Press," 157.

25 For qualitative content analysis see Margrit Schreier, *Qualitative Content Analysis in Practice* (London: Sage, 2012).

26 Kaitlynn Mendes, " 'Feminism Rules! Now, Where's My Swimsuit?' Re-evaluating Feminist Discourse in Print Media 1968–2008," *Media, Culture & Society* 34, no. 5 (2012): 558.

27 Wikipedia categorized *Hürriyet* as "center-left" and *Sabah* as "center-right." These two newspapers, particularly before 2008, are very similar to each other in terms of content. It is hard to argue they represent different political positions.

28 August 2012 was the last month available to users in the library when I collected the data in January 2013.

29 Gevgilili, "Türkiye Basını," 220.

30 Ibid., 222.

31 Ibid., 220.

32 Hürriyet sold 423,974 copies a day in 1975. In 1983 the newspaper sold 738,053 copies a day. See Bülent Özükan, "Basında Tirajlar," *Cumhuriyet Dönemi Türkiye Ansiklopedisi*, Vol. 1 (Istanbul: İletişim Yayınları, 1983), 232 (Table 4).

33 News announcing Özkök's departure from his position: *Sabah*, "Ertuğrul Özkök, Hürriyet'in Genel Yayın Yönetmenliği'nden ayrıldı," December 30, 2009. Available online: http://www.sabah.com.tr/ekonomi/2009/12/30/ertugrul_ozkok_hurriyetin_genel_yayin_yonetmenliginden_ayrildi (accessed December 18, 2018).

34 Bia Haber Merkezi, "Demirören Yazılı Basında Birinci Sıraya Yükseliyor," March 23, 2018. Available online: http://bianet.org/bianet/siyaset/195466-demiroren-yazili-basinda-birinci-siraya-yukseliyor (accessed December 18, 2018).

35 Bia Haber Merkezi, "Vatan ve Milliyet, Demirören-Karacan'a Satıldı," April 21, 2011. Available online: http://bianet.org/bianet/medya/129424-vatan-ve-milliyet-demiroren-karacan-a-satildi (accessed December 18, 2018).

36 Hıfzı Topuz, *Türk Basın Tarihi* (Istanbul: Remzi Kitabevi, 2003), 287.

37 *Hürriyet*, "TMSF Atv ve Sabah'a El Koydu," April 2, 2007. Available online: http://www.hurriyet.com.tr/tmsf-atv-ve-sabaha-el-koydu-6248828 (accessed December 18, 2018).

38 Media Ownership Monitor, Turkey, 2017. Available online: http://turkey.mom-rsf.org/en/owners/companies/detail/company/company/show/kalyon-group/ (accessed December 18, 2018).

39 Media Ownership Monitor, Turkey, 2017. Available online: http://turkey.mom-rsf.org/en/media/detail/outlet/yeni-safak/ (accessed December 18, 2018).

40 Hilâl Kaplan mentioned these names in her last article in *Yeni Şafak*: Hilâl Kaplan, "Benim için Yeni Şafak," *Yeni Şafak*, February 23, 2015.

41 For more information on Ali Bayramoğlu's departure see: *Cumhuriyet*, "Ali Bayramoğlu Yeni Şafak'tan ayrıldı: Beklentilerinizi karşılayamam," September 21, 2016. Available online: http://www.cumhuriyet.com.tr/haber/turkiye/603063/Ali_Bayramoglu_Yeni_Safak_tan_ayrildi__Beklentilerinizi_karsilayamam.html (accessed December 18, 2018).

42 Media Ownership Monitor, Turkey, 2017. Available online: http://turkey.mom-rsf.org/en/owners/individual-owners/detail/owner/owner/show/nuri-albayrak/ (accessed December 18, 2018).

43 Media Ownership Monitor, Turkey, 2017. Available online: http://turkey.mom-rsf.org/en/owners/companies/detail/company/company/show/albayrak-media-group/ (accessed December 18, 2018).

44 *Yeni Şafak*, "Beyaz Saray'ın bize karşı olduğu yalan," August 22, 2002, 10 (photo caption).

45 Metin Gurcan, "Theory or Attitude? A Comparative Analysis of Turkish Newspaper Articles on Turkish Foreign Policy, June 2008–June 2011," *Turkish Studies* 14, no. 2 (2013): 354.

46 There is an extensive academic literature on Fethullah Gülen movement. Among others, see: Berna Turam, *Between Islam and the State: The Politics of Engagement* (Stanford, CA: Stanford University Press, 2007).

47 Topuz, *Türk Basın Tarihi*, 294.

48 See Hakkı Taş and Meral Uğur, comparing Zaman's editorial cartoons with the cartoons in secular newspapers *Milliyet* and *Cumhuriyet*: Hakkı Taş and Meral Uğur, "Roads "Drawn" to Modernity: Religion and Secularism in Contemporary Turkey," *PS: Political Science and Politics* 40, no. 2 (2007): 311–14.

49 For an example see *Zaman*'s issue on July 22, 2005.

50 Nevval Sevindi and Nuriye Akman are other famous female journalists from the liberal democratic camp who wrote for *Zaman*.

51 *Zaman*'s distribution was based on subscription in addition to the sales at the newsstand. In 2005 *Zaman* had a disagreement over its circulation with the Turkish branch of the International Federation of Audit Bureau of Circulations (IFABC). This led to a lawsuit and eventually ended with the closure of the bureau in Turkey. Journalists from the secular media argued that *Zaman*'s figures were fake.

52 The fluctuations in *Sabah* may be partially explained by the change of ownership.

53 For examples on visual research see: Gunther Kress and Theo van Leeuwen, *Reading Images: The Grammar of Visual Design*, 2nd edn (Abingdon: Routledge, 2006); Gillian Rose, *Visual Methodologies: An Introduction to the Interpretation of Visual Materials* (London: Sage, 2001); Shahira Fahmy, "Picturing Afghan Women: A Content Analysis of AP Wire Photographs During the Taliban Regime and After the Fall of the Taliban Regime," *Gazette: The International Journal for Communication Studies* 66, no. 2 (2004): 91–112; Michael Griffin, "Picturing America's 'War on Terrorism' in Afghanistan and Iraq," *Journalism* 5, no. 4 (2004): 381–402; Michael Emmison and Philip Smith, *Researching the Visual: Images, Objects, Contexts and Interactions in Social and Cultural Inquiry* (London: Sage, 2000); Marion G. Müller and Esra Özcan, "The Political Iconography of Muhammad Cartoons: Understanding Cultural Conflict and Political Action," *PS: Political Science and Politics* 40, no. 2 (2007): 287–92.

54 *Yeni Şafak*, "Cem: Halk Vicdanına Göre Oy Kullanacak," November 2, 2002, 12.

55 *Zaman*, "Bu Belediyeye Para Verme, Kanalizasyonu da Sen Yap," June 5, 2011, 11.

56 *Hürriyet*, "Hopa'ya Geldim Ama Eşkiya Göremedim," June 11, 2011, front page. For the image (from an angle different from the print version), see: http://fotogaleri. hurriyet.com.tr/galeridetay/47810/2/1/kilicdaroglu-metin-lokumcunun-evini-ziyaret-etti (accessed December 8, 2018).

57 *Zaman*, "Yaşasın Demokrasi," June 11, 2011, 18–19.

58 *Zaman*, "Demokrasinin Bayramı," June 12, 2011, front page.

59 *Sabah*, "Avrupa Kapılarına Şarkılarla Dayandık," October 28, 2002, 2.

60 Ibid.

61 *Zaman*, "Sezen Aksu Brüksel'de Türkiye'yi Tanıttı," October 29, 2002, front page.

62 Series by Savaş Ay, "Kasımpaşa'dan İktidara," first article published in *Sabah* on November 5, 2002.

63 *Sabah*, "Sümeyye Erdoğan: Shakira Dinlerim Kimse Bana Karışmaz," November 8, 2002, 18.

64 *Sabah*, "Babamla Çatır Çatır Tartışırım," November 9, 2002, 18.

65 Ibid.

66 *Sabah*, "Eşimden Şüphelenirsem Kıskanç Biri Olabilirim," November 5, 2002, 17. For the original interview see Ruşen Çakır and Fehmi Çalmuk, *Recep Tayyip Erdoğan: Bir Dönüşüm Öyküsü* (Istanbul: Metis Yayınları, 2001).

67 Sevilay Yükselir, "Emine Erdoğan: Hakkımı Helal Etmiyorum!" *Sabah*, November 28, 2010. Available online: https://www.sabah.com.tr/yazarlar/yukselir/2010/11/28/emine_erdogan_hakkimi_helal_etmiyorum (accessed December 18, 2018). *Habertürk*, "Türkiye'nin Tartıştığı Kadının Öyküsü," December 21, 2006. Available online: http://www.haberturk.com/gundem/haber/9830-turkiyenin-tartistigi-kadinin-oykusu (accessed December 18, 2018).

68 Yükselir, "Emine Erdoğan: Hakkımı Helal Etmiyorum!"

69 *Hürriyet*, "İran'da Kız Öğrenci Alarmı," October 3, 2002, 23. *Hürriyet*, "İran'da Kadınlara Üniversite Yasağı," August 23, 2012, 12.

70 *Hürriyet*, "Taşlanmaktan Kurtuldu," October 30, 2002, front page.

71 *Hürriyet*, "'İyi Eş Yatakta İtaatkâr ve Fahişe Olabilmeli,'" June 5, 2011, 9.

72 *Sabah*, "İranlılar İç Çamaşırı Kuyruğuna Girdi!" November 8, 2002, 10. For a similar story see: *Hürriyet*, "İran Polisi Türk Fuarını Bastı," July 16, 2007, 4.

73 *Yeni Şafak*, "Suudi Kadınlar Direksiyonda," June 18, 2011, 9.

74 *Zaman*, "Dualar Dile Geldi," July 22, 2007, 13.

75 *Hürriyet*, "Duayı Yanlış Okuyunca İmamın Hışmına Uğradı," July 19, 2007, 3.

76 *Hürriyet*, "İki Yıl Okula Gitti, ÖSS'de 839. Oldu," July 21, 2007, 6.

77 *Sabah*, "Bizi Tutsaklıktan Kurtardınız," October 29, 2002, 10.

78 *Hürriyet*, "İki Yıl Okula Gitti, ÖSS'de 839. Oldu."

79 *Yeni Şafak*, "Türkiye'de Okuyamadı, İngiltere'de Birinci Oldu," July 19, 2007, 10.

80 *Zaman*, "Tuvalden Kaleme Namaz Hikayeleri," Friday supplement, June 10, 2011, 4.

81 Işıl Cinmen, "Nişantaşı'ndaki Başörtülü Ressam," *Habertürk*, July 21, 2014. Available online: https://www.haberturk.com/kultur-sanat/haber/972027-nisantasindaki-basortulu-ressam (accessed December 18, 2018).

82 Berna Turam, *Gaining Freedoms: Claiming Space in Istanbul and Berlin* (Stanford, CA: Stanford University Press, 2015).

83 Şemsinur B. Özdemir, "Yurtdışında Mezun Oldular Türkiye'de Tören Yapacaklar," *Zaman*, August 22, 2002, front page and page 2. Also see Şemsinur B. Özdemir, "Üniversiteyi Yurtdışında Bitiren Başörtülüler Başarılarını Kutladı," *Zaman*, August 24, 2002, 6.

84 Sevim Şentürk, "Kadınlar Eve mi Dönüyor?" *Zaman Pazar*, June 12, 2011, 11.

85 News about "kermes" activities is an example for that. Kermes is a typical female philanthropic activity. It is used for fundraising by selling women's traditional

handwork. For a typical story see: *Zaman*, "Yardım Etmek Huzur Veriyor," October 29, 2002, 19.

86 Zehra Yılmaz, *Dişil Dindarlık: İslâmcı Kadın Hareketinin Dönüşümü* (Istanbul: İletişim Yayınları, 2015), 13–31.

87 Ibid., 27. On AKP's neoliberal policies and gender also see: Saniye Dedeoglu and Adem Yavuz Elveren (eds.), *Gender and Society in Turkey: The Impact of Neoliberal Policies, Political Islam and EU Accession* (London: I.B. Tauris, 2012).

88 Sibel Özbudun, *Kadınlar, İslam, AKP ve Ötesi* (Ankara: Ütopya, 2016), 222.

89 For more information on this magazine, see: Feyda Sayan-Cengiz, "Eroding the Symbolic Significance of Veiling? The Islamic Fashion Magazine *Âlâ*, Consumerism, and the Challenged Boundaries of the 'Islamic neighborhood,'" *New Perspectives on Turkey* 58 (2018): 155–78.

90 Feyda Sayan-Cengiz, *Beyond Headscarf Culture in Turkey's Retail Sector* (Basingstoke: Palgrave Macmillan, 2016).

91 *Yeni Şafak*, "Çiftçiye Destek Ödemesi Başlıyor," October 30, 2002, 7.

92 *Yeni Şafak*, "Yoksulun Sofrasında Peynir Kırık, Ekmek Bayat," October 27, 2002, 7.

93 *Yeni Şafak*, "ATO'dan İki Bin Aileye Gıda Yardımı," November 2, 2002, 8.

94 These visits became very popular and were imitated by other politicians in the party.

95 The *iftar* meal marks the end of the fasting day.

96 *Yeni Şafak*, "İlk İftar Gecekonduda," November 7, 2002, front page and page 13.

97 *Yeni Şafak*, "İşte Tayyip Bebek," July 29, 2007, 11.

98 *Yeni Şafak*, "Kübra'dan Elinizi Çekin," June 6, 2011, front page.

99 *Yeni Şafak*, "Kübramızı Rahat Bırakın," June 6, 2011, 15.

100 *Yeni Şafak*, "İşte Tayyip Bebek," July 29, 2007, 11.

101 Both columnists have been writing in the newspaper at least since 1999. Their columns are available online from 1999 onward.

102 To compare the location of Albayrak's columns in 2002 and 2012, see: *Yeni Şafak*, October 31, 2002, 19 vs. *Yeni Şafak*, August 4, 2012, 15. To compare Barbarosoğlu's columns in 2002 and 2011, see: *Yeni Şafak*, November 1, 2002, 16 vs. *Yeni Şafak*, June 15, 2011, 11.

103 Merve Sena Kılıç, "Başarımın Arkasında Babam ve Türk Silahlı Kuvvetleri Var," *Yeni Şafak Pazar*, June 12, 2011, 8. Other conservative female writers with pictures in my sampling are Emeti Saruhan, Naz Emel Koç, and Cemile Ağaç.

104 Büşra and Kübra Sönmezışık, "Hizmet Ehlinin Aleviliğine Sünniliğine Bakılmaz," *Yeni Şafak Pazar*, June 5, 2011, 6.

105 Özcan, "Visualization of Gender in the Turkish Press," 187.

106 Advertisement for *İkiz Aynası* [*Twin Mirror*], *Yeni Şafak*, June 5, 2011, 24.

107 Advertisements for *Orta Kuşak* and *Muhalif*, *Yeni Şafak*, August 23, 2012, 21.

108 Gülizar Baki, "Ekranların Başarılı Spikeri Orsem Ertingü: Çocukluk Hayallerim Gerçekleşti," *Zaman*, Saturday supplement, June 18, 2011, 4.

109 By liberal-left, I mean those sectors of the Left (mostly the liberal democrats) who were against the headscarf ban.

110 Ayşe Arman, "Siz Şeytan Değilsiniz Biz de Melek Değiliz," *Hürriyet*, August 27, 2006. Available online: http://www.hurriyet.com.tr/siz-seytan-degilsiniz-biz-de-melek-degiliz-4984921 (accessed December 19, 2018).

111 Ertuğrul Özkök, "Sevişmenin Anadili," *Hürriyet*, July 29, 2007, 19.

112 Nihal Bengisu Karaca, "Bir mütesettirin tatil güncesi," *Radikal*, August 11, 2007. Available online: http://www.radikal.com.tr/hayat/bir-mutesettirin-tatil-guncesi-867464/ (accessed December 19, 2018).

113 Mücahit Bilici, "İslam'ın Brozlaşan Yüzü: Caprice Hotel Örnek Olayı," in *İslam'ın Yeni Kamusal Yüzleri*, ed. Nilüfer Göle (Istanbul: Metis Yayınları, 2000), 216–37.

114 For an example see: Ayşe Özyılmazel, "Anlat Nihal Hanım Anlat!" *Sabah*, August 27, 2007. Available online: https://www.sabah.com.tr/yazarlar/gunaydin/ozyilmazel/2007/08/27/anlat_nihal_hanim_anlat (accessed December 19, 2018).

115 Media observers in Turkey widely believe that *Taraf* had the Gülenists' financial support. The newspaper played a critical role in the Ergenekon trials against the military establishment.

116 Ertuğrul Özkök, "Şu Kadınların Adını Bir Yana Yazın," *Hürriyet*, January 15, 2010. Available online: http://www.hurriyet.com.tr/su-kadinlarin-adini-bir-yana-yazin-13483058 (accessed December 19, 2018).

117 Ertuğrul Özkök, "Modern Mahrem Gerçekten Sokağa Çıkıp Halkın Arasına Karıştı mı?" *Hürriyet*, November 11, 2012. Available online: http://www.hurriyet.com.tr/modern-mahrem-gercekten-sokaga-cikip-halkin-arasina-karisti-mi-21897745 (accessed December 19, 2018). Ertuğrul Özkök, "En Etkili 10 Başı Örtülü Kadın," *Hürriyet*, November 12, 2012. Available online: http://www.hurriyet.com.tr/en-etkili-10-basi-ortulu-kadin-21903539 (accessed December 19, 2018). Ertuğrul Özkök, "Başı Örtülü Kadın Aşkı İhmal mı Etti," *Hürriyet*, November 13, 2012. Available online: http://www.hurriyet.com.tr/basi-ortulu-kadin-aski-ihmal-mi-etti-21911485 (accessed December 19, 2018).

118 Ertuğrul Özkök, " 'Eski Kafa'da Yeni Kafa Bir Mülakat," *Hürriyet*, June 7, 2013. Available online: http://www.hurriyet.com.tr/eski-kafada-yeni-kafa-bir-mulakat-23451173 (accessed December 19, 2018). Ertuğrul Özkök, "Muhafazakâr Kadın da Kadınmış," *Hürriyet*, June 9, 2013. Available online: http://www.hurriyet.com.tr/muhafazak-r-kadin-da-kadinmis-23465667 (accessed December 19, 2018).

119 Özkök, "Muhafazakâr Kadın da Kadınmış."

120 Özkök, "Muhafazakâr Kadın da Kadınmış."

121 For one of the articles indicating a crack between conservative women and liberal democrats see: Ayşe Böhürler, "Muhalif Dostlarım!" *Yeni Şafak*, January 9, 2010. I cover the case of Nuray Mert in Chapter 4 of this book.

122 For example, Hilâl Kaplan's article on ISIS was among the headlines of *T24*, a secular liberal online newspaper, following an ISIS attack. See: T24, "Hilâl Kaplan: DAEŞ, 'kontrolden çıkan' ülkeleri 'terbiye etmek' için kullanılan bir kırbaca benziyor!" July 8, 2016. Available online: http://t24.com.tr/haber/hilal-kaplan-daes-kontrolden-cikan-ulkeleri-terbiye-etmek-icin-kullanilan-bir-kirbaca-benziyor,349025 (accessed December 19, 2018).

123 Ertuğrul Özkök mentioned Ayşe Böhürler and Nihal Bengisu Karaca in his list of "the most influential ten women wearing headscarf."

124 Nihal Bengisu Karaca, "Varlık Sebebin 'Şeriat Tehlikesi' Olursa . . . ," *Habertürk*, October 17, 2010.

125 For an example, showing Nihal Bengisu Karaca interviewing Ahmet Davutoğlu, then the minister of foreign affairs, during a trip to Qatar, see: Nihal Bengisu Karaca, "Özrü ABD'ye Bağlamak Aşağılık Kompleksidir," *Habertürk*, March 27, 2013. Journalists critical of AKP are kept out foreign trips by using accreditation procedures.

126 Hilâl Kaplan, "Kılıçdaroğlu'nun 'Ana' Muhalefeti," *Yeni Şafak*, April 29, 2011.

127 Hilâl Kaplan, "Dost musun Düşman mısın?" *Yeni Şafak*, April 15, 2012. Hilâl Kaplan, "Kafesteki Hrant Dink," *Yeni Şafak*, January 18, 2013. Hilâl Kaplan, "Adalet Talebimiz Var!" *Yeni Şafak*, March 11, 2012.

128 "Cumhurbaşkanı Erdoğan, A Haber Gündem Özel'de Soruları Yanıtladı / 30 Temmuz 2016," https://www.youtube.com/watch?v=yJ9yvTE9lr0&t=58s (accessed December 19, 2018).

129 For internet trolling and an incident that involved Hilâl Kaplan, see: Ergin Bulut and Erdem Yörük, "Digital Populism: Trolls and Political Polarization of Twitter in Turkey," *International Journal of Communication* 11 (2017): 4093–117.

130 For Böhürler's television programs in her own words see, Ayşe Böhürler, "Kutuplaşsak mı Kutuplaşmasak mı?" *Yeni Şafak*, April 4, 2009. Ayşe Böhürler, "Her Evden Somali'ye Bir İftar," *Yeni Şafak*, July 30, 2011.

131 For more information on this referendum see Berk Esen and Şebnem Gümüşçü, "A Small Yes for Presidentialism: The Turkish Constitutional Referendum of April 2017," *Journal South European Society and Politics* 2, no. 3 (2017): 303–26.

132 Indeed, on March 14, 2018, Ayşe Çavdar, a scholar who closely observes the AKP's policies and writes a column in the oppositional online newspaper *Artı Gerçek*, published an article analyzing conservative women's ongoing support for Erdoğan. Ayşe Çavdar, "Erdoğan Neyi Güncelliyor?" *Artı Gerçek*, March 14, 2018. Available online: https://www.artigercek.com/erdogan-neyi-guncelliyor?t=1521020412 (accessed December 8, 2018). Hilâl Kaplan and Ayşe Böhürler gave partisan support to AKP during the June 24, 2018 elections. Nihal Bengisu Karaca tried to find an objective position by trying to address a number of criticisms.

Chapter 4: The Rise of the Conservative Female Journalist and the Mainstreaming of the Headscarf

1 Hilâl Kaplan, "Allah Var ve O'nun Gazabından Korkun," *Yeni Şafak*, April 22, 2011.

2 Hilâl Kaplan, "Kavga Etme Hürriyeti," *Yeni Şafak*, May 13, 2011.

3 Hilâl Kaplan, "Üsame ve Mavi Marmara," *Yeni Şafak*, May 4, 2011.

4 Hilâl Kaplan, "Atatürklü Demokrasi Olur mu?" *Yeni Şafak*, November 6, 2011. Hilâl Kaplan, "Yol Ayrımımız İdeolojik Değildir Ağbiler," *Yeni Şafak*, December 16, 2011.

5 Hilâl Kaplan, "Erdoğan: Türkiye'nin Surları," *Sabah*, August 30, 2017. Available online: https://www.sabah.com.tr/yazarlar/hilalkaplan/2017/08/30/erdogan-turkiyenin-surlari (accessed December 8, 2018).

6 Hilâl Kaplan, "248 Kez EVET," *Sabah*, April 14, 2017. Available online: https://www.sabah.com.tr/yazarlar/hilalkaplan/2017/04/14/248-kez-evet (accessed December 8, 2018).

7 Nihal Bengisu Karaca, "Ajan Provakatöre Gerek Yok Heveskarlık da Aynı Sonucu Doğurur," *Habertürk*, March 19, 2010.

8 Nihal Bengisu Karaca, "Başbakanın Milli Söylemleri İşin Kolayına Kaçmak mı?" *Habertürk*, April 22, 2014.

9 For an analysis on conservative women's novels see: Kenan Çayır, *Islamic Literature in Contemporary Turkey: From Epic to Novel* (New York: Palgrave, 2007). Elifhan Köse, *Sessizliği Söylemek* (Istanbul: İletişim Yayınları, 2012).

10 D. Beybin Kejanlıoğlu, Çağla Kubilay, and Nalan Ova, "Islamist Columnists Discussing 'Women in the Public Sphere': A Discourse Analysis of the Turkish Press," *Middle East Journal of Culture and Communication* 5, no. 3 (2012): 282–301. Yeşim Arat, "Islamist Women and Feminist Concerns in Contemporary Turkey," *Frontiers* 37, no. 3 (2016): 125–50.

11 Arat, "Islamist Women and Feminist Concerns."

12 Nihal Bengisu Karaca, "Mevzu Demokrasi ise 'Baraj' Teferruat Değildir," *Habertürk*, March 26, 2010. Nihal Bengisu Karaca, "Biz Hiç Mutabık Olmadık," *Habertürk*, March 15, 2010. Nihal Bengisu Karaca, "Yeni Medya ve Handikapları," *Habertürk*, February 17, 2012. Karaca's writing had numerous references to "pluralism" in 2010.

13 Nihal Bengisu Karaca, "İyi Dediniz, Demokrasi 'Her Şeye Rağmen' İşliyor," *Habertürk*, March 19, 2014. Nihal Bengisu Karaca, "Gezi Ruhu," *Habertürk*, June 3, 2014. Nihal Bengisu Karaca, "Demokrasiye Küresel Test: Sandık," *Habertürk*, August 4, 2013.

14 Nihal Bengisu Karaca, "Hangi Esmanın Aynasısın?" *Habertürk*, January 15, 2012. Arat analyzed this particular piece in detail as an example of "feminist interpretation of Islam." Arat, "Islamist Women and Feminist Concerns," 138.

15 Nihal Bengisu Karaca, "Siyasette 'Anne'nin Yeri ve Önemi," *Habertürk*, March 10, 2010.

16 Arat, "Islamist Women and Feminist Concerns," 135.

17 Ayşe Böhürler, "Haysiyet Cellatlığı," *Yeni Şafak*, December 7, 2013.

18 Ayşe Böhürler, "Frenk Armudu Gibi: Laiklik," *Yeni Şafak*, April 30, 2016.

19 Deniz Kandiyoti, "The Travails of the Secular: Puzzle and Paradox in Turkey," *Economy and Society* 41, no. 4 (2012): 525–6.

20 Ayşe Böhürler, "Ayrımcılık Din Kisvesi Altında Kutsanabilir mi?" *Yeni Şafak*, November 25, 2006. Ayşe Böhürler, "Hem Müslüman, Hem Düşman ...," *Yeni Şafak*, August 15, 2009.

21 Hilâl Kaplan, "'Ape Musa'nın Acısı," *Yeni Şafak*, March 25, 2011.

22 Hilâl Kaplan, "Çevrenin Merkeze Yürüyüşü," *Yeni Şafak*, June 15, 2011.

23 Ayşe Böhürler, "AK Parti'nin Tehlikeli Kurucuları," *Yeni Şafak*, September 22, 2012.

24 Ayşe Böhürler, "13. Yılın Ardından," *Yeni Şafak*, August 16, 2014; Nihal Bengisu Karaca, "Hasar Raporu," *Habertürk*, June 19, 2013.

25 Ayşe Böhürler, "Ezberden İtirazlar ...," *Yeni Şafak*, January 26, 2008.

26 Ayşe Böhürler, "Sağduyu," *Yeni Şafak*, December 28, 2013.

27 Nihal Bengisu Karaca, "27 Nisan: Başlangıç," *Habertürk*, April 27, 2012. Nihal Bengisu Karaca, "Tahliyelerin Anlamı Ne?" *Habertürk*, March 12, 2014. Hilâl Kaplan, "Çıraklıktan Ustalığa Ak Parti'nin Asabiyesi," *Yeni Şafak*, May 18, 2011.

28 Eric Louw, *Media and Political Process*, 2nd edn (London: Sage, 2010).

29 Ayşe Böhürler, "Yazı Yazmak Nedir?" *Yeni Şafak*, March 16, 2013.

30 Ayşe Böhürler, "Vicdanımızın Kör Noktaları," *Yeni Şafak*, November 12, 2011.

31 Ayşe Böhürler, "Kürt Meselesinde Maço İttifak," *Yeni Şafak*, July 3, 2010.

32 Nihal Bengisu Karaca, "Ayarsız Türkiye'nin Abartılı Metaforu: Hitler," *Habertürk*, May 7, 2010. Defending Erdoğan against the accusations of dictatorship is a regular trope in Nihal Bengisu Karaca's columns in *Habertürk*: "Bakla Yağmuru," July 14, 2013; "Diktatörlük Çok Güzel, Gelsene!" July 31, 2013; "Diktatör Dediğin Haddini Bilmeli," October 18, 2013; "'Tayyip İstifa' Meşru Bir Talep midir?" June 30, 2013; "Futbol Sadece Futbol Değilmiş Sahi ...," September 27, 2013; "İyi Dediniz, Demokrasi 'Her Şeye Rağmen' İşliyor," March 19, 2014.

33 Nihal Bengisu Karaca, "Üç Çocuk, Bol Meyve, Çok Demeç ...," *Habertürk*, July 23, 2010.

34 Hilâl Kaplan criticized the infantilization of citizens in relation to Atatürk: Hilâl Kaplan, "Atamızı anıyoruz," *Yeni Şafak*, November 11, 2012.

35 The Blue Marmara (or Mavi Marmara) incident refers to a military operation by Israel against the ship *Blue Marmara* that carried humanitarian aid to the Gaza Strip.

36 Karaca, "Üç Çocuk, Bol Meyve, Çok Demeç ...."

37 Hilâl Kaplan, "Hitler ve Obama," *Yeni Şafak*, October 5, 2011.

38 Hilâl Kaplan, "Atatürk Diktatördür," *Yeni Şafak*, April 16, 2012.

39 Hilâl Kaplan, "Abdülhamit ve Erdoğan," *Sabah*, June 3, 2016. Available online: https://www.sabah.com.tr/yazarlar/hilalkaplan/2016/06/03/abdulhamit-ve-erdogan (accessed December 8, 2018).

40 Hilâl Kaplan, "Ümmeti Birleştirmek Farz, Bölmek Haramdır," *Yeni Şafak*, May 20, 2012.

41 Nihal Bengisu Karaca, "Siyasetçiler Düşünerek Konuşursa Gazeteciler Çok Sıkılır," *Habertürk*, December 4, 2009.

42 Nihal Bengisu Karaca, "Üç Çocuk, Bol Meyve, Çok Demeç . . . ," *Habertürk*, July 23, 2010.

43 Nihal Bengisu Karaca, "Kongre, Manifesto ve 'Üslup,' " *Habertürk*, September 28, 2012.

44 Nihal Bengisu Karaca, "Başbakan Neden Hoş Göremiyor," *Habertürk*, November 12, 2010.

45 Ibid.

46 Nihal Bengisu Karaca, "Koşun Koşun, Taraf'a Çakmak Serbest Olmuş . . . ," *Habertürk*, December 3, 2010.

47 Karaca, "Kongre, Manifesto ve 'Üslup.' "

48 Ayşe Böhürler, "Hep Yeni Bir Erdoğan," *Yeni Şafak*, September 17, 2011. Ayşe Böhürler, "Kan Uyuşmazlığı," *Yeni Şafak*, January 14, 2012. She praised Gül and Erdoğan for always remaining the same in their essence.

49 Ayşe Böhürler, "Çankaya," *Yeni Şafak*, September 20, 2014.

50 Ayşe Böhürler, "Cahiller ve Bedri Baykam," *Yeni Şafak*, September 4, 2010. Ayşe Böhürler, "Ezberden İtirazlar . . . ," *Yeni Şafak*, January 26, 2008.

51 Nihal Bengisu Karaca, "Savcı Davasına Sahip Çıksın," *Habertürk*, April 23, 2009.

52 Nihal Bengisu Karaca, " 'Evet'in Arzusu, 'Hayır'ın Kabusu," *Habertürk*, August 18, 2010. Nihal Bengisu Karaca, " 'Evet' çünkü . . . ," *Habertürk*, September 8, 2010.

53 Ayşe Böhürler, "AK Parti," *Yeni Şafak*, June 14, 2008.

54 Ayşe Böhürler, "Barışçıl Cevaplar . . . ," *Yeni Şafak*, August 4, 2007.

55 Nihal Bengisu Karaca, "Gecikmiş Açılımın Travması Pek Olurmuş," *Habertürk*, June 25, 2010. Ayşe Böhürler, "Düşman Olmak İstemiyoruz," *Yeni Şafak*, June 9, 2007.

56 Ayşe Böhürler, "Bir Gazeteci Siyasete Girerse Gör Başına Neler Gelir!" *Yeni Şafak*, May 29, 2010.

57 Ayşe Böhürler, "Kitap Var, Kitap Var!" *Yeni Şafak*, November 7, 2009.

58 Nihal Bengisu Karaca, " 'Ucube,' " *Habertürk*, January 12, 2011.

59 Nihal Bengisu Karaca, "Çifte Standart: Vekilse Mubah Akademisyense Suçlu," *Habertürk*, January 16, 2016.

60 *Makul* (reasonable) or *mutedil* (moderate) are the terms that women often use.

61 Ayşe Böhürler, "Merhaba," *Yeni Şafak*, October 28, 2006. Ayşe Böhürler, "Kırmızı Çizgiler," *Yeni Şafak*, March 15, 2008. Ayşe Böhürler, "Elalem Korkusu!" *Yeni Şafak*, December 27, 2008. Ayşe Böhürler, "Demokles'in Kılıcı!" *Yeni Şafak*, April 19, 2008.

62 Ayşe Böhürler, "Pilavdan Dönenin Kaşığı Kırılsın," *Yeni Şafak*, August 11, 2007.

63 Böhürler, "Kitap Var, Kitap Var!"

64 Ayşe Böhürler, "Türk Kadını Rejime Karşı Kim Koruyacak!" *Yeni Şafak*, May 12, 2007.

65 Ayşe Böhürler, "Kadınlar Üzerinden Siyaset, Güzellik, Gençlik Faşizmi!" *Yeni Şafak*, December 30, 2006; Ayşe Böhürler, "Filistinlileri Savunan İsrailli Avukat," *Yeni Şafak*, February 24, 2007; Ayşe Böhürler, "28 Şubat En Çok Kadınları Vurdu," *Yeni Şafak*, March 3, 2007; Ayşe Böhürler, "Gazeteciliği Kim Öğretti?" *Yeni Şafak*, October 10, 2009.

66 Ayşe Böhürler, "Yeni Bir Laiklik Anlayışına İhtiyaç Var," *Yeni Şafak*, December 21, 2013.

67 Berk Esen and Sebnem Gumuscu, "Rising Competitive Authoritarianism in Turkey," *Third World Quarterly* 37, no. 9 (2016): 5.

68 For more information on broadcasting in Kurdish see: Ece Algan, "Local Broadcasting as Tactical Media: Exploring Practices of Kurdish Activism and Journalism in Turkey," *Middle East Journal of Culture and Communication* (in press, 2018).

69 Hilâl Kaplan, "Siyasette Her Şey Olabilir," *Yeni Şafak*, April 6, 2011.

70 Hilâl Kaplan, " 'İyi Çocuk'lara Kötü Haber," *Yeni Şafak*, April 17, 2011.

71 Nihal Bengisu Karaca, "Hak Talebi Ne Zamandan Beri 'Pazarlık' Oldu," *Habertürk*, April 15, 2011.

72 Kaplan, " 'İyi Çocuk'lara Kötü Haber."

73 Böhürler was critical too, but not as often. For one of her articles criticizing the party for failing to fulfill its promise of more democracy see: Ayşe Böhürler, "Gündem Yorgunuyuz," *Yeni Şafak*, February 11, 2012.

74 Hilâl Kaplan, "Çıraklıktan Ustalığa AK Parti'nin Asabiyesi," *Yeni Şafak*, May 18, 2011. Nihal Bengisu Karaca, "Aradığınız Adreste Böyle Bir Halk Bulunamadı," *Habertürk*, January 21, 2011. Nihal Bengisu Karaca, "O Kazanacak Çünkü . . . ," *Habertürk*, June 1, 2011.

75 Karaca, " 'Ucube.' "

76 Hilâl Kaplan, "BDP'nin Oyları Neden Arttı?" *Yeni Şafak*, June 17, 2011.

77 Ayşe Böhürler, "Hiç Bir Cinayet Karanlık Dehlizlerde Kaybolmaz," *Yeni Şafak*, January 21, 2012.

78 Nihal Bengisu Karaca, "Mavi Marmaya'ya İkinci Hücum," *Habertürk*, September 14, 2011.

79 Nihal Bengisu Karaca, "Darbe Tehdidiyle Demokrasi İmal Etmek," *Habertürk*, September 26, 2012. Nihal Bengisu Karaca, "Diktatör Dediğin Haddini Bilmeli," *Habertürk*, October 18, 2013.

80 Ayşe Böhürler, "Bayramda Ev Sohbetleri," *Yeni Şafak*, October 27, 2012.

81 Ayşe Böhürler, "Sanatlı mı Bu İş Şimdi?" *Yeni Şafak*, November 24, 2012.

82 Nihal Bengisu Karaca, "Evlad'ı Fatihan'ın Sultanahmet'i Katli Caiz midir?" *Habertürk*, October 23, 2011. Nihal Bengisu Karaca, "Kars'ta Hassasiyet İstanbul'da Reel Politika," *Habertürk*, January 14, 2011. Nihal Bengisu Karaca, "Şehrin Emek'leri," *Habertürk*, December 25, 2011.

83 Kaplan, "BDP'nin Oyları Neden Arttı?"

84 Hilâl Kaplan, "İçişleri Bakanına Birkaç Soru," *Yeni Şafak*, December 19, 2011.

85 Hilâl Kaplan, "Kişi Kültü Olarak Atatürk ve Erdoğan," *Yeni Şafak*, May 30, 2012.

86 Nihal Bengisu Karaca, "İleri Demokrasi mi, İleri Müteahhitlik mi?" *Habertürk*, April 17, 2011.

87 Karaca, "Kars'ta Hassasiyet İstanbul'da Reel Politika."

88 Ibid.

89 Nihal Bengisu Karaca, " 'Korkuyorum Şekerim'den 'Korkuyorum Anne'ye … ," *Habertürk*, March 9, 2011.

90 Böhürler, "Gündem Yorgunuyuz." Hilâl Kaplan, "Nefret Söylemi, Müslümanlar ve İfade Özgürlüğü," *Yeni Şafak*, October 5, 2012. Hilâl Kaplan, "Özür Diliyorum," *Yeni Şafak*, January 1, 2012. Hilâl Kaplan, "Hükümetin Uludere'ye Yaklaşımı," *Yeni Şafak*, January 4, 2012. Hilâl Kaplan, "Kaçakçılık ve İstismar," *Yeni Şafak*, January 6, 2012.

91 Hilâl Kaplan, "Ak Parti'nin Demokratlığı," *Yeni Şafak*, July 30, 2012. Hilâl Kaplan, "Zulüm ve AK Parti," *Yeni Şafak*, February 3, 2012.

92 Hilâl Kaplan, "Savcı Sarıkaya Değil Yalçınkaya Olsaydı," *Yeni Şafak*, February 22, 2012.

93 Nihal Bengisu Karaca, "Ya Sonra," *Habertürk*, June 3, 2011.

94 Ibid.

95 Nihal Bengisu Karaca, "Böyle Giderse Türkler Ülkeyi Böler," *Habertürk*, June 7, 2013.

96 For an extensive analysis of the protests, see: Umut Özkırımlı (ed.), *The Making of a Protest Movement in Turkey: #occupygezi* (New York: Palgrave Macmillan, 2014).

97 Hilâl Kaplan, "Sivil Darbe Nasıl Olur?" *Yeni Şafak*, July 1, 2013. Hilâl Kaplan, " 'Öteki Mahalle'nin Yardıma İhtiyaci Var," *Yeni Şafak*, June 24, 2013. Nihal Bengisu Karaca, "Gezi'den Gayrı!" *Habertürk*, June 9, 2013.

98 Nihal Bengisu Karaca, "Taksim, Tahrir ve Fabrika Ayarlarına Dönüş … ," *Habertürk*, July 5, 2013.

99 Ayşe Böhürler, "Orantısız Güven," *Yeni Şafak*, June 8, 2013. Nihal Bengisu Karaca, "Samimi Müşteki, Organize Müfteri," *Habertürk*, June 5, 2013.

100 Nihal Bengisu Karaca, "Orantısız Mesaj," *Habertürk*, June 12, 2013. Nihal Bengisu Karaca, "Orantısız Efsane," *Habertürk*, June 14, 2013.

101 Nihal Bengisu Karaca, "Böyle Giderse Türkler Ülkeyi Böler," *Habertürk*, June 7, 2013.

102 Nihal Bengisu Karaca, "Diktatör Dediğin Haddini Bilmeli," *Habertürk*, October 18, 2013.

103 Nihal Bengisu Karaca, "Bitmedi," *Habertürk*, June 16, 2013.

104 Nihal Bengisu Karaca, "Hasar Raporu," *Habertürk*, June 19, 2013. Karaca, "Böyle Giderse Türkler Ülkeyi Böler." Nihal Bengisu Karaca, "Millet Olabilmek," *Habertürk*, June 21, 2013.

105 Gene Sharp, *From Dictatorship to Democracy: A Conceptual Framework for Liberation* (East Boston, MA: Albert Einstein Institution, 1994). A later edition was published in 2012, a year before the Gezi protests.

106 Karaca, "Bitmedi."

107 Ayşe Böhürler, "Git Artık Kolum Tutuldu!—Gitti Elhamdulillah!" *Yeni Şafak*, February 12, 2011.

108 Ayşe Böhürler, "Gezi'de Gördüklerim," *Yeni Şafak*, June 15, 2013.

109 Ayşe Böhürler, "Gururumuz İncindi," *Yeni Şafak*, June 22, 2013.

110 Nihal Bengisu Karaca, "'Başörtülü Yazarlar' Meselesi" *Habertürk*, July 21, 2013.

111 Nihal Bengisu Karaca, "Saklı Sevinç," *Habertürk*, April 3, 2013. Hilâl Kaplan had also listed the accomplishments of the government on removing the ban in an article: Hilâl Kaplan, "Başörtüsü Yasağında Neredeyiz?" *Yeni Şafak*, January 27, 2013.

112 Elif Çakır, "Başbakan Erdoğan'ın 'Yerlerde Sürüklediler' Dediği Anne Star'a Konuştu," *Star*, June 13, 2013. Available online: https://www.star.com.tr/guncel/basbakan-erdoganin-yerlerde-surukslediler-dedigi-anne-stara-konustu-haber-762093/ (accessed May 8, 2019).

113 Nihal Bengisu Karaca, "Gelin," *Habertürk*, February 16, 2014.

114 Ibid.

115 İsmet Berkan and Balçiçek İlter faced severe criticism for supporting Elif Çakır's story. Both of them apologized when the recordings were published. Hazal Özvarış (interview with İsmet Berkan), "'Radikal Yaşayabilirdi, En Büyük Sorun Gazetecilerde, Beceremedik,'" *T24*, June 24, 2014. Available online: http://t24.com.tr/haber/radikal-yasayabilirdi-en-buyuk-sorun-gazetecilerde-beceremedik,262158 (accessed December 8, 2018). Balçiçek İlter, "Kabataş," *Türkiye*, February 15, 2014. Available online: https://www.turkiyegazetesi.com.tr/yazarlar/balcicek-ilter/578235.aspx (accessed December 8, 2018).

116 Nihal Bengisu Karaca, "Kırık Bir 'Recm' Hikayesi," *Habertürk*, May 9, 2010.

117 Nihal Bengisu Karaca, "'Tayyip İstifa' Meşru Bir Talep midir?" *Habertürk*, June 30, 2013. Nihal Bengisu Karaca, "Hasar Raporu," *Habertürk*, June 19, 2013. Nihal Bengisu Karaca, "'Kapı Duvar' Devletten, 'Kapıları Açan' Devlete," *Habertürk*, October 2, 2013.

118 Nihal Bengisu Karaca, "Gezi Ruhu," *Habertürk*, June 3, 2014. Karaca, "Hasar Raporu."

119 Karaca, "Gezi Ruhu."

120 Nihal Bengisu Karaca, "Kutuplaşma Değil Mutabakat Var," *Habertürk*, February 5, 2014.

121 Nihal Bengisu Karaca, "Acımadı ki!" *Habertürk*, December 8, 2010. Nihal Bengisu Karaca, "Yumurta ve Yumurtlama," *Habertürk*, December 10, 2010.

122 Karaca, "Hasar Raporu." Nihal Bengisu Karaca, "#Diren Çözüm Süreci!" *Habertürk*, June 28, 2013. Nihal Bengisu Karaca, "Millet Olabilmek," *Habertürk*, June 21, 2013.

123 Nihal Bengisu Karaca, " 'Musaddık'laştırma Planı," *Habertürk*, September 19, 2010. Nihal Bengisu Karaca, " 'Evet'in İntikamı: Yargıtay'ın Tahliye Rövanşı," *Habertürk*, January 7, 2011. Here Karaca refers to an intelligence, "that justifies all the means to produce results against the government."

124 Nihal Bengisu Karaca, "Asıl Hedef Suriye mi?" *Habertürk*, August 22, 2012.

125 Ayşe Böhürler, "Türkiye'nin Başı Dönerken Ak Saçlılar Dinlenmeli," *Yeni Şafak*, January 4, 2014.

126 Nihal Bengisu Karaca, " 'Evet' Çünkü . . . ," *Habertürk*, September 8, 2010. Nihal Bengisu Karaca, " 'Evet'in Arzusu 'Hayır'ın Kabusu," *Habertürk*, August 18, 2010.

127 Ayşe Böhürler, "Cahiller ve Bedri Baykam," *Yeni Şafak*, September 4, 2010. Ayşe Böhürler, "Demokrasi Engeli: Ne İdüğü Belirsiz Halk," *Yeni Şafak*, September 11, 2010.

128 With some exceptions. According to Nil Mutluer the reformist branch of Kemalist women were against the headscarf ban. See Nil Mutluer, "Kemalist Feminists in the Era of the AK Party," *The Turkish AK Party and Its Leader: Criticism, Opposition and Dissent*, ed. Ümit Cizre (New York: Routledge, 2016), 53.

129 At the end of the 1990s, Göle had called the Islamist writers the counter-elites. See Nilüfer Göle, "Secularism and Islamism in Turkey: The Making of Elites and Counter-Elites," *The Middle East Journal* 51, no. 1 (1997): 46–58.

130 Ayşe Böhürler, "Türban Tartışmalarının Yan Faydaları!" *Yeni Şafak*, March 8, 2008.

131 Ayşe Böhürler, "Türkiye'de Farklı Olmak," *Yeni Şafak*, December 20, 2008.

132 Ayşe Böhürler, "Türkiye'de Farklı Olmak," *Yeni Şafak*, December 20, 2008.

133 Ayşe Böhürler, "Oyunuzun Kıymetini Bilin," *Yeni Şafak*, March 29, 2014.

134 Ayşe Böhürler Interviews Hüsamettin Arslan: "Gezi Devrime Veda Ağıtıdır," *Yeni Şafak*, March 28, 2014.

135 Hilâl Kaplan, " 'Modern Mahrem'den "İslami Teröristler'e," *Yeni Şafak*, April 9, 2012.

136 Nihal Bengisu Karaca, "Vicdanı Sömürgeleştirilmiş," *Habertürk*, October 21, 2015. Nihal Bengisu Karaca, "İttifakı Tanıyalım," *Habertürk*, June 11, 2014.

137 Ayşe Böhürler, "Zihin İşgaline Direnmek," *Yeni Şafak*, January 1, 2011. In this piece Böhürler referred to Frantz Fanon as an author who helped Islamists like her resist Western thought. Even though Turkey was never officially colonized, references to anti-colonialist theorists is common in women's writing.

138 Nihal Bengisu Karaca, "Birlik ya da Beraberlik," *Habertürk*, October 8, 2009. She defined belonging to the same religion as "the spiritual core of this geography" ("bu coğrafyanın ruhsal mayası").

139 Ayşe Böhürler, "Müslüman Olmaktan Utanıyor muyuz?" *Yeni Şafak*, September 29, 2007.

140 Ayşe Böhürler, "Tu-Kaka," *Yeni Şafak*, February 23, 2008.

141 Nihal Bengisu Karaca, "Liberal Vesayet mi?" *Habertürk*, September 18, 2011.

142 Hilâl Kaplan, "Profesyonel Müslüman ve İman," *Yeni Şafak*, November 21, 2011.

143 Nihal Bengisu Karaca, "Rövanşizmin Panzehiri Başörtüsü Yasaklarını Kaldırmaktır," *Habertürk*, February 27, 2010.

144 Hilâl Kaplan, "Bir İslamsızlaştırma Hamlesi Olarak 1915," *Yeni Şafak*, April 23, 2012.

145 In a rather exceptional article, Karaca defended the nonbelievers' right to be buried as they wish: Nihal Bengisu Karaca, "Ölüm Tarzı," *Habertürk*, August 26, 2011.

146 Ayşe Böhürler, "Frenk Armudu Gibi: Laiklik," *Yeni Şafak*, April 30, 2016.

147 Nihal Bengisu Karaca, "Zorbalık," *Habertürk*, April 1, 2012.

148 *Bianet*, "Dindar Gençlik Yetiştirmek İstiyoruz," *BIA Ankara News Desk*, February 1, 2012. Available online: https://bianet.org/english/din/135875-dindar-genclik-yetistirmek-istiyoruz (accessed December 8, 2018).

149 For an example of these discussions continued into 2015 see: Yılmaz Murat Bilican, "Hükümetin Zorunlu Din Dersi İnadı," *T24*, February 21, 2015. Available online: http://t24.com.tr/yazarlar/yilmaz-murat-bilican/hukumetin-zorunlu-din-dersi-inadi,11310 (accessed December 8, 2018).

150 Karaca, "Zorbalık."

151 Nihal Bengisu Karaca did not support the Kurd's demands to receive education in Kurdish. Nihal Bengisu Karaca, "Takvim Savaşları," *Habertürk*, November 9, 2012.

152 Hilâl Kaplan, "4+4+4'e Muhalifler Neden Kaybetti?" *Yeni Şafak*, April 1, 2012.

153 Gamze Bal, "İçki İmalatı Eve Taşındı: 50 Liraya 10 Şişe Rakı," *Cumhuriyet*, October 21, 2017. Available online: http://www.cumhuriyet.com.tr/haber/ekonomi/850034/icki_imalati_eve_tasindi__50_liraya_10_sise_raki.html (accessed December 8, 2018).

154 Hülya Özmen Karabağlı, "Meclis'te Alkolsüz Resepsiyon," *Gazete Duvar*, October 1, 2016. Available online: https://www.gazeteduvar.com.tr/politika/2016/10/01/mecliste-alkolsuz-resepsiyon/ (accessed December 8, 2018).

155 *Hürriyet Daily News*, "Turkey's Main Opposition CHP Seeks Probe into 'Alcohol in Mosque' Gezi protest claim," December 9, 2013. Available online: http://www.hurriyetdailynews.com/turkeys-main-opposition-chp-seeks-probe-into-alcohol-in-mosque-gezi-protest-claim-59301 (accessed December 8, 2018).

156 Ayşe Böhürler, "İki Taraf-Tek Mantık," *Yeni Şafak*, May 17, 2008.

157 Nihal Bengisu Karaca, "Hani Bir Kadeh Rakı Hayal Oluyordu," *Habertürk*, April 25, 2009.

158 Hilâl Kaplan, "Alkol Riyakarlığı," *Yeni Şafak*, May 26, 2013.

159 Ayşe Böhürler, "Türkiye'nin Sekülerliği," *Yeni Şafak*, January 13, 2007.

160 Nihal Bengisu Karaca, " 'Tayyip İstifa' Meşru Bir Talep Midir?" *Habertürk*, June 30, 2013.

161 Esen and Gumuscu talked about three waves of mass firings of critical journalists, Esen and Gumuscu, "Rising Competitive Authoritarianism," 1591. Liberal democrats' firings/departure from conservative newspapers preceded these waves and signaled what was to come.

162 Ayşe Böhürler, "AK Parti Seçmeni," *Yeni Şafak*, January 22, 2011.

163 Ayşe Böhürler, "Havlama Hürriyeti," *Yeni Şafak*, January 29, 2011.

164 Ibid.

165 Nuray Mert was hired by *Cumhuriyet*, the voice of the Kemalist constituents in 2015. This uneasy partnership ended in 2017 when Mert questioned the seculars' criticisms of the legislation that granted legally binding status to marriages performed by muftis and religious officials. *Cumhuriyet*'s readers celebrated the firing of Mert, whom they had long regarded as responsible for strengthening Islamism and the AKP in Turkey.

166 Nuray Mert, " 'Mertlik' Meselesi," *Milliyet*, June 4, 2011. Available online: http://www.milliyet.com.tr/yazarlar/nuray-mert/-mertlik--meselesi-1398572/ (accessed December 8, 2018).

167 Ibid.

168 Nihal Bengisu Karaca, "İki Zalimden Birini Seçmek Zorunda mıyız?" *Habertürk*, June 10, 2011.

169 Nihal Bengisu Karaca, "Yeni Medya ve Handikapları," *Habertürk*, February 17, 2012.

170 Ayşe Böhürler, "Ergenekon'a AİHM Darbesi," *Yeni Şafak*, February 18, 2012.

171 The first article is: Hilâl Kaplan, "Yeni Kandil Muhipleri," *Yeni Şafak*, July 24, 2011. Also see: Hilâl Kaplan, "Halis Niyetlerle …," *Yeni Şafak*, July 27, 2011. Hilâl Kaplan, "Masum Değiliz Hiç Birimiz," *Yeni Şafak*, July 29, 2011.

172 Kaplan, "Yeni Kandil Muhipleri—2," July 25, 2011.

173 For a later example see: Nihal Bengisu Karaca, "İttifakı Tanıyalım," *Habertürk*, June 11, 2014.

174 Kaplan, "Yeni Kandil Muhipleri—2."

175 Hilâl Kaplan, " 'Bay Vijdan' ve Saz Arkadaşları," *Yeni Şafak*, August 17, 2011.

176 Hilâl Kaplan, "Yeni Kandil Muhipleri," *Yeni Şafak*, July 24, 2011.

177 Kaplan, "Yeni Kandil Muhipleri—2."

178 Hilâl Kaplan, "Hedef Göstermeyi Hafifletenlere Cevap," *Yeni Şafak*, August 21, 2011.

179 Hilâl Kaplan, "Ji Bo Min Nekuje! Ji Bo Min Nemire!" *Yeni Şafak*, September 28, 2011. Karaca, "İttifakı Tanıyalım."

180 For more information on the peace process see Tanıl Bora, *Cereyanlar: Türkiye'de Siyasi İdeolojiler* (Istanbul: İletişim Yayınları, 2017), 881–4.

181 Ayşe Böhürler, "Kahramanlar, Katiller …," *Yeni Şafak*, June 26, 2010. For Kaplan's articles supporting the process see: Hilâl Kaplan, "Yakarız Bu Barışı Yakarız!" *Yeni Şafak*, May 23, 2011. Hilâl Kaplan, "Milliyetçi Başbakan ve BDP," *Yeni Şafak*, November 26, 2012.

182 Hilâl Kaplan, "Ahmet Kaya ve Tayyip Erdoğan," *Yeni Şafak*, November 14, 2011. Hilâl Kaplan, "Uludere'deki Günaha Ortak Olmayın," *Yeni Şafak*, May 25, 2012. Hilâl Kaplan, "Dokunulmazlıkları Kaldırmak 1990'Lara Dönmektir," *Yeni Şafak*, September 10, 2012. Ayşe Böhürler, "Karışan İzler," *Yeni Şafak*, December 31, 2011.

183 Hilâl Kaplan, "Kürtlerin Izdırabı, Müslümanlar ve Fethullah Gülen," *Yeni Şafak*, October 28, 2011. Hilâl Kaplan, "Üniter Devlet İslam'ın Şartı mıdır?" *Yeni Şafak*, May 14, 2012. Hilâl Kaplan, "Müslüman Kürtler Ne İster?" *Yeni Şafak*, November 21, 2012.

184 Kaplan, "Ahmet Kaya ve Tayyip Erdoğan." Kaplan, "Uludere'deki Günaha Ortak Olmayın." Kaplan, "Dokunulmazlıkları Kaldırmak 1990'lara Dönmektir." Böhürler, "Karışan İzler."

185 Hilâl Kaplan, "Özür Diliyorum," *Yeni Şafak*, January 1, 2012. Hilâl Kaplan, "Hükümetin Uludere'ye Yaklaşımı," *Yeni Şafak*, January 4, 2012. Hilâl Kaplan, "Kaçakçılık ve İstismar," *Yeni Şafak*, June 1, 2012.

186 Bora, *Cereyanlar*, 882. For more information on the Kurdish peace process, see July 2018 Special Issue of *Turkish Studies* on "Repression and Resistance—Fragments of Kurdish Politics in Turkey under the AKP Regime." Also see: Kumru F. Toktamis, "A Peace That Wasn't: Friends, Foes, and Contentious Re-entrenchment of Kurdish Politics in Turkey," *Turkish Studies* 19, no. 5 (2018): 697–722.

187 Ayşe Böhürler, "Düşman Olmak İstemiyoruz," *Yeni Şafak*, June 9, 2007. According to Böhürler, Kurdish politicians' sincerity were shadowed by their belonging. For some of the other articles that she discusses the Kurdish issue in relation to sincerity and authenticity see: Ayşe Böhürler, "Kürt Meselesini Konuşmak," *Yeni Şafak*, December 8, 2007; Ayşe Böhürler, "Barışa Çakılan Çivi," *Yeni Şafak*, June 18, 2011.

188 Hilâl Kaplan was critical of the distinction between the Good and the Bad Kurds. Hilâl Kaplan, "Kötü Başörtülüler," *Yeni Şafak*, March 27, 2011. The theme of "sincerity" did not show up in her columns during the discussion of the Kurdish issue.

189 Ayşe Böhürler, "Adilos Bebe," *Yeni Şafak*, November 8, 2008. Ayşe Böhürler, "Çocuklara Kan Sıçratmak," *Yeni Şafak*, August 18, 2012.

190 Ayşe Böhürler, "Taşın Altındaki El!" *Yeni Şafak*, June 16, 2012. Böhürler "Karışan İzler."

191 Ayşe Böhürler, "Kürt Kimliğinin Alt Başlıkları Neler?" *Yeni Şafak*, December 22, 2007. Ayşe Böhürler, "Kürt Anaları mı, Kürt Beyleri mi?" *Yeni Şafak*, August 8, 2009.

192 Kaplan, "Müslüman Kürtler Ne İster?"

193 Nihal Bengisu Karaca, "Türkiye Sizinle Utanç Duyuyor," *Habertürk*, April 14, 2010. Nihal Bengisu Karaca, "Burun Farkıyla Önde," *Habertürk*, April 16, 2010.

194 Nihal Bengisu Karaca, "Adrese Teslim . . . ," *Habertürk*, July 23, 2009.

195 Nihal Bengisu Karaca, "Dokunulur," *Habertürk*, April 30, 2016.

196 Nihal Bengisu Karaca, "Asıl Şirk 'Kürtçe'yi Putlaştırmak Değil Miydi?" *Habertürk*, December 29, 2010. Nihal Bengisu Karaca, "Demirtaş'ın Savaş Çağrısı," *Habertürk*, September 20, 2014. Nihal Bengisu Karaca, "Pek İddiali Bay Demirtaş," *Habertürk*, May 22, 2015. Nihal Bengisu Karaca, "Demirtaş'tan Gizli Erdoğan Propagandası," *Habertürk*, December 18, 2015. Karaca, "Dokunulur."

197 For the website of Academics for Peace, see: https://barisicinakademisyenler.net/ English. For their public statement in Turkish, see: "Barış İçin Akademisyenler'in 1128 İmzayla Açıkladığı Bildirinin Tam Metni," *T24*, January 16, 2016. Available online: http://t24.com.tr/haber/baris-icin-akademisyenlerin-1128-imzayla-acikladigi-bildirinin-tam-metni,324471 (accessed December 8, 2018).

198 "Hilâl Kaplan: Bu Kadar Rezil Bir Çağri Olamaz," YouTube, January 14, 2016. Available online: https://www.youtube.com/watch?v=5JBSSUVWNJM (accessed December 8, 2018).

199 Nihal Bengisu Karaca, "Çifte Standart: Vekilse Mubah Akademisyense Suçlu," *Habertürk*, January 16, 2016.

200 Ayşe Böhürler, "82 Anayasasına Evet Diyene Hayır!" *Yeni Şafak*, April 7, 2012.

201 Ayşe Böhürler, "Otoriteye Boyun Eğmek!" *Yeni Şafak*, June 12, 2010. Böhürler, "82 Anayasasına Evet Diyene Hayır!"

202 Ayşe Böhürler, "Siyaset Simyacıları," *Yeni Şafak*, July 21, 2012.

203 Ayşe Böhürler, "Kahire Konuşmasından Bu Yana . . . ," *Yeni Şafak*, September 29, 2012.

204 Böhürler, "Siyaset Simyacıları." Liberal democrats can be seen in these terms as well: they constituted the wing of the Left in Turkish politics that stood closer to the Right on a number of issues.

205 Ayşe Böhürler, "Suriye'ye Müdahaleci Bak!" *Yeni Şafak*, April 21, 2012.

206 Ayşe Böhürler, "Saatleri Ayarlama Enstitüsü," *Yeni Şafak*, October 6, 2012.

207 Hilâl Kaplan, "Sağcı Müslüman," *Yeni Şafak*, December 30, 2011.

208 Nick Tattersall, "Turkey Calls Syria Security Leak 'Villainous,' Blocks YouTube," *Reuters*, March 27, 2014. Available online: https://www.reuters.com/article/us-syria-crisis-turkey/turkey-calls-syria-security-leak-villainous-blocks-youtube-idUSBREA2Q17420140327 (accessed December 9, 2018).

209 Gul Tuysuz and Ivan Watson, "Turkey Blocks YouTube Days After Twitter Crackdown," *CNN*, March 28, 2014. Available online: https://www.cnn.com/2014/03/27/world/europe/turkey-youtube-blocked/index.html (accessed December 9, 2018).

210 Nihal Bengisu Karaca, "Topyekun Hainlik," *Habertürk*, March 28, 2014. Nihal Bengisu Karaca, "2014 Biterken," *Habertürk*, December 28, 2014.

211 Ayşe Böhürler, "Gündem Yorgunuyuz," *Yeni Şafak*, February 11, 2012.

212 Ayşe Böhürler, "Akil İnsanlar ve Medya," *Yeni Şafak*, April 20, 2013.

213 Ayşe Böhürler, " 'Dava Arkadaşı,' " *Yeni Şafak*, October 12, 2013. Ayşe Böhürler, "Hakkı Teslim Etmek Gerekir," *Yeni Şafak*, November 29, 2014.

214 One of the leading figures of the Turkish Right, a female journalist Nazlı Ilıcak (born 1944), was a long-time ally both for the AKP and its predecessor, the Virtue Party. Ilıcak was not a religious conservative and did not wear a headscarf. Yet she became an MP from the Virtue Party in 1999 and was the strongest defender of

Merve Kavakçı. Ilıcak walked with Kavakçı into the parliament to support her during the oath-taking ceremony. Nazlı Ilıcak went to jail following the July 15, 2016 coup attempt for siding with the Gülenists after the AKP parted ways with them.

215 Feyda Sayan-Cengiz, *Beyond Headscarf Culture in Turkey's Retail Sector* (Basingstoke: Palgrave Macmillan, 2016), 50. For the original reference on romanticizing resistance see: Lila Abu-Lughod, "The Romance of Resistance: Tracing Transformations of Power Through Bedouin Women," *American Ethnologist* 17, no. 1 (1990): 41–55.

216 Ertuğrul Özkök, "Sevişmenin Anadili," *Hürriyet*, July 29, 2007, 19.

217 Hilâl Kaplan, "Müslümanlar ve Sekülerizm," *Yeni Şafak*, April 10, 2011.

218 There are conservative writers who have admitted that they found it legitimate to do *takiyye*. Nuray Mert was furious when a leading male Islamist writer admitted that the AKP always remained true to its conservative ideals and as conservatives they knew about it even when the AKP's discourse seemed to diverge from religious conservatism during the party's early years in power. Nuray Mert, "İslamcılık, Çirkin İtiraf," *Cumhuriyet*, May 8, 2017. Available online: http://www.cumhuriyet.com.tr/koseyazisi/735899/islamcilik__cirkin_itiraf.html (accessed December 9, 2018).

219 D. Beybin Kejanlıoğlu and her colleagues tried to understand women's position vis-à-vis the Kemalists in terms of a hegemonic struggle and discursive struggle. See: Kejanlıoğlu et al., "Islamist Columnists Discussing 'Women in the Public Sphere.'"

220 Nihal Bengisu Karaca, "Yetti de Arttı Bile! . . . ," *Habertürk*, October 20, 2010.

221 Thomas F. Pettigrew, "The Ultimate Attribution Error: Extending Allport's Cognitive Analysis of Prejudice," *Personality and Social Psychology Bulletin* 5 (1979): 461–76. For contemporary applications of the concept see: Bradley W. Gorham, "News Media's Relationship with Stereotyping: The Linguistic Intergroup Bias in Response to Crime News," *Journal of Communication* 56 no. 2 (2006): 289–308.

222 Ayşe Böhürler, "Çevre Baskısı," *Yeni Şafak*, June 2, 2007.

223 Ayşe Böhürler, "Önce İlke . . . ," *Yeni Şafak*, April 9, 2011.

224 Nihal Bengisu Karaca, "Parlamento Dışı Muhalefetin Yeni Adresi," *Habertürk*, June 13, 2012. Nihal Bengisu Karaca, "'Gettoların Kapılarını Açıyoruz,'" *Habertürk*, June 5, 2011. The Has Party annulled itself and joined the AKP in 2012. Its story lasted only a very short time.

225 Nihal Bengisu Karaca, "Asıl Hedef Suriye mi?" *Habertürk*, August 22, 2012.

226 Hilâl Kaplan, "Başı Açıklık, Siyasal Simgedir," *Yeni Şafak*, February 6, 2013.

227 Symbolizing "not wearing headscarf" this way can have dire consequences for women who do not wear a headscarf, particularly in an increasingly conservative

environment where not covering the hair is associated with lax morals and sexual availability. The following misogynist statement often coming from AKP members has become a disturbing remainder of misogyny toward not-religions women: "A woman without headscarf is like a house without curtains: either for rent or for sale." The conservative women in this study do not condone such statements.

Chapter 5: Loss of Sisterhood: Challenges for the Progressive Feminist Movement in Turkey

1 Elifhan Köse argues that after the 1990s, conservative women's criticisms of the male public sphere indicate a new fault line within patriarchy, rather than a break from it. Elifhan Köse, *Sessizliği Söylemek* (Istanbul: İletişim Yayınları, 2012), 9.

2 *Bianet* is funded by the European Union and has managed to escape the government's heavy hand and did not suffer from closure. Yet the site's chief editor, Nadire Mater, has faced charges because of her support for the pro-Kurdish newspaper *Özgür Gündem*.

3 Handan Koç extensively delineated the antifeminist trends in conservative men and women's writing. Handan Koç, *Muhafazakarlığa Karşı Feminizm* (Istanbul: Güldünya Yayınları, 2015). Tanıl Bora in *Cereyanlar: Türkiye'de Siyasi İdeolojiler* (Istanbul: İletişim Yayınları, 2017), 801, also reminded the readers of how Muslim women tried to refute the claims of the famous feminist Duygu Asena during the 1980s. Asena had authored a very popular book, *The Woman Has No Name* [*Kadının Adı Yok*] in 1987. A conservative female author, Şerife Katırcı, responded to Asena's book by publishing *The Muslim Woman Has a Name* in 1989. In other words, feminists have regularly faced a backlash led by conservative women.

4 Their support for conservative women distinguishes Turkey's progressive feminists from the feminists in the United States. For American feminists, it has been always clear that they do not share common ground with America's conservative women. On American feminists' position toward conservative women in the United States, see Ronnee Schreiber, *Righting Feminism: Conservative Women and American Politics* (New York: Oxford University Press, 2008).

5 Ayşe Saktanber, "Whose Virtue Is This?" In *Right-Wing Women: From Conservatives to Extremists Around the World*, ed. Paola Bacchetta and Margaret Power (New York: Routledge, 2002), 76.

6 I borrow the term "housewife populism" from Michelle M. Nickerson, *Mothers of Conservatism: Women and the Postwar Right* (Princeton, NJ: Princeton University Press, 2012), 2. Sevinç Doğan's *Mahalledeki AKP: Parti İşleyişi, Taban Mobilizasyonu ve Siyasal Yabancılaşma* (Istanbul: İletişim Yayınları, 2016), gives a lot of insight about how the AKP mobilized the housewives in lower-class neighborhoods.

7 Nesrin Tuna (Interview with Sibel Eraslan), "Ben İmanlı Feministim," *Pazartesi: Special Issue on Religion*, July–September 2007, 84, a compilation of previously published articles on religion. This interview originally appears in September 1995, issue 6.

8 *Pazartesi*, 92.

9 *Pazartesi*, 87.

10 Interview with Sibel Eraslan: *Haber Diyarbakır*, Sibel Eraslan Başörtülüleri Kızdıracak, March 1, 2011. Formerly available online: http://www.haberdiyarbakir. net/sibeleraslanbasortululerikizdiracak40699h/. The website is now defunct.

11 *Pazartesi*, 83.

12 For more information on how lower-class women navigate the connotations of headscarf and how their narratives challenge "a politics of identity frame," see Feyda Sayan-Cengiz, *Beyond Headscarf Culture in Turkey's Retail Sector* (Basingstoke: Palgrave Macmillan, 2016), 147.

13 For an example of fieldwork done in Ümraniye, one of these neighborhoods, see: Jenny White, *Islamist Mobilization in Turkey: A Study in Vernacular Politics* (Seattle, WA: University of Washington Press, 2002).

14 Aksu Bora and Asena Günal mention how, in the 1990s, feminists got outside of big cities. Aksu Bora and Asena Güral, "Önsöz," in *90'larda Türkiye'de Feminizm* (Istanbul: İletişim Yayınları, 2002), 8.

15 Şirin Tekeli's compilation, *Women in Modern Turkish Society: A Reader* (London: Zed Books, 1995) provides a very good entry point to the feminist debates during the 1980s. An earlier work with a similar title edited by Nermin Abadan-Unat, Deniz Kandiyoti, and Mübeccel Kıray, *Women in Turkish Society* (Leiden: E.J. Brill, 1981), is an invaluable resource on the feminist debates during the 1970s.

16 S. Nazik Işık, "1990'larda Kadına Yönelik Aile İçi Şiddetle Mücadele Hareketi İçinde Oluşmuş Bazı Gözlem ve Düşünceler," in *90'larda Türkiye'de Feminizm*, ed. Aksu Bora and Asena Güral (Istanbul: İletişim Yayınları, 2002), 41–72.

17 Ibid., 47.

18 Ibid., 48–9. To visit Mor Çatı, see: https://www.morcati.org.tr/en/ (accessed December 13, 2018). For feminist institutions in Turkey, also see: Ömer Çaha, *Women and Civil Society in Turkey: Women's Movements in a Muslim Society* (Farnham: Ashgate, 2013), 93–119.

19 Yeşim Arat, "Rethinking the Political: A Feminist Journal in Turkey, Pazartesi," *Women's Studies International Forum* 27, no. 3 (2004): 281–92. For earlier feminist women's magazines in Turkey, see Süheyla Kırca, "Turkish Women's Magazines: The Popular Meets the Political," *Women's Studies International Forum* 24, no. 3/4 (2001): 457–68.

20 To visit KA.DER, see: http://ka-der.org.tr/en/ (accessed December 13, 2018). See also Aksu Bora, "Bir Yapabilirlik olarak Ka-Der," *90'larda Türkiye'de Feminizm*, ed. Aksu Bora and Asena Güral (Istanbul: İletişim Yayınları, 2002), 109–24.

21 Ayşe Gül Altınay, "Bedenimiz ve Biz: Bekaret ve Cinselliğin Siyaseti," In *90'larda Türkiye'de Feminizm*, ed. Aksu Bora and Asena Güral (Istanbul: İletişim Yayınları, 2002), 324.

22 Women for Women's Human Rights, *Turkish Civil and Penal Code Reforms from a Gender Perspective: The Success of Two Nationwide Campaigns* (Istanbul: Women for Women's Human Rights, 2005), 1.

23 Ibid., 4.

24 Berrin Yenice, in a conversation, told me that she once went to a movie session that started at midnight in Beyoğlu during the 1980s. She and her sister were the only women around. That changed in the 1990s.

25 For information about Kaos GL, see: http://www.kaosgldernegi.org/belge. php?id=tarihce (accessed December 13, 2018). Please also see: Yıldız Tar, "Kaos GL 23 Yaşında!" *Bia Haber Merkezi*, September 20, 2017. Available online: http://bianet. org/bianet/lgbti/189983-kaos-gl-23-yasinda (accessed December 8, 2018). For more information on LBGT communities in Turkey, see: Eser Selen, "The Stage: A Space for Queer Subjectification in Contemporary Turkey," *Gender, Place & Culture* 19, no. 6 (2012): 730–49; Burçak Cürül and Rasim Özgür Dönmez, "Transsexuals in Turkey: Between Disciplining and Eradicating," in *Gendered Identities: Criticizing Patriarchy in Turkey*, ed. Rasim Özgür Dönmez and Fazilet Ahu Özmen (Lanham, MD: Lexington Books, 2013), 67–77. Please also see, Pınar İlkkaracan, "Democratization in Turkey from a Gender Perspective," in *Turkey's Democratization Process*, ed. Carmen Rodríguez, Antonio Ávalos, Hakan Yılmaz, and Ana I. Planet (Abingdon: Routledge, 2014), 169–71.

26 Even though the 1990s were a period of expansion for women and LGBTQ activism, this did not translate into the recognition of the Kurdish citizens' rights in Turkey. The 1990s have been remembered as one of the worst decades, during which time the government brutally suppressed Kurdish demands.

27 This phase of feminism in Turkey emerged out of the leftist movements after the 1980 military coup. Nükhet Sirman and others called it the third wave of feminism in Turkey. Nükhet Sirman, "Feminism in Turkey: A Short History," *New Perspectives on Turkey* 3 (1989): 1–34. Cagla Diner and Şule Toktaş, "Waves of Feminism in Turkey: Kemalist, Islamist and Kurdish Women's Movements in an Era of Globalization," *Journal of Balkan and Near Eastern Studies* 12, no. 1 (2010): 41–57.

28 Yeşim Arat, "Islamist Women and Feminist Concerns in Contemporary Turkey," *Frontiers* 37, no. 3 (2016): 131.

29 Women for Women's Human Rights, *Turkish Civil and Penal Code Reforms*, 14.

30 Deniz Kandiyoti, "Locating the Politics of Gender: Patriarchy, Neo-liberal Governance and Violence in Turkey," *Research on Policy on Turkey* 1, no. 2 (2016): 109. Binnaz Toprak also pointed at the gap between AKP's discourse and practice: Binnaz Toprak, *Türkiye'de Farklı Olmak* (Istanbul: Metis, 2009).

31 Doğan, *Mahalledeki AKP*, 225–37. For more information on AKP's Women's Branches also see: Zana Çitak and Özlem Tür, "Women Between Tradition and Change: The Justice and Development Party Experience in Turkey," *Middle Eastern Studies* 44, no. 3 (2008): 455–69.

32 Sibel Eraslan explicitly mentioned People's Houses in *Pazartesi* interview: "Our [Welfare Party] municipalities try to do the things that the People's Houses used to do earlier," 83. Erdoğan continued the emphasis on municipal services initiated during the Welfare Party.

33 For more information on ISMEK, see: http://ismek.ist/eng/default.aspx (accessed December 13, 2018).

34 Erdoğan's hostility toward the Turkish feminists and progressive women's rights organizations that aim to strengthen gender equality in Turkey has not been a secret. See: İlkkaracan, "Democratization in Turkey from a Gender Perspective."

35 *The Guardian*, "Turkish President Says Childless Women Are 'Deficient, Incomplete,'" June 5, 2016. Available online: https://www.theguardian.com/world/2016/jun/06/turkish-president-erdogan-childless-women-deficient-incomplete (accessed December 13, 2018).

36 Burçin Belge, "Kadınlar 'Aile ve Sosyal Politika' değil 'Eşitlik Bakanlığı' İstiyor," *BİA Haber Merkezi*, May 16, 2011. Available online: https://bianet.org/bianet/kadin/130027-kadinlar-aile-ve-sosyal-politika-degil-esitlik-bakanligi-istiyor (accessed December 13, 2018).

37 Ayşe Böhürler, "Üç Bakan, Üç Dönem," *Yeni Şafak*, July 9, 2011.

38 The AKP had an up-and-down relationship with the LGBT movement as well. The course of party's relationship with the LGBT movement is similar to that of the liberals, Kurds, and the feminists. One of the founders of Kaos GL was detained because of his social media posts in February 2018. For LGBT rights under the AKP, see Feride Acar and Gülbanu Altunok, "The 'Politics of Intimate' at the Intersection of Neo-liberalism and Neo-conservatism in Contemporary Turkey," *Women's Studies International Forum* 41 (2013): 14–23.

39 İlkkaracan, "Democratization in Turkey from a Gender Perspective," 172.

40 Bülent Arınç, "Kadın Herkesin İçerisinde Kahkaha Atmayacak," YouTube, July 29, 2014. Available online: https://www.youtube.com/watch?v=DjWpj3L3IsM (accessed December 13, 2018).

41 Ömer Tuğrul İnançer, "Hamile Kadının Sokakta Gezmesi Uygun Değildir," YouTube, July 25, 2013. Available online: https://www.youtube.com/watch?v=V5_fkRlw0lc (accessed December 13, 2018).

42 Kandiyoti, "Locating the Politics of Gender," 111.

43 Kandiyoti's analysis is also based on the same report. For the organization's website, see: http://kadincinayetlerinidurduracagiz.net/for-english (accessed December 13, 2018).

44 We will Stop Femicide Platform, "Kadın Cinayetlerini Durduracağız Platformu, 2016 Yılı Raporu," January 1, 2017. Available online: http://kadincinayetlerinidurduracagiz. net/veriler/2786/kadin-cinayetlerini-durduracagiz-platformu-2016-yili-raporu (accessed December 13, 2018). The website http://kadincinayetleri.org/ (accessed December 13, 2018) keeps a database on women's murders and the "excuses" provided by the perpetrators.

45 Didem Unal, "Vulnerable Identities: Pious Women's Columnists' Narratives on Islamic Feminism and Feminist Self-Identification in Contemporary Turkey," *Women's Studies International Forum* 53 (2015): 15.

46 In fact, women wearing the headscarf and critical toward the AKP are aware that women not wearing headscarf are becoming vulnerable. Hadiye Yolcu, a young woman with headscarf from Anti-Capitalist Muslims, said that she will be ready to fight for women not wearing the headscarf if/when that day comes. She argued that many women covered their hair during their husbands' time in the parliament as the headscarf has become a precondition to get to higher positions. Büşra Cebeci, " 'Başörtüsüzler Ayrıştırılırsa, Onları da Biz Savunacağız,' " *Bia Haber Merkezi*, February 13, 2018. Available online: https://bianet.org/bianet/toplumsal-cinsiyet/194058-basortusuzler-ayristirilirsa-onlari-da-biz-savunacagiz (accessed December 13, 2018).

47 *Bianet*, "Aggressor Who Kicked Woman For Wearing Shorts Sentenced to Prison," *BIA News Desk*, September 8, 2017. Available online: https://bianet.org/english/ women/189663-aggressor-who-kicked-woman-for-wearing-shorts-sentenced-to-prison (accessed December 13, 2018).

48 *Bianet*, "PM on Man Who Attacked Woman Wearing Shorts: He Could Have Just Mumbled to Himself," *BIA News Desk*, September 22, 2016. Available online: http:// bianet.org/english/women/178913-pm-on-man-who-attacked-woman-wearing-shorts-he-could-have-just-mumbled-to-himself (accessed December 13, 2018).

49 *Bianet*, "Metroda Kadına Tekme, Bu Sefer Bahane 'Bacak Bacak Üstüne Atmak,' " *BİA Haber Merkezi* November 30, 2016. Available online: https://m.bianet.org/bianet/ kadin/181244-metroda-kadina-tekme-bu-sefer-bahane-bacak-bacak-ustune-atmak (accessed December 13, 2018).

50 Tolga Korkut, "Kadın: Sokakta Cinsel Tacize Uğradım. Polis: Uzlaşmak İster misiniz?" *BIA News Center*, Van, Turkey, August 26, 2008. Available online: https:// bianet.org/bianet/kadin/109285-kadin-sokakta-cinsel-tacize-ugradim-polis-uzlasmak-ister-misiniz (accessed December 13, 2018).

51 Kandiyoti, "Locating the Politics of Gender," 106.

52 *Gazete Karınca*, "Kayyumların İlk Hedefi Kadın Kurumları: İşte Kapatılan 52 Kadın Merkezi," March 2, 2017. Available online: http://gazetekarinca.com/2017/03/ kayyumlarin-ilk-hedefi-kadin-kurumlari-iste-kapatilan-52-kadin-merkezi/ (accessed December 13, 2018). See also: Bianet, "Feminist Aktivist Zozan

Özgökçe Gözaltında," *Bia Haber Merkezi*, January 27, 2017. Available online: https://m.bianet.org/bianet/insan-haklari/183097-feminist-aktivist-zozan-ozgokce-gozaltinda (accessed December 13, 2018).

53 Çiçek Tahaoğlu, "Kadın Dernekleri Kapatıldı, Hangi Çalışmalar Yarıda Kaldı?" *BİA Haber Merkezi*, November 16, 2016. Available online: https://m.bianet.org/bianet/ toplumsal-cinsiyet/180798-kadin-dernekleri-kapatildi-hangi-calismalar-yarida-kaldi (accessed December 13, 2018).

54 *Gazete Karınca*, "DİHA ve JINHA Dahil 15 Yayın Kapatıldı," October 29, 2016. Available online: http://gazetekarinca.com/2016/10/diha-ve-jinha-dahil-15-yayin-kapatildi/ (accessed December 13, 2018).

55 *Bianet*, "Erdoğan: Bu Feministler Filan Var Ya . . . ," *Bia News Desk*, February 17, 2015. Available online: https://bianet.org/bianet/kadin/162367-erdogan-bu-feministler-filan-var-ya (accessed December 13, 2018).

56 Sibel Eraslan writes in the pro-government newspaper *Star* and is committed to the AKP and the Erdoğan family. See her columns for her partisanship in numerous issues. For the interview, see: Nesrin Tuna (Interview with Sibel Eraslan), "Ben İmanlı Feministim," *Pazartesi: Special Issue on Religion*, July–September 2007, a compilation of previously published articles on religion. This interview originally appears in September 1995, issue 6.

57 Handan Koç, Elifhan Köse, İpek Merçil, and Sibel Özbudun are among the writers who pointed at the antifeminism in conservative women's writings. See the references section for their work.

58 Ayşe Böhürler, "Ayrı Dünyalar Aynı Yollar," *Yeni Şafak*, November 9, 2013.

59 Ibid.

60 Ibid.

61 Ayşe Böhürler, "Demokrasi Engeli: Ne İdüğü Belirsiz Halk," *Yeni Şafak*, September 11, 2010.

62 Böhürler, "Ayrı Dünyalar Aynı Yollar."

63 Ayşe Böhürler, "Hakkı Teslim Etmek Gerekir," *Yeni Şafak*, November 29, 2014. In this article, while defending Erdoğan, Böhürler argues that Erdoğan always rejected the "women centered, aggressive language of feminist ideology," yet this did not prevent him from pursuing policies that improved women's rights.

64 Nihal Bengisu Karaca, "Fıtrat, Tekâmüle Mani midir?" *Habertürk*, November 29, 2014.

65 Pınar Tremblay, "How Erdoğan won the women's vote," *Al-Monitor*, August 19, 2014. Available online: http://www.al-monitor.com/pulse/originals/2014/08/turkey-women-akp-vote-presidential-elections.html# (accessed December 13, 2018).

66 Böhürler traveled extensively and made a documentary about women in other Muslim countries.

67 Ayşe Böhürler, "Hakkı Teslim Etmek Gerekir," *Yeni Şafak*, November 29, 2014.

68 Ayşe Böhürler, "Her Kadın Artık Milletvekili Olabilir," *Yeni Şafak*, November 2, 2013.

69 Ayşe Böhürler, "Bir Zamanlar Türkiye," *Yeni Şafak*, October 5, 2013.

70 Ibid.

71 Ayşe Böhürler, "Şark Cephesinde Kadın," *Yeni Şafak*, November 29, 2008. Ayşe Böhürler, "Ahkam Kesmek mi—Çözüm Bulmak mı?" *Yeni Şafak*, May 9, 2009. Ayşe Böhürler, "Başörtüsü Üzerinden Siyaset," *Yeni Şafak*, March 7, 2009. Ayşe Böhürler, "İki Taraf-Tek Mantık," *Yeni Şafak*, May 17, 2008.

72 Ayşe Böhürler, "İnsan mı Devlet mi?" *Yeni Şafak*, May 26, 2012.

73 Ayşe Böhürler, "AK Parti'nin Tehlikeli Kurucuları," *Yeni Şafak*, September 22, 2012. Böhürler's point conflict with research on women's roles in the AKP, at least during the party's first term. See Ayşe Gunes Ayata and Fatma Tütüncü, "Party Politics of the AKP (2002–2007) and the Predicaments of Women at the Intersection of the Westernist, Islamist and Feminist Discourses in Turkey," *British Journal of Middle Eastern Studies* 35, no. 3 (2008): 363–84. For a later study, see: Zeynep Şahin-Mencütek, "Gender Politics of the Justice and Development Party in Turkey," in *Gender, Conservatism and Political Representation*, ed. Karen Celis and Sarah Childs (Colchester: ECPR Press, 2014), 83–102.

74 Ayşe Böhürler, "AK Parti Seçmeni," *Yeni Şafak*, January 22, 2011. Ayşe Böhürler, "Seçim Mutfağı," *Yeni Şafak*, June 11, 2011. Ayşe Böhürler, "Barışa Çakılan Çivi," *Yeni Şafak*, June 18, 2011.

75 Ayşe Böhürler, "Sağduyu," *Yeni Şafak*, August 20, 2011. Ayşe Böhürler, "Teşhirde Unutulanlar," *Yeni Şafak*, May 14, 2011.

76 Ayşe Böhürler, "Tepkili Olmak, Vicdanlı Olmaya Engel Degil," *Yeni Şafak*, April 18, 2009. Ayşe Böhürler, "Üç Bakan, Üç Dönem," *Yeni Şafak*, July 9, 2011.

77 Ayşe Böhürler, "Eğitimde Doğruculuk/4+4+4," *Yeni Şafak*, February 25, 2012.

78 Ayşe Böhürler refers to Betül Mardin, famous public relations guru, to support her point. According to Böhürler, Mardin complained about how her republican Kemalist father did not let her attend the university because of its mixed-gender nature, and there were no women-only universities. Instead of seeing the father as the problem, Böhürler sees the secular republican system as the problem, "as a male project that disregarded women's thoughts and feelings" by not providing gender-segregated universities: Ayşe Böhürler, "Kıyamet mi Kopar . . . ," *Yeni Şafak*, September 1, 2007. For Böhürler's writing on girls' schools also see: Ayşe Böhürler, "Harran'da Feminism," *Yeni Şafak*, April 16, 2011. Böhürler, "Ahkam Kesmek mi—Çözüm Bulmak mı?"

79 For Harran Technical and Vocational School's website, see: http://harrankml.meb.k12.tr/ (accessed December 13, 2018).

80 Ayşe Böhürler, "Ezberden İtirazlar . . . ," *Yeni Şafak*, January 26, 2008.

81 *Bianet*, "Davutoğlu'ndan 'Çeyiz Hesabı'," *Bia News Desk*, January 8, 2015. Available online: https://m.bianet.org/bianet/siyaset/161392-davutoglu-ndan-ceyiz-hesabi (accessed December 13, 2018). Haberler, "Devletten Anne Olana 4 Bin 500 Lira!"

Haberler.com, September 4, 2016. Available online: https://www.haberler.com/anne-olana-4-bin-500-lira-8752776-haberi/ (accessed December 13, 2018). *Vatan*, "Anne Olana 4 Bin 500 Lira," September 4, 2016. Available online: http://www.gazetevatan.com/anne-olana-4-bin-500-lira-983144-ekonomi/ (accessed December 13, 2018).

82 *Vatan*, "Yeni Anneye Devletten En Az 6 Bin 622 TL Maaş," September 25, 2017. Available online: http://www.gazetevatan.com/yeni-anneye-devletten-en-az-6-bin-622-tl-maas-1105060-ekonomi/ (accessed December 13, 2018).

83 Gülay Toksöz, "Yeni Aile Nüfus Yasasının Amacı Doğurganlığı Artırmak," *Bia News Desk*, February 6, 2015. Available online: https://m.bianet.org/bianet/toplum/162081-yeni-aile-nufus-yasasinin-amaci-dogurganligi-artirmak (accessed December 8, 2018). Gülay Toksöz, "Yarı Zamanlı Çalışma: İşini Kaybeden Kadınların Yerini Güvencesiz Çalışan Alacak," *Bia News Desk*, February 6, 2016. Available online: https://m.bianet.org/bianet/kadin/172146-yari-zamanli-calisma-isini-kaybeden-kadinlarin-yerini-guvencesiz-calisan-alacak (accessed December 13, 2018). Çiçek Tahaoğlu, " 'Yarı Zamanlı Çalışma, Maaşınızı ve Haklarınızı da Yarıya Düşürüyor,' " *Bia News Desk*, November 10, 2016. Available online: https://m.bianet.org/bianet/toplumsal-cinsiyet/180629-yari-zamanli-calisma-maasinizi-ve-haklarinizi-da-yariya-dusuruyor (accessed December 13, 2018).

84 Hilâl Kaplan, "Cumhurbaşkanı Erdoğan ve Kadın Hakları," *Sabah*, October 23, 2015. Available online: https://www.sabah.com.tr/yazarlar/hilalkaplan/2015/10/23/cumhurbaskani-erdogan-ve-kadin-haklari (accessed December 13, 2018).

85 İlkkaracan, "Democratization in Turkey from a Gender Perspective," 165–7.

86 Gülay Toksöz, "Kentli Kadın İstihdamı Gerçekten Artıyor mu?" *BİA Haber Merkezi*, February 3, 2014. Available online: http://bianet.org/bianet/kadin/153221-kentli-kadin-istihdami-gercekten-artiyor-mu (accessed December 13, 2018). For her work in English see, Gülay Toksöz, "The State of Female Labour in the Impasse of the Neoliberal Market and the Patriarchal Family," in *Gender and Society in Turkey: The Impact of Neoliberal Policies, Political Islam and EU Accession*, ed. Saniye Dedeoglu and Adem Yavuz Elveren (London: I.B. Tauris, 2012), 47–64.

87 Mehveş Evin, "Kadını İstihdama Katıyoruz Oyunları," *Milliyet*, June 4, 2014. Available online: http://www.milliyet.com.tr/yazarlar/mehves-evin/kadini-istihdama-katiyoruz-oyunlari-1892165/ (accessed December 13, 2018).

88 Saniye Dedeoglu and Adem Yavuz Elveren (eds.), *Gender and Society in Turkey: The Impact of Neoliberal Policies, Political Islam and EU Accession* (London: I.B. Tauris, 2012). See also work by, Sibel Özbudun, *Kadınlar: İslam, AKP ve Ötesi* (Ankara: Ütopya, 2016); Zehra Yılmaz, *Dişil Dindarlık: İslâmcı Kadın Hareketinin Dönüşümü* (Istanbul: İletişim Yayınları, 2015); Zafer Yılmaz, "Strengthening the Family Policies in Turkey: Managing the Social Question and Armoring Conservative–Neoliberal Populism," *Turkish Studies* 16, no. 3 (2015): 371–90.

89 Ayşe Böhürler, "Hakkı Teslim Etmek Gerekir," *Yeni Şafak*, November 29, 2014. Böhürler argued that there were four women's shelters when AKP came to power, and the number increased to seventy-eight.

90 Çiçek Tahaoğlu, "Polisten Şiddet Gören Kadına: 'Ben de Öldürürüm Diyorum Ama Öldürmüyorum,'" *Bia News Desk*, March 8, 2016. Available online: https://m.bianet. org/bianet/kadin/172822-polisten-siddet-goren-kadina-ben-de-oldururum-diyorum-ama-oldurmuyorum (accessed December 13, 2018).

91 Ayşe Arman, "Şimdi de Hedef Kadın Sığınma Evleri mi? Onları da Kapatınca Rahat mı Edeceksiniz?!" *Hürriyet*, June 1, 2017. Available online: http://www.hurriyet.com. tr/yazarlar/ayse-arman/simdi-de-hedef-kadin-siginma-evleri-mi-onlari-da-kapatinca-rahat-mi-edeceksiniz-40476197 (accessed December 13, 2018).

92 *T24*, "Kadın Hareketi Aktivisiti Avukat Hülya Gülbahar: Kadınlar Ne Ailede Ne de Devlette 'Reisli' Bir Yaşam İstemiyor," March 8, 2016. Available online: http://t24. com.tr/haber/kadin-hareketi-aktivisiti-avukat-hulya-gulbahar-kadinlar-ne-ailede-ne-de-devlette-reisli-bir-yasam-istemiyor,331245 (accessed December 13, 2018).

93 Berrin Sönmez, "Sığınacak Yer Bulamayan Kadınlar Ölüme Mahkum," *Gazete Duvar*, March 18, 2017. Available online: https://www.gazeteduvar.com.tr/yazarlar/ 2017/03/18/siginacak-yer-bulamayan-kadinlar-olume-mahkum/ (accessed December 13, 2018).

94 Hilâl Kaplan, "Çokeşlilik Meselesi," *Yeni Şafak*, May 29, 2011.

95 Kareem Shaheen and Gokce Saracoglu, "Turkish Marriage Law a Blow to Women's Rights, Say Activists," *The Guardian*, November 14, 2017. Available online: https:// www.theguardian.com/world/2017/nov/14/turkish-marriage-law-a-blow-to-womens-rights-say-activists (accessed December 13, 2018).

96 Ayşe Böhürler, "Muhafazakar Erkekler," *Yeni Şafak*, March 21, 2009.

97 Ayşe Böhürler, "Başörtüye Gül Takmak," *Yeni Şafak*, May 3, 2008. Ayşe Böhürler, "Hüseyin Üzmez Vakası!" *Yeni Şafak*, November 1, 2008. Ayşe Böhürler, "Başörtüsü Üzerinden Siyaset," *Yeni Şafak*, March 7, 2009. Ayşe Böhürler, "Müslüman Erkek Medyası!" *Yeni Şafak*, January 30, 2010. Ayşe Böhürler, "Tecavüzden Korunma Dini Tavsiyeler . . . ," *Yeni Şafak*, February 19, 2011. Ayşe Böhürler, "Zavallı Zalim!" *Yeni Şafak*, February 26, 2011. Ayşe Böhürler, "Bir Zamanlar Türkiye," *Yeni Şafak*, October 5, 2013. Ayşe Böhürler, "Allah Yüzünüzü Güldürsün," *Yeni Şafak*, August 2, 2014. Hilâl Kaplan, "'Muhafazakar' Erkek Tipolojisi," *Yeni Şafak*, October 19, 2011. Hilâl Kaplan, "Üstü Kalsın," *Yeni Şafak*, April 4, 2011.

98 Nihal Bengisu Karaca, "Hamile Kadınlar ve Tuğrul İnançer," *Habertürk*, August 2, 2013.

99 Ibid., translation mine.

100 Ayşe Böhürler, "Darbeleri Araştırma Komisyonunun Başında İyi ki Bir Kadın Var," *Yeni Şafak*, June 9, 2012. See also the discussion program "Yeni Bakışlar Özel—29 Mayıs 2016 (Toplumda Kadın)," from *Habertürk* television, published on YouTube,

May 30, 2016. Available online: https://www.youtube.com/watch?v=s390Bhlf0WY (accessed December 13, 2018). In the program Nihal Bengisu Karaca talked about women in Muslim society and emphasized that Muslim women see their bodies as belonging to God.

101 Many scholars pointed to this difference. For a study pointing to it, see: Köse, *Sessizliği Söylemek*. For conservative writers' stance on abortion, see: Çağla Kubilay, "İslami Muhafazakâr Kadın Yazarların Perspektifinden Kürtaj Tartışması: Eleştirel Bir Değerlendirme," *Alternatif Politika* 6, no. 3 (2014): 387–421.

102 Ayşe Böhürler, "Televizyon, Din ve Biz," *Yeni Şafak*, July 27, 2013.

103 Hilâl Kaplan, "Namussuzlar!" *Yeni Şafak*, December 30, 2012. Hilâl Kaplan, "Ağrı'da Bir Melek Öldürüldü," *Yeni Şafak*, July 29, 2012. Ayşe Böhürler, "Cami Cemaati," *Yeni Şafak*, July 4, 2009. Ayşe Böhürler, "Seçkinci Olunur mu, Doğulur mu?" *Yeni Şafak*, May 1, 2010.

104 Hilâl Kaplan, "Çokeşlilik ve Haklı Arayış," *Yeni Şafak*, May 27, 2011.

105 Feminists saw Turkey's leadership in the Istanbul Convention as a significant achievement and supported it. The Istanbul Convention was one moment where feminists and conservative women worked together to prevent violence against women. For more information on this convention see Arat, "Islamist Women and Feminist Concerns," 131–2.

106 Nihal Bengisu Karaca, "Fatma Salman'ın Şiddet Görmesi," *Habertürk*, December 9, 2012. Ayşe Böhürler, "Arz Etmek ve Değerler," *Yeni Şafak*, July 23, 2011. Hilâl Kaplan, "Özgecan'ın Babası: 'Allah'ın İpine Sarılalım'," *Yeni Şafak*, February 18, 2015.

107 Ayşe Böhürler, "Zulmü Alkışlayamam/Zalimi Asla Sevemem," *Yeni Şafak*, March 17, 2012.

108 Ayşe Böhürler, "Hakkı Teslim Etmek Gerekir," *Yeni Şafak*, November 29, 2014.

109 I have adopted this term from Kandiyoti, "Locating the Politics of Gender," 106.

110 Nihal Bengisu Karaca, "Erkek Erkeğe Açılım . . . ," *Habertürk*, August 16, 2009. The following two articles are examples from her foreign travels with Recep Tayyip Erdoğan and Ahmet Davutoğlu. Both columns included pictures showing Karaca with AKP leaders: Nihal Bengisu Karaca, "Özrü ABD'ye Bağlamak Aşağılık Kompleksidir," *Habertürk*, March 27, 2013; Nihal Bengisu Karaca, "'Ekonomik Bağımsızlığımıza Müdahale Ettirmeyiz,'" *Habertürk*, October 25, 2013.

111 Hazal Özvarış (Interview with Hidayet Şefkatli Tuksal) "'AKP'li Kadınlar Erdoğan'ı Masal Dinler Gibi Dinliyor, Parti Yönetiminde 3–5 Çocuk Doğuran Kim Var?'," *T24*, February 24, 2015. Available online: https://t24.com.tr/haber/17-25-aralik-cemaatin-hukumeti-devirme-girisimi-tapeler-dogru-teror-orgutu-suclamasi-agir,288335 (accessed December 13, 2018).

112 I have borrowed this term from Ronnee Schreiber, yet, slightly modified it. The exact phrase that she has used is "institutionalizing antifeminism." Schreiber, *Righting Feminism*, 22.

113 TÜRGEV is another organization that works toward establishing a conservative gender ideology in Turkey. In the summer of 2017, many billboards in Istanbul featured a young female student wearing the headscarf who had received a scholarship from TÜRGEV.

114 This is a familiar religious-right strategy: During the 1990s, with reference to the popular leftist café Kaktüs, the activists from the religious right opened their alternative coffee house named Kaknüs.

115 Ayşe Böhürler, "Bir Zihniyet Prototipi Olarak Kamer Genç," *Yeni Şafak*, November 30, 2013. Ayşe Böhürler, "Hakkı Teslim Etmek Gerekir," *Yeni Şafak*, November 29, 2014. Hilâl Kaplan, "Erkeksen . . . ," *Yeni Şafak*, November 27, 2013. Nihal Bengisu Karaca, "Yakup Köse İçin Adalet Tecelli Eder Mi?" *Habertürk*, November 27, 2013.

116 *Diken*, "Kadına Şiddete Karşı 'Hükümete Yakınlık Kotası' Uygulandı, 77 Örgüt Hiçe Sayıldı," December 23, 2014. Available online: http://www.diken.com.tr/kadina-siddete-karsi-hukumete-yakinlik-kotasi-uygulandi-77-orgut-hice-sayildi/ (accessed December 13, 2018).

117 Dasha Afanasieva and Jonny Hogg, "Erdogan Divides Turkish Women with Approach to Tackling Violence," *Reuters*, April 20, 2015. Available online: https://www.reuters.com/article/us-turkey-women/erdogan-divides-turkish-women-with-approach-to-tackling-violence-idUSKBN0NB15M20150420 (accessed December 13, 2018).

118 Feminists supported not only women's right to wear the headscarf at universities but also their right to hold public office, a contentious issue even within the AKP government: *T24*, "Feministlerden Başörtülü Kadınlara Destek," March 2, 2013. Available online: https://t24.com.tr/haber/feministlerden-basortulu-kadinlara-destek,224855 (accessed December 13, 2018). Böhürler had recognized support coming from *Pazartesi* magazine: Ayşe Böhürler, "AK Parti'nin Tehlikeli Kurucuları," *Yeni Şafak*, September 22, 2012.

119 Nil Mutluer pointed out how the "reformist" branch of Kemalist women, who also supported women wearing the headscarf in the 1990s, could not make sense of such claims, Nil Mutluer, "Kemalist Feminists in the Era of the AK Party," *The Turkish AK Party and Its Leader: Criticism, Opposition and Dissent*, ed. Ümit Cizre (New York: Routledge, 2016), 68, fn. 33.

120 Some LGBT groups in North America also use the term "gender justice," but this should not be confused with KADEM's usage. KADEM does not support LGBT rights.

121 YouTube channel by KADEM, "KADEM Kadın ve Demokrasi Buluşması 2 Filmi," March 6, 2017. Available online: https://www.youtube.com/watch?v=GKlbWxqh2ao (accessed December 13, 2018).

122 Schreiber, *Righting Feminism*.

123 Kristin Blakely, "Transnational Anti-Feminist Networks: Canadian Right-Wing Women and the Global Stage," in *New Perspectives on the Transnational Right*, ed.

Martin Durham and Margaret Power (New York: Palgrave Macmillan, 2010), 171–86.

124 Hilâl Kaplan, "Dindarlar Arası Diyalog," *Yeni Şafak*, October 2, 2011. In this article, Kaplan talks about her participation in a seminar organized by Liberty Fund, a radical right-wing foundation in the United States.

125 Yılmaz, *Dişil Dindarlık*, 13–31.

126 Ibid.

127 Ayşe Böhürler, "Türkiye'nin İran Üzerinde Etkisi Var mı?" *Yeni Şafak*, July 10, 2010. Nihal Bengisu Karaca, "Kadına Şiddete Karşı: TR İman ve İkna Kuvvetleri," *Habertürk*, March 8, 2013.

128 Arat, "Islamist Women and Feminist Concerns."

129 In an earlier work in 2010, Arat herself argued that AKP cadres find liberal and secular justifications for their conservative policies: Yeşim Arat, "Religion, Politics and Gender Equality in Turkey: Implications of a Democratic Paradox?" *Third World Quarterly* 31, no. 6 (2010): 869–84. In that sense, her 2010 article is much more illuminating on the topic of how conservatives utilize these arguments toward realizing their own vision of society. Arat did not extend her argument to the utilization of feminism toward conservative ends by pro-AKP women. I believe that's because of her ongoing focus on sisterhood, and her search for common ground between different groups of women.

130 For an example see the discussion program: "Yeni Bakışlar Özel—29 Mayıs 2016 (Toplumda Kadın)," from *Habertürk* television, published on YouTube, May 30, 2016. Available online: https://www.youtube.com/watch?v=s390Bhlf0WY (accessed December 13, 2018). Even if the title of the program was "Women in Society," the program approached "women in society" from a religious perspective.

131 Özbudun, *Kadınlar*, 133.

132 Arat, "Islamist Women and Feminist Concerns," 143.

133 Antonio Gramsci, *Selections from the Prison Notebooks* (London: Lawrence & Wishart, 1971). See also Steve Jones, *Antonio Gramsci* (Abingdon: Routledge, 2006) for "war of position" and "war of manoeuvre."

134 Arat, "Islamist Women and Feminist Concerns," 126.

135 Ali Çarkoğlu and Binnaz Toprak, *Türkiye'de Din, Toplum ve Siyaset* (Istanbul: Tesev, 2000). Available online: http://tesev.org.tr/wp-content/uploads/2015/11/Turkiyede_Din_Toplum_Ve_Siyaset.pdf (accessed December 8, 2018). Ali Çarkoğlu and Binnaz Toprak, *Değişen Türkiye'de Din, Toplum ve Siyaset* (Istanbul: Tesev Yayınları, 2006). Available online: http://tesev.org.tr/wp-content/uploads/2015/11/Degisen_Turkiyede_Din_Toplum_Ve_Siyaset.pdf (accessed December 13, 2018). The 2006 study is available also in English: Ali Çarkoğlu and Binnaz Toprak, *Religion, Society and Politics in a Changing Turkey*, trans. Çiğdem Aksoy Fromm, ed. Jenny Sanders (Istanbul: Tesev, 2007). Available online: http://research.sabanciuniv.

edu/5854/1/2007_08_Religon,_Society_and_Politics_in_a_Changing_Turkey.pdf (accessed December 8, 2018).

136 Çarkoğlu and Toprak, *Değişen Türkiye'de Din, Toplum ve Siyaset*, 24. The authors reported the percentage of women who do not wear the headscarf.

137 Çarkoğlu and Toprak, *Değişen Türkiye'de Din, Toplum ve Siyaset*, 26.

138 Localization of secularism does not mean undermining the violence that the secularization of Turkish society has entailed for some devout Muslims.

139 Çarkoğlu and Toprak, *Türkiye'de Din, Toplum ve Siyaset*, 16.

140 İpek Çalışlar, "'30 Yıl Sonra' Kadının Adı Yok," *Bia News Desk*, April 19, 2016. Available online: http://m.bianet.org/bianet/kadin/174010-30-yil-sonra-kadinin-adi-yok (accessed December 13, 2018).

141 For a criticism of essentialism in Turkey's feminist organizations see the interview with feminist scholar Serpil Sancar: Yasemin Akis and Ülkü Özakın (Interview with Serpil Sancar), "Türkiye'de Feminizm ve Kadın Hareketi," *Cogito*, May 16, 2009. Available online: https://bianet.org/kurdi/diger/114551-turkiye-de-feminizm-ve-kadin-hareketi (accessed December 13, 2018). For Sancar's work, see: Serpil Sancar, *Türk Modernleşmesinin Cinsiyeti: Erkekler Devlet, Kadınlar Aile Kurar* (Istanbul: İletişim Yayınları, 2014).

142 Mutluer, "Kemalist Feminists in the Era of the AK Party," in *The Turkish AK Party and Its Leader: Criticism, Opposition and Dissent*, ed. Ümit Cizre (New York: Routledge, 2016), 53.

143 Berna Turam, *Gaining Freedoms: Claiming Space in Istanbul and Berlin* (Stanford, CA: Stanford University Press, 2015), 10.

144 To avoid conceptual confusion, I would prefer the term "Kemalist hardliners" over "conservative." This branch of Kemalism is nationalist and modernist, and the term "conservative" may not be suitable to describe their position in Turkish politics.

145 Mutluer, "Kemalist Feminists in the Era of the AK Party," 45.

146 Ibid., 46.

147 The government ended the state of emergency on July 18, 2018, yet the state of emergency has become the new normal in Turkey. See: *Human Rights Watch*, "Turkey: Normalizing the State of Emergency," July 20, 2018. Available online: https://www.hrw.org/news/2018/07/20/turkey-normalizing-state-emergency (accessed December 13, 2018).

148 I do not include the Fethullah Gülen organization's clandestine network among these conservative groups critical of the government. I approach Gülenists, once close allies of the AKP, as a distinct case.

149 *Gazete Duvar*, "Ömer Faruk Gergerlioğlu'na 2,5 Yıl Hapis," February 21, 2018. Available online: https://www.gazeteduvar.com.tr/gundem/2018/02/21/omer-faruk-gergerliogluna-25-yil-hapis/ (accessed December 13, 2018).

150 Hidayet Şefkatli Tuksal, *Kadın Karşıtı Söylemin İslam Geleneğindeki İzdüşümleri* (Ankara: Kitabiyat, 2000).

151 Later, Erdoğan was heard in a leaked tape reprimanding Tuksal's editor for her critical article. Tuksal argued that her editor did not mention this conversation to her: Hidayet Şefkatli Tuksal, "Star'dan Nasıl Ayrıldım? Gerçekler ve Yalanlar," *Serbestiyet*, March 18, 2014. Available online: http://serbestiyet.com/yazarlar/hidayet-s.-tuksal/stardan-nasil-ayrildim-gercekler-ve-yalanlar-131780 (accessed December 13, 2018). See also: *Radikal*, "Hidayet Şefkatli Tuksal Tapelere Yanıt Verdi," March 18, 2014. Available online: http://www.radikal.com.tr/turkiye/hidayet-sefkatli-tuksal-tapelere-yanit-verdi-1181916/ (accessed December 13, 2018).

152 *Taraf* was shut down following the July 15, 2016 failed coup attempt. The newspaper was known to be financed by Fethullah Gülen's organization.

153 Berrin Sönmez, "15 Temmuz Gibi 16 Nisan'da da 'Hayır' Diyenler: Hak Ve Adalet Platformu," *Gazete Duvar*, April 14, 2017. Available online: https://www.gazeteduvar.com.tr/yazarlar/2017/04/14/15-temmuz-gibi-16-nisanda-da-hayir-diyenler-hak-ve-adalet-platformu/ (accessed December 13, 2018).

154 Tanıl Bora, *Cereyanlar*, 809.

155 Mona Tajali, "The Promise of Gender Parity: Turkey's People's Democratic Party (HDP)," *openDemocracy*, October 29, 2015. Available online: https://www.opendemocracy.net/5050/mona-tajali/promise-of-gender-parity-turkey-s-people-s-democratic-party-hdp (accessed December 13, 2018).

156 Ibid.

157 Bora, *Cereyanlar*, 814.

158 Feyza Akınerdem, "Dindar Kadınlar ve Feminizm—Yakınlıklar ve Uzaklıklar," in *Amargi, Feminizm Tartışmaları* (Istanbul: Kumbara Sanat Atölyesi Araştırma Dizisi—2, 2012), 96.

159 Ibid., 97.

160 Ayşe Böhürler, "Yaşamı Tersten Yaşamak," *Yeni Şafak*, October 9, 2010.

161 Sandra Lee Bartky, *Femininity and Domination: Studies in the Phenomenology of Oppression* (London: Routledge, 1990), 80.

162 Çarkoğlu and Toprak, *Değişen Türkiye'de Din, Toplum ve Siyaset*, 26, 63.

163 Feyza Akınerdem, "Dindar Kadınlar ve Feminizm—Yakınlıklar ve Uzaklıklar," in *Amargi, Feminizm Tartışmaları* (Istanbul: Kumbara Sanat Atölyesi Araştırma Dizisi—2, 2012), 114–15.

164 *Reçel* blog (article by "Feyza," last name not provided), "Anlattığın Benim Hikâyem Değil," May 4, 2015. Available online: http://recel-blog.com/anlattigin-benim-hikayem-degil/ (accessed December 13, 2018). For an interview with Reçel's editors, see: Ayşe Özsoy, "Reçel Blog'un Gündemini Okurları Belirliyor," *Sivil Sayfalar*, March 6, 2018. Available online: http://www.sivilsayfalar.org/2018/03/06/recel-blogun-gundemini-okurlari-belirliyor/ (accessed December 13, 2018).

165 *Reçel* blog (article by the author with the nickname: Başörtülü Bir Dost), "Başı Açık Akademisyen Olur mu?" November 19, 2015. Available online: http://recel-blog.com/basi-acik-akademisyen-olur-mu/ (accessed December 13, 2018).

166 Ibid.

167 For more information on conservative women's blogs see: Melike Aslı Sim, "Unveiling the Secret Stories: Conservative Female Blogosphere in Turkey," *İleti-ş-im: Galatasaray University Journal of Communication* 26 (2017): 39–63. Available online: http://iletisimdergisi.gsu.edu.tr/download/article-file/322267 (accessed December 13, 2018).

168 Büşra Cebeci (Interview with Hadiye Yolcu), "Başörtüsü Mücadelesinin Değişen Yolculuğu, 'Başörtüsüzler Ayrıştırılırsa, Onları da Biz Savunacağız,'" *Bia News Desk*, February 13, 2018. Available online: http://bianet.org/bianet/toplumsal-cinsiyet/194058-basortusuzler-ayristirilirsa-onlari-da-biz-savunacagiz (accessed December 13, 2018).

169 Emine Uçak (Interview with Nil Mutluer), "Yrd. Doç. Dr Nil Mutluer: 'İçe Kapanmak Yerine Dayanışarak Var Olmalıyız,'" *Sivil Sayfalar*, March 2, 2017. Available online: http://www.sivilsayfalar.org/2017/03/02/yrd-doc-dr-nil-mutluer-ice-kapanmak-yerine-dayanisarak-var-olmaliyiz/ (accessed December 13, 2018).

170 Emek ve Adalet Platformu, webpage: http://www.emekveadalet.org/biz-kimiz/; Twitter page: https://twitter.com/emekadalet (both accessed December 13, 2018).

171 Twitter page of Kadına Şiddete Karşı Müslümanlar: https://twitter.com/KSKMuslumanlar (accessed December 13, 2018).

172 Emek ve Adalet Platformu, "Yeni Türkiye'de Kadın Politikaları ve Kadın Mücadelesi," March 8, 2018. Available online: http://www.emekveadalet.org/yayin/yeni-turkiyede-kadin-politikalari-ve-kadin-mucadelesi/ (accessed December 13, 2018).

173 Twitter page of Eşitiz Kadın Grubu: https://twitter.com/esitiz (accessed December 13, 2018).

Chapter 6: Conclusion—Toward a New Gender Equilibrium

1   Esra Özcan, "Conservative Women in Power: A New Predicament for Transnational Feminist Media Research," in *Feminist Approaches to Media Theory and Research*, ed. Dustin Harp, Jaime Loke, and Ingrid Bachmann (Cham: Palgrave Macmillan, 2018), 167–81.

2   Alec Tyson and Shiva Maniam, "Behind Trump's Victory: Divisions by Race, Gender, Education," *Pew Research Center*, November 9, 2016. Available online: http://www.pewresearch.org/fact-tank/2016/11/09/behind-trumps-victory-divisions-by-race-gender-education/ (accessed December 14, 2018).

3 Kathleen M. Blee and Sandra McGee Deutsch (eds.), *Women of the Right: Comparisons and Interplay Across Borders* (University Park, PA: Pennsylvania State University Press, 2012).

4 For more information on Saba Ahmed and the Republican Muslim Coalition, see: http://www.sabaahmed.com/ (accessed December 14, 2018).

5 Sena Karasipahi, *Muslims in Modern Turkey: Kemalism, Modernism and the Revolt of the Islamic Intellectuals* (London: I.B. Tauris, 2009). For example, "Islamic intellectuals" covered in Karasipahi's work are all men.

6 Hilâl Kaplan, "Hedefteki Ben ve Cevaplar," *Yeni Şafak*, December 12, 2012.

7 Ayşe Çavdar, "Erdoğan neyi güncelliyor?" *Artı Gerçek*, March 14, 2018. Available online: https://www.artigercek.com/erdogan-neyi-guncelliyor?t=1521020412 (accessed December 8, 2018).

8 *Bianet*, "Aggressor Who Kicked Woman For Wearing Shorts Sentenced to Prison," *BIA News Desk*, September 8, 2017. Available online: https://bianet.org/english/women/189663-aggressor-who-kicked-woman-for-wearing-shorts-sentenced-to-prison (accessed December 14, 2018).

9 Ayşe Böhürler, "Başörtüsünde Zamanlama Manidar," *Yeni Şafak*, April 12, 2014.

10 Feyda Sayan-Cengiz, *Beyond Headscarf Culture in Turkey's Retail Sector* (Basingstoke: Palgrave Macmillan, 2016), 109–19.

11 Zehra Yılmaz, *Dişil Dindarlık: İslâmcı Kadın Hareketinin Dönüşümü* (Istanbul: İletişim Yayınları, 2015), 13.

12 YouTube, "Şafak Pavey'in Mecliste 'Türban' Konuşması 31 Ekim 2013," between 2:45 and 3:00. Available online: https://www.youtube.com/watch?v=nYqyKc1DqoI (accessed May 8, 2019).

13 Hayrettin Karaman, "Başörtülü Sigara," *Yeni Şafak*, August 3, 2017. Available online: https://www.yenisafak.com/yazarlar/hayrettinkaraman/basortulu-sigara-2039345 (accessed December 14, 2018).

14 Ayşe Böhürler, "Yüksek Performanslı Dindarlık Beklentisi," *Yeni Şafak*, August 30, 2008.

15 Ayşe Böhürler, "Baş Örtme Rahatlığı İle Özgürlük Arasındaki Fark," *Yeni Şafak*, October 13, 2012.

16 Ayşe Böhürler, "Konvansiyon Kartı ve Koz Oyunu," *Yeni Şafak*, October 4, 2014.

17 Ayşe Böhürler, "Mualla Alışverişte," *Yeni Şafak*, November 5, 2011.

18 Hilâl Kaplan, "Güzel Ahlaktan Güzel Yaşam Tarzına," *Yeni Şafak*, July 10, 2011.

19 Ayşe Böhürler, "Mütercim Aydınların Türkiyesi . . . ," *Yeni Şafak*, August 6, 2011. Ayşe Böhürler, "Başörtüye Gül Takmak," *Yeni Şafak*, May 3, 2008.

20 Haşime Kılıçarslan, "Kaldı Bu Silinmez Başörtülü/Şortlu Suçu Üzerimizde," *Reçel* blog, November 20, 2017. Available online: http://recel-blog.com/kaldi-bu-silinmez-basortulu-sortlu-sucu-uzerimizde/ (accessed December 14, 2018).

21 Nil Mutluer, "Kemalist Feminists in the Era of the AK Party," *The Turkish AK Party and Its Leader: Criticism, Opposition and Dissent*, ed. Ümit Cizre (New York: Routledge, 2016), 46.

22 Ayşe Böhürler, "Neden Şimdi?" *Yeni Şafak*, October 23, 2010; Nihal Bengisu Karaca, "Lisede Başörtüsü," *Habertürk*, September 28, 2014. Ayşe Böhürler was not happy about young schoolgirls wearing headscarf. Nihal Bengisu Karaca on the other hand, discussed this issue with reference to a family's right to raise their children however they want.

Select Bibliography

Abadan-Unat, Nermin. *Women in the Developing World: Evidence from Turkey*, Monograph Series in World Affairs, 22/1. Denver, CO: University of Denver, 1986.

Abadan-Unat, Nermin, Deniz Kandiyoti, and Mübeccel Kıray (eds.). *Women in Turkish Society*. Leiden: Brill, 1981.

Abu-Lughod, Lila. "The Romance of Resistance: Tracing Transformations of Power Through Bedouin Women." *American Ethnologist* 17, no. 1 (1990): 41–55.

Acar, Feride. "Women in the Ideology of Islamic Revivalism in Turkey: Three Islamic Women's Journals." In *Islam in Modern Turkey, Religion, Politics and Literature in a Secular State*, edited by Richard Tapper, 280–303. London: I.B. Tauris, 1991.

Acar, Feride, and Gülbanu Altunok. "The 'Politics of Intimate' at the Intersection of Neo-liberalism and Neo-conservatism in Contemporary Turkey." *Women's Studies International Forum* 41 (2013): 14–23.

Ahmed, Feroz. *The Making of Modern Turkey*. London: Routledge, 1993.

Ahmed, Leila. *A Quiet Revolution: The Veil's Resurgence, from the Middle East to America*. New Haven, CT: Yale University Press, 2011.

Akınerdem, Feyza. "Dindar Kadınlar ve Feminizm—Yakınlıklar ve Uzaklıklar," in *Amargi, Feminizm Tartışmaları*, 84–120. Istanbul: Kumbara Sanat Atölyesi Araştırma Dizisi—2, 2012.

Akser, Murat, and Banu Baybars-Hawks. "Media and Democracy in Turkey: Toward a Model of Neoliberal Media Autocracy." *Middle East Journal of Culture and Communication* 5, no. 3 (2012): 302–21.

Akşit, Bahattin. "Imam-Hatip and Other Secondary Schools in the Context of Political and Cultural Modernization of Turkey." *Journal of Human Sciences* 5, no. 1 (1986): 25–41.

Algan, Ece. "Local Broadcasting as Tactical Media: Exploring Practices of Kurdish Activism and Journalism in Turkey." *Middle East Journal of Culture and Communication* (in press, 2018).

Altınay, Ayşe Gül. "Bedenimiz ve Biz: Bekaret ve Cinselliğin Siyaseti." In *90'larda Türkiye'de Feminizm*, edited by Aksu Bora and Asena Güral, 323–43. Istanbul: İletişim Yayınları, 2002.

Altınay, Rustem Ertug. "Şule Yüksel Şenler: An Early Style Icon of Urban Islamic Fashion in Turkey." In *Islamic Fashion and Anti-Fashion: New Perspectives from Europe and North America*, edited by Emma Tarlo and Annelies Moors. London: Bloomsbury Academic, 2013.

Arat, Yeşim. "Feminism and Islam: Considerations on the Journal Kadın ve Aile." In *Women in Modern Turkish Society*, edited by Şirin Tekeli, 66–78. London: Zed Books, 1991.

Arat, Yeşim. "Islamist Women and Feminist Concerns in Contemporary Turkey." *Frontiers* 37, no. 3 (2016): 125–50.

Arat, Yeşim. "Religion, Politics and Gender Equality in Turkey: Implications of a Democratic Paradox?" *Third World Quarterly* 31, no. 6 (2010): 869–84.

Arat, Yeşim. *Rethinking Islam and Liberal Democracy: Islamist Women in Turkish Politics*, Albany, NY: State University of New York Press, 2005.

Arat, Yeşim. "Rethinking the Political: A Feminist Journal in Turkey, Pazartesi." *Women's Studies International Forum* 27, no. 3 (2004): 281–92.

Arsan, Esra. "Killing Me Softly with His Words: Censorship and Self-Censorship from the Perspective of Turkish Journalists." *Turkish Studies* 14, no. 3 (2013): 447–62.

Aslan-Akman, Canan. "Islamic Women's Ordeal with the New Face(s) of Patriarchy in Power: Divergence or Convergence over Expanding Women's Citizenship." In *Gendered Identities: Criticizing Patriarchy in Turkey*, edited by Rasim Özgür Dönmez and Fazilet Ahu Özmen, 113–45. Lanham, MD: Lexington Books, 2013.

Atacan, Fulya. *Cerrahiler*. Istanbul: Hil Yayınları, 1990.

Ayata, Ayşe Gunes, and Fatma Tütüncü. "Party Politics of the AKP (2002–2007) and the Predicaments of Women at the Intersection of the Westernist, Islamist and Feminist Discourses in Turkey." *British Journal of Middle Eastern Studies* 35, no. 3 (2008): 363–84.

Aygül, Cenk. "Electoral Manipulation in March 30, 2014 Turkish Local Elections." *Turkish Studies* 17, no. 1 (2016): 181–201.

Badran, Margot. *Feminism in Islam: Secular and Religious Convergences*. Oxford: Oneworld, 2009.

Badran, Margot. *Samyukta: A Journal of Gender and Culture* 17, no. 1 (2017): special issue on Islamic feminism.

Badran, Margot. "Understanding Islam, Islamism, and Islamic Feminism," *Journal of Women's History* 13, no. 1 (2001): 47–52.

Bartky, Sandra Lee. *Femininity and Domination: Studies in the Phenomenology of Oppression*. London: Routledge, 1990.

Bayram, Salih. "Reporting Hijab in Turkey: Shifts in the Pro- and Anti-Ban Discourses." *Turkish Studies* 10, no. 4 (2009): 511–38.

Bele, Tansu. *Necla Arat, Cumhuriyet Kadının Aydınlık Yüzü*. Istanbul: Kaynak Yayınları, 2013.

Berthezène, Clarisse, and Julie V. Gottlieb (eds.). *Rethinking Right-Wing Women: Gender and the Conservative Party, 1880s to the Present*. Manchester: Manchester University Press, 2018.

Bilici, Mücahit. "İslam'ın brozlaşan yüzü: Caprice Hotel örnek olayı." In *İslam'ın Yeni Kamusal Yüzleri*, edited by Nilüfer Göle, 216–37. Istanbul: Metis Yayınları, 2000.

Blakely, Kristin. "Transnational Anti-Feminist Networks: Canadian Right-Wing Women and the Global Stage." In *New Perspectives on the Transnational Right*, edited by Martin Durham and Margaret Power, 171–86. New York: Palgrave Macmillan, 2010.

Blee, Kathleen M., and Sandra McGee Deutsch (eds.). *Women of the Right: Comparisons and Interplay Across Borders.* University Park, PA: Pennsylvania State University Press, 2012.

Bloom, Peter. "Authoritarian Capitalism in Modern Times: When Economic Discipline Really Means Political Disciplining." *openDemocracy*, July 22, 2015. Available online: https://www.opendemocracy.net/can-europe-make-it/peter-bloom/authoritarian-capitalism-in-modern-times-when-economic-discipline-rea (accessed December 15, 2018).

Bora, Aksu. "Bir Yapabilirlik Olarak Ka-Der." In *90'larda Türkiye'de Feminizm*, edited by Aksu Bora and Asena Günal, 109–24. Istanbul: İletişim Yayınları, 2002.

Bora, Aksu, and Asena Günal (eds.). *90'larda Türkiye'de Feminizm.* Istanbul: İletişim Yayınları, 2002.

Bora, Tanıl. *Cereyanlar: Türkiye'de Siyasi İdeolojiler.* Istanbul: İletişim Yayınları, 2017.

Bulut, Ergin, and Erdem Yörük. "Digital Populism: Trolls and Political Polarization of Twitter in Turkey." *International Journal of Communication* 11 (2017): 4093–117.

Büyüksaraç, Güldem Baykal. "'All Dominion Belongs to Allah . . . Capital Get Out': The Issue of Social Justice and Muslim Anti-Capitalists in Turkey." *Crosscurrents* 66, no. 2 (2016): 239–52.

Çaha, Ömer. *Women and Civil Society in Turkey: Women's Movements in a Muslim Society.* Farnham: Ashgate, 2013.

Çakır, Ruşen, and Fehmi Çalmuk. *Recep Tayyip Erdoğan, Bir Dönüşüm Öyküsü.* Istanbul: Metis, 2001.

Cangöz, İncilay. *Değişen Anlam ve Değerleriyle Gazelecilik.* Ankara: Sınırsız, 2015.

Çarkoğlu, Ali, and Binnaz Toprak. *Değişen Türkiye'de Din, Toplum ve Siyaset.* Istanbul: Tesev, 2006. Available online: http://tesev.org.tr/wp-content/uploads/2015/11/Degisen_Turkiyede_Din_Toplum_Ve_Siyaset.pdf (accessed December 13, 2018).

Çarkoğlu, Ali, and Binnaz Toprak. *Religion, Society and Politics in a Changing Turkey*, translated by Çiğdem Aksoy Fromm and edited by Jenny Sanders. Istanbul: Tesev, 2007. Available online: http://research.sabanciuniv.edu/5854/1/2007_08_Religon,_Society_and_Politics_in_a_Changing_Turkey.pdf (accessed December 8, 2018).

Çarkoğlu, Ali, and Binnaz Toprak. *Türkiye'de Din, Toplum ve Siyaset.* Istanbul: Tesev, 2000. Available online: http://tesev.org.tr/wp-content/uploads/2015/11/Turkiyede_Din_Toplum_Ve_Siyaset.pdf (accessed December 8, 2018).

Çatalbaş, Dilruba. "Freedom of Press and Broadcasting." In *Human Rights in Turkey*, edited by Zehra F. Kabasakal Arat, 19–34. Philadelphia, PA: University of Pennsylvania Press, 2007.

Çayır, Kenan. "The Emergence of Turkey's Contemporary 'Muslim Democrats.'" In *Secular and Islamic Politics in Turkey: The Making of the Justice and Development Party*, edited by Ümit Cizre, 62–79. New York: Routledge, 2008.

Çayır, Kenan. *Islamic Literature in Contemporary Turkey: From Epic to Novel.* New York: Palgrave, 2007.

Cetin, Iclal. "Veiled Representations: Political Battles Around Female Sexuality in Turkish Print Media." *Feminist Media Studies* 10, no. 4 (2010): 409–19.

Christensen, Christian. "Concentration of Ownership, the Fall of the Unions and Government Legislation in Turkey." *Global Media and Communication* 3, no. 2 (2007): 179–99.

Çınar, Alev. *Modernity, Islam, and Secularism in Turkey: Bodies, Places, and Time.* Minneapolis, MN: University of Minnesota Press, 2005.

Cindoğlu, Dilek, and Gizem Zencirci. "The Headscarf in Turkey in the Public and State Spheres." *Middle Eastern Studies* 44, no. 5 (2008): 791–806.

Çitak, Zana, and Özlem Tür. "Women Between Tradition and Change: The Justice and Development Party Experience in Turkey." *Middle Eastern Studies* 44, no. 3 (2008): 455–69.

Cizre, Ümit (ed.). *Secular and Islamic Politics in Turkey: The Making of the Justice and Development Party.* New York: Routledge, 2008.

Cunningham, Karla J. "Gender, Islam, and Conservative Politics." In *Women of the Right: Comparisons and Interplay Across Borders*, edited by Kathleen M. Blee and Sandra McGee Deutsch, 81–97. University Park, PA: The Pennsylvania State University Press, 2012.

Cürül, Burçak, and Rasim Özgür Dönmez. "Transsexuals in Turkey: Between Disciplining and Eradicating." In *Gendered Identities: Criticizing Patriarchy in Turkey*, edited by Rasim Özgür Dönmez and Fazilet Ahu Özmen, 67–77. Lanham, MD: Lexington Books, 2013.

Dedeoglu, Saniye, and Adem Yavuz Elveren (eds.). *Gender and Society in Turkey: The Impact of Neoliberal Policies, Political Islam and EU Accession.* London: I.B. Tauris, 2012.

Diner, Cagla, and Şule Toktaş. "Waves of Feminism in Turkey: Kemalist, Islamist and Kurdish Women's Movements in an Era of Globalization." *Journal of Balkan and Near Eastern Studies* 12, no. 1 (2010): 41–57.

Doğan, Sevinç. *Mahalledeki AKP: Parti İşleyişi, Taban Mobilizasyonu ve Siyasal Yabancılaşma.* Istanbul: İletişim Yayınları, 2016.

Dursun, Çiler. "The Struggle Goes On: The Discursive Strategies of the Islamist Press in Turkey." *Journal of Contemporary European Studies* 14, no. 2 (2006): 161–82.

Eisenstadt, Shmuel Noah. "Multiple Modernities." *Daedalus* 129, no. 1 (2000): 1–29.

Elver, Hilal. *The Headscarf Controversy: Secularism and Freedom of Religion.* Oxford: Oxford University Press, 2012.

Emmison, Michael, and Philip Smith. *Researching the Visual: Images, Objects, Contexts and Interactions in Social and Cultural Inquiry.* London: Sage, 2000.

Esen, Berk, and Sebnem Gumuscu. "Building a Competitive Authoritarian Regime: State–Business Relations in the AKP's Turkey." *Journal of Balkan and Near Eastern Studies* 20, no. 4 (2018): 349–72.

Esen, Berk, and Sebnem Gumuscu. "Rising Competitive Authoritarianism in Turkey." *Third World Quarterly* 37, no. 9 (2016): 1581–606.

Esen, Berk, and Şebnem Gümüşçü. "A Small Yes for Presidentialism: The Turkish Constitutional Referendum of April 2017." *Journal South European Society and Politics* 22, no. 3 (2017): 303–26.

Fahmy, Shahira. "Picturing Afghan Women: A Content Analysis of AP Wire Photographs During the Taliban Regime and After the Fall of the Taliban Regime." *Gazette: The International Journal for Communication Studies* 66, no. 2 (2004): 91–112.

Fallon, Kathleen M., and Julie Moreau, "Righting Africa? Contextualizing Notions of Women's Right-Wing Activism in Sub-Saharan Africa." In *Women of the Right: Comparisons and Interplay across Borders*, edited by Kathleen M. Blee and Sandra McGee Deutsch, 68–80. University Park, PA: The Pennsylvania State University Press, 2012.

Farris, Sara R. *In the Name of Women's Rights: The Rise of Femonationalism*. Durham, NC: Duke University Press, 2017.

Finkel, Andrew. "Who Guards the Turkish Press." *Journal of International Affairs* 54, no. 1 (2000): 147–66.

Gallagher, Margaret. *Who Makes the News? Global Media Monitoring Project 2005*. London: WACC, 2005. Available online: http://cdn.agilitycms.com/who-makes-the-news/Imported/reports_2005/gmmp-report-en-2005.pdf (accessed December 18, 2018).

Gallagher, Margaret, Amie Joof, Nidya Pesántez, and Mindy Ran. *Who Makes the News? Global Media Monitoring Project 2010*. London: WACC, 2010. Available online: http://cdn.agilitycms.com/who-makes-the-news/Imported/reports_2010/global/gmmp_global_report_en.pdf (accessed December 18, 2018).

Gevgilili, Ali. "Türkiye Basını." *Cumhuriyet Dönemi Türkiye Ansiklopedisi*, Vol. 1, 202–22. Istanbul: İletişim Yayınları, 1983.

Gökarıksel, Banu, and Anna Secor. " 'Even I Was Tempted': The Moral Ambivalence and Ethical Practice of Veiling-Fashion in Turkey." *Annals of the Association of American Geographers* 102, no. 4 (2012): 847–62.

Göle, Nilüfer. "Islam in Public: New Visibilities and New Imaginaries." *Public Culture* 14, no. 1 (2002): 173–90.

Göle, Nilüfer. "Secularism and Islamism in Turkey: The Making of Elites and Counter-Elites." *The Middle East Journal* 51, no. 1 (1997): 46–58.

Göle, Nilüfer. *The Forbidden Modern: Civilization and Veiling*. Ann Arbor, MI: University of Michigan Press, 1996.

Göle, Nilüfer, and Ludwig Ammann (eds.). *Islam in Public: Turkey, Iran and Europe*. Istanbul: Bilgi Publishing, 2006.

Goodnow, Trischa. "Using Narrative Theory to Understand the Power of News Photographs." In *Handbook of Visual Communication: Theory, Methods and Media*, edited by Ken Smith, Sandra Moriarty, Gretchen Barbatsis, and Keith Kenney, 351–61. Mahwah, NJ: Lawrence Erlbaum Associates, 2005.

Gorham, Bradley W. "News Media's Relationship with Stereotyping: The Linguistic Intergroup Bias in Response to Crime News." *Journal of Communication* 56, no. 2 (2006): 289–308.

Gözaydın, İştar. *Diyanet: Türkiye Cumhuriyeti'nde Dinin Tanzimi.* Istanbul: İletişim Yayınları, 2009.

Gramsci, Antonio. *Selections from the Prison Notebooks.* London: Lawrence & Wishart, 1971.

Griffin, Michael. "Picturing America's 'War on Terrorism' in Afghanistan and Iraq: Photographic Motifs as News Frames." *Journalism* 5, no. 4 (2004): 381–402.

Gül, Songül Sallan, and Hüseyin Gül. "The Question of Women in Islamic Revivalism in Turkey: A Review of the Islamic Press." *Current Sociology* 48, no. 2 (2000): 1–26.

Gurcan, Metin. "Theory or Attitude? A Comparative Analysis of Turkish Newspaper Articles on Turkish Foreign Policy, June 2008–June 2011." *Turkish Studies* 14, no. 2 (2013): 346–71.

Gürsoy, Yaprak. "From Tutelary Powers and Interventions to Civilian Control: An Overview of Turkish Civil–Military Relations Since the 1920s." In *Turkey's Democratization Process*, edited by Carmen Rodríguez, Antonio Ávalos, Hakan Yılmaz, and Ana I. Planet, 253–73. Abingdon: Routledge, 2014.

Hall, Stuart. "The Determinations of News Photographs." In *The Manufacture of News: Deviance, Social Problems and the Mass Media*, edited by Stanley Cohen and Jock Young, 226–43. London: Constable, 1982.

Heper, Metin. "A 'Democratic-Conservative' Government by Pious People: The Justice and Development Party in Turkey." In *The Blackwell Companion to Contemporary Islamic Thought*, edited by Ibrahim M. Abu-Rabiʿ, 345–61. Malden, MA: Blackwell, 2006.

Hortaçsu, Nuran, and Elvan Melek Ertürk. "Women and Ideology: Representations of Women in Religious and Secular Turkish Media." *Journal of Applied Social Psychology* 33, no. 10 (2003): 2017–39.

İlkkaracan, Pınar. "Democratization in Turkey from a Gender Perspective." In *Turkey's Democratization Process*, edited by Carmen Rodríguez, Antonio Ávalos, Hakan Yılmaz, and Ana I. Planet, 154–76. Abingdon: Routledge, 2014.

İlyasoğlu, Aynur. *Örtülü Kimlik: İslamcı Kadın Kimliğinin Oluşum Öğeleri.* Istanbul: Metis Yayınları, 1994.

İmamoğlu, Olcay E., Yeşim (Yasak) Gültekin, Bahar Köseoğlu, and Afife Çebi. "Representation of Women and Men in Turkish Newspapers." *Journal of Human Sciences* 9, no. 2 (1990): 57–67.

İncirlioğlu, Emine Onaran. "Images of Village Women in Turkey: Models and Anomalies." In *Deconstructing the Images of "the Turkish Woman,"* edited by Zehra F. Arat, 199–223. New York: St. Martin's Press, 1998.

Irak, Dağhan. "A Close-Knit Bunch: Political Concentration in Turkey's Anadolu Agency Through Twitter Interactions." *Turkish Studies* 17, no. 2 (2016): 336–60.

Işık, S. Nazik. "1990'larda Kadına Yönelik Aile İçi Şiddetle Mücadele Hareketi İçinde Oluşmuş Bazı Gözlem ve Düşünceler." In *90'larda Türkiye'de Feminizm*, edited by Aksu Bora and Asena Güral, 41–72. Istanbul: İletişim Yayınları, 2002.

Jones, Steve. *Antonio Gramsci*. Abingdon: Routledge, 2006.

Kadıoğlu, Ayşe. "Coup d'État Attempt: Turkey's Reichstag Fire?" *openDemocracy*, July 16, 2016. Available online: https://www.opendemocracy.net/ay-e-kad-o-lu/coup-d-tat-attempt-turkey-s-reichstag-fire (accessed December 8, 2018).

Kandiyoti, Deniz. "Locating the Politics of Gender: Patriarchy, Neo-liberal Governance and Violence in Turkey." *Research on Policy on Turkey* 1, no. 2 (2016): 103–18.

Kandiyoti, Deniz. "The Travails of the Secular: Puzzle and Paradox in Turkey." *Economy and Society* 41, no. 4 (2012): 513–31.

Kandiyoti, Deniz, and Zühre Emanet. "Education as Battleground: The Capture of Minds in Turkey." *Globalizations* 14, no. 6 (2017): 869–76.

Kaplan, Carla. "Identity." In *Keywords for American Cultural Studies*, edited by Bruce Burgett and Glenn Hendler, 123–7. New York: New York University Press, 2007. Available online: https://keywords.nyupress.org/american-cultural-studies/essay/identity/ (accessed December 15, 2018).

Karasipahi, Sena. *Muslims in Modern Turkey: Kemalism, Modernism and the Revolt of the Islamic Intellectuals*. London: I.B. Tauris, 2009.

Kejanlıoğlu, D. Beybin, Çağla Kubilay, and Nalan Ova. "Islamist Columnists Discussing 'Women in the Public Sphere': A Discourse Analysis of the Turkish Press." *Middle East Journal of Culture and Communication* 5, no. 3 (2012): 282–301.

Kılıçbay, Barış, and Mutlu Binark. "Consumer Culture, Islam and the Politics of Lifestyle." *European Journal of Communication* 17, no. 4 (2002): 495–511.

Kırca, Süheyla. "Turkish Women's Magazines: The Popular Meets the Political." *Women's Studies International Forum* 24, no. 3/4 (2001): 457–68.

Koç, Handan. *Muhafazakârlığa Karşı Feminizm*. Istanbul: Güldünya Yayınları, 2015.

Korteweg, Anna C., and Gökçe Yurdakul. *The Headscarf Debates: Conflicts of National Belonging*. Stanford, CA: Stanford University Press, 2015.

Köse, Elifhan. *Sessizliği Söylemek*. Istanbul: İletişim Yayınları, 2012.

Kress, Gunther, and Theo van Leeuwen. *Reading Images: The Grammar of Visual Design*. 2nd edn. Abingdon: Routledge, 2006.

Kubilay, Çağla. "İslami Muhafazakâr Kadın Yazarların Perspektifinden Kürtaj Tartışması: Eleştirel Bir Değerlendirme." *Alternatif Politika* 6, no. 3 (2014): 387–421. Available online: http://alternatifpolitika.com/makale/islami-muhafazak-r-kadin-yazarlarin-perspektifinden-kurtaj-tartismasi-elestirel-bir-degerlendirme (accessed December 19, 2018).

Kuzmanovic, Daniella. "Imbued with Agency: Contesting Notions of the Extraordinariness of Türkan Saylan." In *Politics of Worship in the Contemporary Middle East: Sainthood in Fragile States*, edited by Andreas Bandak and Mikkel Bille, 171–90. Leiden Brill, 2013.

Louw, Eric. *The Media and Political Process*. 2nd edn. London: Sage, 2010.

Macharia, Sarah. *Who Makes the News? Global Media Monitoring Project 2015*. London: WACC, 2015. Available online: http://cdn.agilitycms.com/who-makes-the-news/ Imported/reports_2015/global/gmmp_global_report_en.pdf (accessed December 18, 2018).

MEDIZ—Women's Media Watch Group. *End to Sexism in the Media*. Istanbul: Çağın Matbaacılık, 2008. Available online [in Turkish]: http://www.bianet.org/bianet/ medya/107742-mediz-raporu-medyada-yonetimde-olmayan-kadin-haberlerde- nesne (accessed December 18, 2018).

Mendes, Kaitlynn. " 'Feminism Rules! Now, Where's My Swimsuit?' Re-evaluating Feminist Discourse in Print Media 1968–2008." *Media, Culture & Society* 34, no. 5 (2012): 554–70.

Mengü, Seda, Murat Mengü, and Necla Odyakmaz. "Ideological Formation in Turkish Newspapers: An Analysis of the News About the Headscarf Issue." *Journal of Arab & Muslim Media Research* 2, no. 3 (2009): 223–39.

Menon, Kalyani Devaki. *Everyday Nationalism: Women of the Hindu Right in India*. Philadelphia, PA: University of Pennsylvania Press, 2010.

Merçil, İpek. "İslam ve Feminizm." In *Cinsiyetli Olmak: Sosyal Bilimlere Feminist Bakışlar*, edited by Zeynep Direk, 106–17. Istanbul: Yapı Kredi Yayınları, 2007.

Messaris, Paul, and Abraham Linus. "The Role of Images in Framing News Stories." In *Framing Public Life: Perspectives on Media and Our Understanding of the Social World*, edited by Stephen D. Reese, Oscar H. Gandy, and August E. Grant, 215–26. Mahwah, NJ: Lawrence Erlbaum Associates, 2001.

Müller, Marion G., and Esra Özcan. "The Political Iconography of Muhammad Cartoons: Understanding Cultural Conflict and Political Action." *PS: Political Science and Politics* 40, no. 2 (2007): 287–92.

Mutluer, Nil. "Kemalist Feminists in the Era of the AK Party." In *The Turkish AK Party and Its Leader: Criticism, Opposition and Dissent*, edited by Ümit Cizre, 40–74. New York: Routledge, 2016.

Navaro-Yashin, Yael. "The Market for Identities: Secularism, Islamism, Commodities." In *Fragments of Culture: The Everyday of Modern Turkey*, edited by Deniz Kandiyoti and Ayşe Saktanber, 221–53. New Brunswick, NJ: Rutgers University Press, 2002.

Nickerson, Michelle M. *Mothers of Conservatism: Women and the Postwar Right*. Princeton, NJ: Princeton University Press, 2012.

Ohm, Britta. "Organizing Popular Discourse With and Against the Media: Notes on the Making of Narendra Modi and Recep Tayyip Erdoğan as Leaders-Without- Alternative." *Television & New Media* 16, no. 4 (2015): 370–7.

Onar, Nora. "Kemalists, Islamists, and Liberals: Shifting Patterns of Confrontation and Consensus 2002–06." *Turkish Studies* 8, no. 2 (2007): 273–88.

Öncü, Ayşe. "Turkish Women in the Professions: Why So Many?" In *Women in Turkish Society*, edited by Nermin Abadan-Unat, Deniz Kandiyoti, and Mübeccel Kıray, 181–93. Leiden: E.J. Brill, 1981.

Özbudun, Ergun. "Democracy, Tutelarism, and the Search for a New Constitution." In *Turkey's Democratization Process*, edited by Carmen Rodríguez, Antonio Ávalos, Hakan Yılmaz, and Ana I. Planet, 293–311. Abingdon: Routledge.

Özbudun, Sibel. *Kadınlar: İslam, AKP ve Ötesi*. Ankara: Ütopya, 2016.

Özcan, Ayşe Esra. "The New Configurations of Islam in Contemporary Turkey: The Case of Yaşar Nuri Öztürk." Unpublished MA thesis, Boğaziçi University, Istanbul, 2000.

Özcan, Ayşe Esra. "Visualization of Gender in the Turkish Press: A Comparative Analysis of Six Turkish Newspapers." IRC-Library. Bremen: Information Resource Center der Jacobs University Bremen, 2010. Available online: https://opus.jacobs-university.de/frontdoor/index/index/docId/279 (accessed December 8, 2018).

Özcan, Esra. "Conservative Women in Power: A New Predicament for Transnational Feminist Media Research." In *Feminist Approaches to Media Theory and Research*, edited by Dustin Harp, Jaime Loke, and Ingrid Bachmann, 167–81. Cham: Palgrave Macmillan, 2018.

Özcan, Esra. "Turkish Women in Islamism: Gender and the Mirage of 'Islamic Feminism.'" *Samyukta: A Journal of Gender and Culture* 17, no. 1 (2017): 182–92.

Özcan, Esra. "Women's Headscarves in News Photographs: A Comparison Between the Secular and Islamic Press During the AKP Government in Turkey." *European Journal of Communication* 30, no. 6 (2015): 698–713.

Özkırımlı, Umut. "How to Liquidate a People? Academic Freedom in Turkey and Beyond." *Globalizations* 14, no. 6 (2017): 851–6.

Özkırımlı, Umut (ed.). *The Making of a Protest Movement in Turkey: #occupygezi*. New York: Palgrave Macmillan, 2014.

Özükan, Bülent. "Basında Tirajlar." *Cumhuriyet: Dönemi Türkiye Ansiklopedisi*, Vol. 1, 229–32. Istanbul: İletişim Yayınları, 1983.

Pettigrew, Thomas F. "The Ultimate Attribution Error: Extending Allport's Cognitive Analysis of Prejudice." *Personality and Social Psychology Bulletin* 5 (1979): 461–76.

Power, Margaret. *Right-Wing Women in Chile: Feminine Power and the Struggle Against Allende, 1964–1973*. University Park, PA: Penn State University Press, 2002.

Rose, Gillian. *Visual Methodologies: An Introduction to the Interpretation of Visual Materials*. London: Sage, 2001.

Şahin-Mencütek, Zeynep. "Gender Politics of the Justice and Development Party in Turkey." In *Gender, Conservatism and Political Representation*, edited by Karen Celis and Sarah Childs, 83–102. Colchester: ECPR Press, 2014.

Saktanber, Ayşe. *Living Islam: Women, Religion and the Politicization of Culture in Turkey*. London: I.B. Tauris, 2002.

Saktanber, Ayşe. "Whose Virtue Is This? The Virtue Party and Women in Islamist Politics in Turkey." In *Right-Wing Women: From Conservatives to Extremists Around the World*, edited by Paola Bacchetta and Margaret Power, 71–83. New York: Routledge, 2002.

Saktanber, Ayşe. "Women in the Media in Turkey: The Free, Available Woman or the Good Wife and Selfless Mother." In *Women in Turkish Society: A Reader*, edited by Şirin Tekeli, 153–69. Atlantic Heights, NJ: Zed Books, 1991.

Sancar, Serpil. *Türk Modernleşmesinin Cinsiyeti: Erkekler Devlet, Kadınlar Aile Kurar.* Istanbul: İletişim Yayınları, 2014.

Sandıkçı, Özlem, and Güliz Ger. "Veiling in Style: How Does a Stigmatized Practice Become Fashionable?" *Journal of Consumer Research* 37, no. 1 (2010): 15–36.

Sarkar, Tanika, and Urvashi Butalia. *Women and Right-Wing Movements: Indian Experiences.* London: Zed Books, 1995.

Sayan-Cengiz, Feyda. *Beyond Headscarf Culture in Turkey's Retail Sector.* Basingstoke: Palgrave Macmillan, 2016.

Sayan-Cengiz, Feyda. "Eroding the Symbolic Significance of Veiling? The Islamic Fashion Magazine *Âlâ*, Consumerism, and the Challenged Boundaries of the 'Islamic neighborhood.'" *New Perspectives on Turkey* 58 (2018): 155–78.

Scheck, Raffael. *Mothers of the Nation: Right-Wing Women in Weimar Germany.* Oxford: Berg, 2004.

Schreiber, Ronnee. *Righting Feminism: Conservative Women and American Politics.* New York: Oxford University Press, 2008.

Schreier, Margrit. *Qualitative Content Analysis in Practice.* London: Sage, 2012.

Selen, Eser. "The Stage: A Space for Queer Subjectification in Contemporary Turkey." *Gender, Place & Culture* 19, no. 6 (2012): 730–49.

Sever, Metin, and Cem Dizdar. *2. Cumhuriyet Tartışmaları: Yeni Arayışlar, Yeni Yönelimler.* Istanbul: Başak Yayınları, 1993.

Sharp, Gene. *From Dictatorship to Democracy: A Conceptual Framework for Liberation.* East Boston, MA: Albert Einstein Institution, 1994.

Sim, Melike Aslı. "Unveiling the Secret Stories: Conservative Female Blogosphere in Turkey." *İleti-ş-im: Galatasaray University Journal of Communication* 26 (2017): 39–63. Available online: http://iletisimdergisi.gsu.edu.tr/download/article-file/322267 (accessed December 13, 2018).

Sirman, Nükhet. "Feminism in Turkey: A Short History." *New Perspectives on Turkey* 3 (1989): 1–34.

Sözeri, Ceren, and Zeynep Güney. *The Political Economy of the Media in Turkey: A Sectoral Analysis.* Istanbul: Tesev, 2011.

Tambar, Kabir. *The Reckoning of Pluralism: Political Belonging and the Demands of History in Turkey.* Stanford, CA: Stanford University Press, 2014.

Tanrıöver, Hülya Uğur. "Medyada Kadınların Temsil Biçimleri ve Kadın Hakları İhlalleri." In *Kadın Odaklı Habercilik*, edited by Sevda Alankuş, 151–68. Istanbul: IPS İletişim Vakfı Yayınları, 2007. Available online: http://bianet.org/files/static/bia_kitaplar/kadinodaklihabercilik.pdf (accessed December 18, 2018).

Taş, Hakkı, and Meral Uğur. "Roads 'Drawn' to Modernity: Religion and Secularism in Contemporary Turkey." *PS: Political Science and Politics* 40, no. 2 (2007): 311–14.

Tekeli, Şirin (ed.). *Women in Modern Turkish Society: A Reader.* London: Zed Books, 1995.

Tılıç, Doğan L. *Media Ownership Structure in Turkey.* Ankara: Çağdaş Gazeteciler Derneği, 2000.

Toksöz, Gülay. "The State of Female Labour in the Impasse of the Neoliberal Market and the Patriarchal Family." In *Gender and Society in Turkey: The Impact of Neoliberal Policies, Political Islam and EU Accession*, edited by Saniye Dedeoglu and Adem Yavuz Elveren, 47–64. London, I.B. Tauris, 2012.

Toktamis, Kumru F. "A Peace That Wasn't: Friends, Foes, and Contentious Re-entrenchment of Kurdish Politics in Turkey." *Turkish Studies* 19, no. 5 (2018): 697–722.

Toprak, Binnaz. *Türkiye'de Farklı Olmak*. Istanbul: Metis, 2009.

Topuz, Hıfzı. *Türk Basın Tarihi*. Istanbul: Remzi Kitabevi, 2003.

Tugal, Cihan. "In Turkey, the Regime Slides from Soft to Hard Totalitarianism." *openDemocracy*, February 17, 2016. Available online: https://www.opendemocracy.net/cihan-tugal/turkey-hard-totalitarianism-erdogan-authoritarian (accessed December 8, 2018).

Tuksal, Hidayet Şefkatli. *Kadın Karşıtı Söylemin İslam Geleneğindeki İzdüşümleri*. Ankara: Kitabiyat, 2000.

Turam, Berna. *Between Islam and the State: The Politics of Engagement*. Stanford, CA: Stanford University Press, 2007.

Turam, Berna. *Gaining Freedoms: Claiming Space in Istanbul and Berlin*. Stanford, CA: Stanford University Press, 2015.

Turam, Berna. "Turkish Women Divided by Politics: Secularist Activism Versus Pious Non-resistance." *International Feminist Journal of Politics* 10, no. 4 (2008): 475–94.

Unal, Didem. "Vulnerable Identities: Pious Women Columnists' Narratives on Islamic Feminism and Feminist Self-Identification in Contemporary Turkey." *Women's Studies International Forum* 53 (2015): 12–21.

White, Jenny. *Islamist Mobilization in Turkey: A Study in Vernacular Politics*. Seattle, WA: University of Washington Press, 2002.

Women for Women's Human Rights. *Turkish Civil and Penal Code Reforms from a Gender Perspective: The Success of Two Nationwide Campaigns*. Istanbul: Women for Women's Human Rights, 2005.

Yesil, Bilge. *Media in New Turkey: The Origins of an Authoritarian Neoliberal State*. Urbana, IL: University of Illinois Press, 2016.

Yılmaz, Ferruh. "From Immigrant Worker to Muslim Immigrant: Challenges for Feminism." *European Journal of Women's Studies* 22, no. 1 (2015): 37–52.

Yılmaz, Ferruh. *How the Workers Became Muslims: Immigration, Culture, and Hegemonic Transformation in Europe*. Ann Arbor, MI: University of Michigan Press, 2016.

Yılmaz, Zafer. "'Strengthening the Family' Policies in Turkey: Managing the Social Question and Armoring Conservative–Neoliberal Populism." *Turkish Studies* 16, no. 3 (2015): 371–90.

Yılmaz, Zehra. *Dişil Dindarlık: İslâmcı Kadın Hareketinin Dönüşümü*. Istanbul: İletişim Yayınları, 2015.

Index

Lightning Source UK Ltd.
Milton Keynes UK
UKHW021429281119
354321UK00004B/290/P